MANAGING MARKETING
IN THE 21ST CENTURY:

Developing & Implementing The Market Strategy

3rd edition

www.axcesscapon.com

To access O-codes, go to **www.ocodes.com**

STUDENT
STUDY GUIDE

Noel Capon

with

Andrew Yap

Library of Congress Cataloging-in-Publication Data

Capon, Noel
   Managing Marketing in the 21st Century (3rd edition) – Student Study Guide / Noel Capon with
Andrew Yap
      p. cm.
   ISBN 978-0-9833300-9-7

Editor: Noel Capon
Copy Editor: Christy Goldfinch
Book/Cover Design: Anna Botelho

TABLE OF CONTENTS

SECTION I
MARKETING
AND THE FIRM

Managing Marketing in the 21ˢᵗ Century

SECTION I: MARKETING AND THE FIRM

> **CHAPTER 1**
> **Introduction to Managing Marketing**

> **CHAPTER 2**
> **The Value of Customers**

SECTION II: FUNDAMENTAL INSIGHTS FOR STRATEGIC MARKETING

> **CHAPTER 3**
> Market Insight

> **CHAPTER 4**
> Customer Insight

> **CHAPTER 6**
> Marketing Research

TRANSITION TO STRATEGIC MARKETING

> **CHAPTER 5**
> Insight about Competitors, Company, and Complementers

SECTION III: STRATEGIC MARKETING

IMPERATIVE 1
Determine and Recommend Which Markets to Address

> **CHAPTER 7**
> Identifying and Choosing Opportunities

IMPERATIVE 2
Identify and Target Market Segments

> **CHAPTER 8**
> Market Segmentation and Targeting

IMPERATIVE 3
Set Strategic Direction and Positioning

> **CHAPTER 9**
> Market Strategy – Integrating Firm Efforts for Marketing Success

> **CHAPTER 10**
> Managing through the Life Cycle

> **CHAPTER 11**
> Managing Brands

SECTION IV: IMPLEMENTING THE MARKET STRATEGY

IMPERATIVE 4
Design the Market Offer

PART A: PROVIDING CUSTOMER VALUE

PART B: COMMUNICATING CUSTOMER VALUE

PART C: DELIVERING CUSTOMER VALUE

PART D: GETTING PAID FOR CUSTOMER VALUE

> **CHAPTER 12**
> Managing the Product Line

> **CHAPTER 15**
> Integrated Marketing Communications

> **CHAPTER 18**
> Distribution Decisions

> **CHAPTER 19**
> Critical Underpinnings of Pricing Decisions

> **CHAPTER 13**
> Managing Services and Customer Service

> **CHAPTER 16**
> Mass and Digital Communication

> **CHAPTER 20**
> Setting Prices

> **CHAPTER 14**
> Developing New Products

> **CHAPTER 17**
> Directing and Managing the Field Sales Effort

IMPERATIVE 5
Secure Support from Other Functions

> **CHAPTER 21**
> Ensuring the Firm Implements the Market Offer as Planned

IMPERATIVE 6
Monitor and Control

> **CHAPTER 22**
> Monitoring and Controlling Firm Functioning and Performance

SECTION V: SPECIAL MARKETING TOPICS

> **CHAPTER 23**
> International, Regional, and Global Marketing

CHAPTER 1

INTRODUCTION TO MANAGING MARKETING

WHAT DOES MARKETING MEAN TODAY?

Marketing plays a critical role in today's business environment where maximizing shareholder value is an increasingly important goal. The essence of marketing focuses on how firms attract, retain, and grow customers.

MARKETING AS A PHILOSOPHY Firms with a marketing philosophy embrace the view that marketing is the guiding force or orientation for the entire organization. They operate with an external orientation by focusing their attention and resources outside the corporation — to acquire, retain, and grow customers — but take careful account of competitors and the broader environment in which they do business. By contrast, internally oriented companies focus on internal issues like products, services, and processes.

MARKETING IMPERATIVES These are the must-dos of marketing. Executives with marketing or product management titles generally implement six imperatives. They are:

STRATEGIC MARKETING

- Imperative 1: Determine and recommend which markets to address.
- Imperative 2: Identify and target market segments.
- Imperative 3: Set strategic direction and positioning.

IMPLEMENTING THE MARKET STRATEGY

- Imperative 4: Design the market offer.
- Imperative 5: Secure support from other functions.
- Imperative 6: Monitor and control execution and performance.

As a broader framework when thinking about markets and marketing, marketers must also consider the **four principles** of marketing. These principles form the basis of marketing decision-making. They act as guidelines for implementing the six imperatives:

- Principle 1: Selectivity and Concentration
- Principle 2: Customer Value

- Principle 3: Differential Advantage
- Principle 4: Integration

THE CHANGING VIEW

OLD WAY	NEW WAY
Accounting profit is critical	Shareholder value is critical
Core of marketing job is the marketing mix	The marketing job encompasses six marketing imperatives
Customers are a *necessary evil*	Customers are the firm's *core assets*
Firm must manage the *status quo*	Firm must manage change
Firm operates to suit managers' goals	Firm operates to deliver value to customers
Internal orientations are acceptable	An external orientation is critical for success
Marketing department does the marketing	All firm employees have a marketing orientation
Marketing is one of the firm's functions	Marketing is a philosophy as well as a function
Organizational survival is a major firm objective	Shareholder value is the major firm objective
Seller power dominates	Customer power dominates
Shareholder value is an issue for finance	Shareholder value is an issue for marketing
Suppliers choose options	Customers choose options

> ### *Marketing Question*
>
> Choose two familiar firms, one that exemplifies the *old way* and one that exemplifies the *new way*. What criteria led you to identify these firms? Why?

THE MARKETING JOB

Marketing is the firm's fundamental activity. When marketing delivers **customer value** to satisfy customer needs, the firm *attracts*, *retains*, and *grows customers*. If costs are in line, *profits* follow. Profits help the firm survive and grow as an independent entity and secure the resources to grow and enhance **shareholder value**.

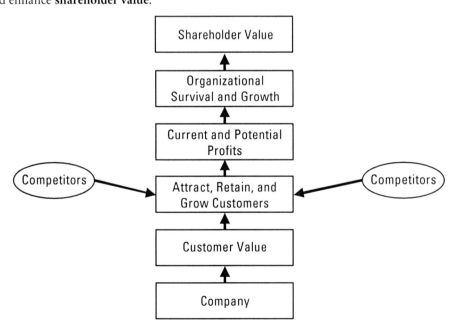

FIGURE 1.1

THE FUNDAMENTAL BUSINESS MODEL

Marketing's role includes identifying opportunities, figuring out customers' needs, understanding the competition, developing appealing products and services, and communicating value to potential customers. When these tasks are done well, shareholder value increases. The competitive battle to attract, retain, and grow customers is at the heart of all business activity.

The firm must deliver to **customers** greater **value** than **competitors** do. Customers reward firms that deliver customer value by purchasing their products and services, today and tomorrow. This **exchange** is the basis of all markets. In sum, when the firm delivers greater customer value than competitors, it should earn profits, survive and grow, and make shareholders very happy. If customers perceive that competitors deliver greater value, ultimately the firm will perish.

MARKETING AND SHAREHOLDER VALUE

The shareholder-value perspective defines management's job as maximizing returns for the firm's owners — its shareholders. When this perspective dominates, government regulations tend to favor the owners. Active shareholder opposition, and sometimes-unfriendly takeover bids, tend to occur when the firm underperforms in increasing shareholder value.

The firm only increases shareholder value if its incoming cash flows earn a return on investment at least equal to its **cost of capital** (the weighted average of the firm's cost of equity and cost of debt). When the firm fails to earn its cost of capital, it destroys shareholder value. Customers provide revenues and cash flow when they believe the firm's products and services offer better value than competitive alternatives.

If marketing fails to deliver superior value, the firm will go out of business — by bankruptcy, merger, or acquisition. Today, customer value and shareholder value are closely intertwined. Increased acceptance of the shareholder-value perspective has raised the stakes considerably. If marketing does not perform consistently well, the firm should anticipate a bleak future.

MARKETING AS A PHILOSOPHY: EXTERNAL AND INTERNAL ORIENTATIONS

THE EXTERNAL ORIENTATION

The externally oriented firm looks outward to the environment and knows that customers are central to its future. This firm knows that its current products, services, and processes are the reasons for past and present success. It also knows that, as its external environment changes, its products, services, and processes must also change. The externally oriented firm does not fear change but invests in new capabilities and competencies to exploit opportunities and create and serve customers.

INTERNAL ORIENTATIONS

In contrast to the external orientation, internally oriented firms focus on their own internal functions, and delivering customer value takes a back seat. Specific internal orientations include:

OPERATIONS ORIENTATION
The firm with an *operations orientation* typically focuses upon reducing unit costs. There is nothing wrong with cutting costs, but cost-cutting should not be a priority when the firm introduces a new product or when product varieties, promotional effort, and short delivery times are crucial for attracting, retaining, and growing customers.

SALES ORIENTATION

Firms with a *sales orientation* focus on short-term sales volume. They are less concerned with profits and long-run customer relationships. They set prices too low and offer excessive discounts and/or too-favorable credit terms — and may create a perception of low quality. They spend little on marketing research and planning, target customers indiscriminately, offer too many products, and over-invest in finished-goods inventories.

FINANCE ORIENTATION

The firm with a *finance orientation* focuses too heavily on short-term profits. When a firm *manages by the numbers*, it tends to avoid expenditures with long-term payoffs. The finance-oriented firm mortgages its future by indiscriminately cutting back on R&D, capital investment, marketing research, and/or advertising. Pricing focuses on short-term profits, and planning processes are weak or nonexistent.

TECHNOLOGY ORIENTATION

A firm with a *technology orientation* focuses on RD&E (research, development, and engineering) and pays little attention to customer value. The firm's products are often over-engineered, but customers will not pay for unneeded features. First-class products are critical for attracting, retaining, and growing customers, but the firm's product development efforts must center on customer requirements.

Marketing Exercise

Interview an executive. Identify examples where functional silos hurt performance — and where different functions worked well together. Why did these different behaviors occur?

THE SIX MARKETING IMPERATIVES

These imperatives are the must-dos of marketing.

STRATEGIC MARKETING — IMPERATIVE 1: DETERMINE AND RECOMMEND WHICH MARKETS TO ADDRESS

The first imperative requires the firm to answer critical questions about its business and market portfolio:

- In which new businesses and markets shall we invest — people, time, dollars?
- From which businesses and markets shall we withdraw?
- In which current businesses and markets shall we continue to invest?
- How much investment shall we make in these various businesses and markets?

For Imperative 1, marketing plays two key roles:

- **Identify opportunities.** Marketing personnel should research the environment to identify potential opportunities and bring these to top management's attention. They should also collect and analyze data that bear on the entry decision. Marketing should also be intimately involved with the firm's current markets and businesses and advise on investment and exit decisions.

- **Advise on proposed strategic actions.** Many parts of the firm develop strategic initiatives. Marketing has the responsibility to insert itself into these decisions. The firm should fully explore the marketing ramifications of its decisions or disaster may ensue.

STRATEGIC MARKETING — IMPERATIVE 2: IDENTIFY AND TARGET MARKET SEGMENTS

Imperative 2 states that marketing must identify **market segments** — groups of customers with similar needs that value similar benefits, with similar levels of priority. Once the firm has identified segments, it must decide which to target. Note the two elements of Marketing Imperative 2: a *creative and analytic* part — identifying market segments; and a *decision-making* part — choosing which segments to target, based on the firm's ability to deliver value. Effective segmentation and targeting drive profits.

FIGURE 1.2

MARKET SEGMENTATION AND TARGETING

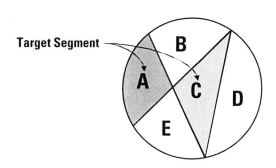

Note: The entire *pie* represents the population of existing and potential customers. Each *slice* or target segment — A,B,C,D,E — reflects specific needs and required benefits of the population. Note that each segment may contain *sub-segments*.

STRATEGIC MARKETING — IMPERATIVE 3: SET STRATEGIC DIRECTION AND POSITIONING

In Imperative 3, the firm decides how to compete in those market segments it has targeted. For each target segment, marketing must formulate performance objectives. The firm must also decide on its positioning for each segment — target customers, target competitors, value proposition, and reasons to believe. Together with Marketing Imperative 2, positioning completes the STP triumvirate — segmentation, targeting, and positioning.

Typically, individual market segments are at different developmental stages and hence require different approaches. Finally, decisions about strategic direction also include questions of branding — how the firm wants customers to view the corporate entity and its products — brand identity. The firm must continually assess its strategic direction and make necessary course corrections.

Marketing Exercise

Identify three examples each of well-integrated and poorly integrated market offers.

IMPLEMENTING THE MARKET STRATEGY — IMPERATIVE 4: DESIGN THE MARKET OFFER

Imperative 4 focuses on design of the **market offer.** The market offer is the total benefit package the firm provides its customers. Tools for designing the offer are the most well-known part of marketing. The **marketing mix** elements (aka the **4Ps**) comprise the basic building blocks of the firm's offer:

- **Product.** In general, the product embodies the major benefits the firm offers to satisfy customer needs — these benefits provide value to customers. The term *product* embraces both physical products and services.

- **Promotion.** Promotion embraces the various ways the firm communicates with customers — informing and persuading customers to purchase its products. Promotion includes *mass* and *digital communications* like traditional advertising and the Internet, and *personal communications* like the sales force.

- **Distribution.** Distribution focuses on how and where the customer secures the product. To conform to the 4Ps framework, marketers sometimes refer to *distribution* as *place.*

- **Price.** Price is what customers pay. The firm establishes its feasible price by the equivalent amount of value it offers through its products and services, promotion, and distribution.

IMPLEMENTING THE MARKET STRATEGY — IMPERATIVE 5: SECURE SUPPORT FROM OTHER FUNCTIONS

Imperative 5 focuses on how the firm's functions work together to ensure the firm makes the *right* market offer. Marketing requires two very different types of support:

- **Support for design** — relates to technical, operational, and economic feasibility. When the *best* design for customers requires product features the firm cannot make, marketing must develop extraordinary strength to keep the firm focused on satisfying customer needs — and pushing specific functions to evolve their capabilities.

- **Support for implementation** — assumes the design is agreed upon and fixed. Often called *internal marketing*, or getting *buy-in*, marketers must possess the leadership and interpersonal skills to encourage and stimulate cooperation across multiple functions.

> *Marketing Question*
>
> How good a job has Google done in implementing the six marketing imperatives?

IMPLEMENTING THE MARKET STRATEGY — IMPERATIVE 6: MONITOR AND CONTROL EXECUTION AND PERFORMANCE

Imperative 6 focuses on monitor and control — Is the firm achieving its desired results? If results are not on track, the firm should make changes.

Essentially, marketing should continually secure answers to three questions and act accordingly:

- Are the firm's various functions and departments *implementing* the market offer?

- Is the firm's market and financial *performance* reaching planned objectives?

- Based on the current *environment*, are the firm's objectives, strategies, and implementation plans on track, or should the firm make changes?

THE FOUR PRINCIPLES OF MARKETING

Four marketing principles serve as guidelines for acting on the six marketing imperatives.

PRINCIPLE 1: SELECTIVITY AND CONCENTRATION

Providing advice on market selection — Imperative 1 — and deciding which market segments to target — Imperative 2 — are among marketing's primary responsibilities. The basic principle underlying these imperatives is the Principle of Selectivity and Concentration. Two aspects comprise the Selectivity and Concentration principle:

- **Selectivity.** Marketing must carefully choose targets for the firm's efforts.

- **Concentration.** The firm should concentrate its resources against those targets.

PRINCIPLE 2: CUSTOMER VALUE

According to the Principle of Customer Value, the firm's marketplace success depends on providing value to customers. This principle is central to marketing's job. Customer insight should drive design and implementation of market offers. Customer value should drive the firm's product and investment decisions — and its performance evaluations.

PRINCIPLE 3: DIFFERENTIAL ADVANTAGE

The Principle of Differential Advantage is closely related to the Principle of Customer Value. Differential advantage is similar to having a *competitive advantage*, a *unique selling proposition*,

Marketing Question

Apple's success has made it one of the world's most admired firms. How do you assess Apple's adherence to the four marketing principles?

or an *edge*. The Principle of Differential Advantage asserts that the firm *should offer customers something they value and are willing to pay for but cannot get, or believe they cannot get, elsewhere.* This principle leads to several implications:

- **Competition.** The principle emphasizes competition. To avoid competitive parity, the firm's offer must be better than competitors' offers. The firm must create and re-create its differential advantage to beat competitors.

- **Superiority of differential advantages.** Some differential advantages are better than others. A differential advantage based on product design or product availability may be more sustainable than a differential advantage based on communications.

- **Eroding differential advantages.** Competition will eventually erode away even the apparently most sustainable differential advantage. Maintaining differential advantage is marketing's most fundamental challenge; the search for differential advantage must be ongoing.

- **Cannibalizing a differential advantage.** To stay ahead of competition, the firm must be willing to cannibalize its own offerings.

- **Differential advantage and difference.** A *differential advantage* is not the same as a *difference*. The firm's differences must create benefits that customers recognize, value, and are willing to pay for.

PRINCIPLE 4: INTEGRATION

Successful integration — critical for all marketing efforts — has two dimensions:

- **At the customer.** The firm must carefully integrate and coordinate all design and executional elements of the offer it makes to customers.

- **In the firm.** To achieve integration at the customer, the firm must integrate and coordinate all internal functional activities; this is often very difficult.

Firms with an external orientation are more likely to achieve integration, because the shared value of serving customers promotes a common purpose. Responsibility for designing and implementing market offers drives agreement on priorities, together with close and cooperative working relationships.

....

TRUE / FALSE QUESTIONS

1. The firm only increases shareholder value if its incoming cash flows earn a return on investment at least equal to its cost of capital. ❏ **TRUE** ❏ **FALSE**

2. Firms with a sales orientation focus on short-term sales volume and are less concerned with profits and long-run customer relationships. ❏ **TRUE** ❏ **FALSE**

3. A firm with a finance orientation focuses on research, development, and engineering and pays little attention to customer value. ❏ **TRUE** ❏ **FALSE**

4. The marketing offer is the total benefit package the firm provides to its customers. ❏ **TRUE** ❏ **FALSE**

5. Firms with an internal orientation are more likely to achieve integration because the shared value of serving customers promotes a common purpose. ❏ **TRUE** ❏ **FALSE**

....

MULTIPLE CHOICE QUESTIONS

1. All of the following represent critical questions required to be answered about a firm's business and market portfolio for Imperative 1 EXCEPT:

   a. In which businesses and markets shall we invest?
   b. From which businesses and markets shall we withdraw?
   c. Is the firm's market and financial performance reaching planned objectives?
   d. In which current businesses and markets shall we continue to invest?

2. The firm with a(n) _____ is typically less concerned with profits and long-run customer relationships.

   a. sales orientation
   b. operations orientation
   c. finance orientation
   d. technology orientation

3. Which of the following is NOT one of the marketing mix elements that comprise the basic building blocks of a firm's offer?

   a. product
   b. promotion
   c. position
   d. price

4. Which of the following four Principles of Marketing emphasizes competition?

   a. The Principle of Selectivity and Concentration
   b. The Principle of Customer Value
   c. The Principle of Differential Advantage
   d. The Principle of Integration

Answers on page 205

CHAPTER 2

THE VALUE
OF CUSTOMERS

CUSTOMERS ARE THE FIRM'S CORE ASSETS. By attracting, retaining, and growing customers, the firm makes profits today and promises profits tomorrow. We can measure the value that customers bring to the firm by means of customer lifetime value (CLV).

THE CHANGING VIEW

OLD WAY	NEW WAY
Accept that some customers are difficult to address	Strive to give customers consistently good experiences
Acquiring customers is critical	Retaining and growing profitable customers and acquiring new customers are critical
Customer databases nonexistent	Customer databases pivotal
Firm manages products	Firm manages customers
Firm should attract, retain, and grow all customers	Firm should *fire* some current customers and be selective in acquiring new customers
Fragmented information on customers	Sophisticated CRM systems and data mining
Measure product profitability	Measure customer profitability and customer lifetime value
Plant and equipment are the firm's core assets	Customers are the firm's core assets
Product and sales territory considerations dominate resource allocation	Customer and customer segment considerations dominate resource allocation
Product profitability drives incentive systems	Customer profitability drives incentive systems
Products are at the heart of firm decision-making	Customers are at the heart of firm decision-making
Zero or negative reward for customer loyalty	Loyalty incentives very common

CUSTOMER LIFETIME VALUE (CLV)

Customer lifetime value (CLV) depends on just three factors — profit margin (m), retention rate (r), and discount rate (d). **Profit margin** is the annual value the customer brings to the firm. CLV also takes into account profit margins the firm earns in future years. When the firm has many customers, **retention rate** is simply the number of customers at the end of the year, divided by the number of customers at the start of the year. Retention is the inverse of **defection** or **churn**. The **discount rate** allows us to combine present and future profit margins.

CALCULATING CUSTOMER LIFETIME VALUE (CLV)

In each year, a firm earns a portion of its CLV. In the first year, the firm earns CLV (1):

$$\text{CLV (1)} = m \times r/(1 + d)$$

Restating this simple expression in words, CLV (1) is:

- the *margin (m)* the firm earns in year 1,
- multiplied by the *retention rate (r)* — the probability that a customer at the start of the year will still be a customer at the end of the year,
- *discounted* back to the start of the year, using the term *1/(1+d)*. The *discount rate, d*, is the firm's cost of capital.

We simplify the calculation by assuming that each term — *margin (m), discount rate (d)*, and *retention rate (r)* — is constant year to year.

The **margin multiple** = $r/(1 + d - r)$, so that:

$$\text{CLV} = m \times r/(1 + d - r)$$

> ### *Marketing Question*
>
> How do you assess CLV for customers of Apple, Facebook. Google, Hershey, Nokia, Pfizer, and Walmart? If CLV is high — why? If CLV is low — why?

INCREASING CUSTOMER LIFETIME VALUE

The firm has only three, and only three, ways to increase CLV:

- Increase the profit margin (m) the firm earns from customers
- Increase customer retention rate (r) (reduce customer defection rate)
- Reduce discount rate (d)

INCREASE PROFIT MARGIN THE FIRM EARNS FROM CUSTOMERS

The firm has several options for raising CLV by increasing profit margins from current customers:

- **Customer selection.** Well-selected current customers provide a base level of profit margin.
- **Customer satisfaction and loyalty.** Well-served customers increase purchases over time.
- **Customization.** Targeted offers to defined segments provide greater customer value.
- **Pricing.** If customer satisfaction is high, the firm may be able to set higher prices.
- **Operating costs.** As the firm learns to serve customers, it reduces operating costs and may reap scale economies with individual customers.

In addition, satisfied customers may help the firm secure revenues from other customers:

- **Learning.** The firm learns by working closely with customers and becomes better able to attract new customers.
- **Network externalities.** In some markets, customers bring value to other customers.
- **Positive word of mouth and referrals.** Satisfied customers generate positive word of mouth and provide referrals to potential customers.
- **Signals.** Securing a high-profile customer may provide the firm with credibility among other potential customers.

Marketing Question

Suppose a firm's annual revenue growth goal was 15 percent. Consider two situations:

- Customer retention rate = 80 percent

- Customer retention rate = 95 percent

What would the firm's customer acquisition rate have to be in each case? What would be the implications for the firm?

INCREASE CUSTOMER RETENTION RATE — REDUCE CUSTOMER DEFECTION RATE

Customer retention rate has an important impact on CLV. A 5 percent increase in customer retention rate enhances CLV by over 50 percent in several industries.

HOW CUSTOMER RETENTION WORKS

As retention rate increases, the firm's steady-state market share increases. Indeed, relatively small differences in customer retention can lead to large differences in long-run market share. Further, at high retention rates, small increases in retention have a disproportionate impact on the average length of time (tenure) a customer stays with the firm. As customer tenure increases, the customer provides sales revenues and profit margins for a longer period.

ACQUIRING NEW CUSTOMERS

In order to attract new customers, the firm has to incur an **acquisition cost (AC)**; this must be part of the CLV calculation. Using the same approach as before, we account for the costs to acquire these new customers:

$$CLV = m \times r/(1 + d - r) - AC$$

The firm should acquire a customer if the first term in the CLV expression, $m \times r/(1 + d - r)$, is greater than the acquisition cost (AC). If the acquisition cost were greater, the firm would lose money by acquiring the customer. The actual cost to acquire a new customer varies widely by company and industry.

OPTIONS FOR ADDRESSING CUSTOMERS

Much of *Managing Marketing in the 21st Century* focuses on enhancing CLV from current customers and acquiring profitable new customers. Here, we identify a broad set of options.

FIGURE 2.1

APPROACHES TO IMPROVING CUSTOMER LIFETIME VALUE

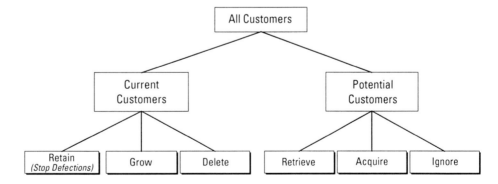

CURRENT CUSTOMERS

The firm has three options for current customers — retain, grow, and delete.

RETAIN

The firm's customer base is like a leaky bucket; the firm should plug its holes. By updating products and services to meet evolving customer needs and by taking other actions to bind customers more closely, the firm enhances satisfaction, increases loyalty, and reduces defections. Satisfied and delighted customers are more likely to continue buying than dissatisfied customers. On average, multiple-product customers have higher retention. Some firms budget **maintenance expenses** for extra services so as to offer current customers greater value. Maintenance expenses reduce the firm's profit margin from current customers, but they are often more cost-effective than having customers defect.

GROW

Satisfied customers may also be willing to buy more. The firm may increase customer margins by **cross-selling**. Amazon is a good Internet example of increasing revenues through cross-selling. Actually, Amazon has two types of marketing effort: Type 1 attracts customers to its website through targeted offerings; type 2 encourages visitors to explore the site for new items, driving multiple purchases and enhanced customer satisfaction.

DELETE

Some customers are not worth having. Most firms have unprofitable customers and should seriously consider ending these relationships, taking care to avoid potentially negative word of mouth.

POTENTIAL CUSTOMERS

The firm has three options for potential customers — retrieve, acquire, and ignore.

RETRIEVE

All firms have customers that defect; the prior relationship makes them **winback** opportunities. These customers are a special category because the firm often has information about them than about other potential customers. The firm knows (or can find out) what they purchased, what they spent, how they make decisions, why they left, and other data that can help the firm serve them again.

ACQUIRE

To reach sales and profit goals, most firms must acquire profitable new customers. Sometimes the firm seeks customers with similar characteristics to current customers — other times, it wants very different customers. The firm has four major approaches for acquiring customers:

- **Independent marketing activities.** Most firms use communications to reach potential customers and persuade them to buy their products and services.
- **Affiliations.** The firm makes formal or informal relationships with individuals or other organizations to feed it customers. Informal relationships are very common in the service sector.
- **Channel strategies.** Rather than approach potential customers directly, the firm works through third parties like agents, brokers, and distributors.
- **Firm and business-unit acquisitions.** Whenever the firm completes a merger or acquisition, it acquires customers, regardless of purpose.

IGNORE

The firm must decide on desirable customer characteristics and make investments in potential customers that bring positive CLV. By the same token, the firm should ignore customers that do not possess these favorable characteristics.

Marketing Question

Think of a local business. What approaches does it use to acquire customers? What alternative approaches could it implement?

BEING SELECTIVE ABOUT CUSTOMERS

Many customers bring value to the firm, but some do not. Quantifying the *value of a customer* is important in understanding how to identify valuable customers, and develop options to address unwelcome customers.

CUSTOMER PROFITABILITY

Most firms invest heavily in sophisticated accounting systems and data analysis tools that help answer questions like:

- Are our current products profitable?
- Shall we discontinue this old product and, if so, when?
- Shall we introduce a new product?

By contrast, few firms can answer equivalent questions about customers. This failure is especially critical in multi-business and multinational firms. Profitability data typically reside in individual businesses and geographies whose systems do not interface with one another. Several different businesses and/or geographics may have the same customer, but not know it! A firm's inability to measure customer profitability is in sharp contrast to treating customers as assets and CLV.

Firms use a variety of methods and systems to gather and assess data relevant to customer activity and profitability, notably customer relationship management *(CRM)* systems. When firms examine revenues, costs, and profits by customer, they often find an **80:20 rule**: 80 percent of revenues come from 20 percent of customers. Many firms have installed strategic (or key) account management systems to serve their most important customers.

The converse analogue of the 80:20 rule is the **20:80 rule**; 20 percent of revenues come from 80 percent of customers. This rule raises two critical yet related questions:

- What does it cost the firm to serve these customers?
- Is it profitable to serve these customers? If not, what action should the firm take?

Firms with this sort of revenue and profit distribution have three major options for addressing low-profit or unprofitable customers:

- **Invest for the future.** Two types of customer may have significant potential: small organizations that may grow, and large organizations where the firm is currently unsuccessful.
- **Reduce resource commitment.** The firm may develop a new communications strategy like switching an on-the-road sales force to telesales, or using Internet and e-mail approaches. Another option is to hand off customers to third parties like distributors, agents, brokers, contract sales forces, and value-added resellers.
- **Fire customers!** The firm stops selling to loss-making customers with little potential.

Marketing Question

Which companies do you believe affirmatively seek to fire and/or reject customers? Are they successful in pursuing these activities? What firms inadvertently fire and/or reject *good* customers?

CUSTOMER SUITABILITY

The firm may cease doing business with a current customer or forgo a relationship with a potential customer for other reasons:

- **Capacity constraints.** The firm may have insufficient ability — expertise, physical capacity, financial resources — to serve all its customers.
- **Competition.** The customer is a current or potential competitor.
- **Evolving strategy.** If the firm shifts direction, drops products, or divests a business, it sheds customers as a byproduct of its strategic change.
- **Foreclosing options.** The customer prohibits the firm from serving other customers.

- **Impact on the offer.** In many service businesses, fellow customers are integral to the offer. Bad behavior by some customers reduces the value for all customers.
- **Impact on the firm's reputation.** A firm/customer relationship negatively affects the firm's brand image.
- **Instability.** The customer may be profitable but purchase widely varying amounts, causing organizational dislocation.
- **Non-payer.** This customer would be profitable if it paid, but it doesn't.
- **Potential costs.** Future costs of doing business with this customer are too high.

CUSTOMER RELATIONSHIP MANAGEMENT

A customer relationship comprises the series of over-time interactions or *touch points* between the customer and the firm. **Customer relationship management (CRM)** (relationship marketing) is a synthesis of marketing, customer service, and quality management that manages these touch points. More precisely, CRM is the ongoing process of identifying and creating new value with individual customers and sharing these benefits over a lifetime of association with them. Three issues are crucial for success:

- **Objectives.** The firm must be very clear about CRM system objectives. Without good direction, the firm cannot select from myriad initiatives, and costs can easily spiral out of control.
- **Customer benefits.** The CRM system must provide benefits to customers — new products and services, high customer service levels — and to the firm. The CRM system must drive *mutually* beneficial relationships with customers.
- **Technology.** Many people believe extensive databases and advanced information technology underpin CRM systems. Of course, technology, customer databases, and **data-mining** often play important roles. But CRM is not about technology. CRM is about forming *mutually beneficial relationships* with customers.

DEVELOPING A CRM SYSTEM

Customer databases for effective CRM systems must be accessible, accurate, complete, consistent, current, relevant, secure, and structured. Many firms spend highly to develop customer databases. Key characteristics of successful systems are:

- **Customer characteristics.** Demographic data independent of the firm: B2C — name, gender, age, family size (birth dates), and address. B2B — sales revenues, number of employees, age of organization, industry, decision-makers, influencers.
- **Customer responses to firm decisions.** Purchases following sales promotions, direct marketing offers, and price changes — also perceptions and preferences (from research).
- **Customer contact history.** B2C — phone calls for product information, customer service requests. B2B — deliveries, sales calls, technical service calls.
- **Customer purchase history.** What was purchased — by SKU; when; by what method — cash or credit; through what intermediary (if any); what price and/or price discounts; how and when delivered. Data should include firm profit margin per purchase.
- **Customer value to the firm.** Data for assessing customer lifetime value (CLV), like purchase history. The database should be sufficiently flexible to follow individuals and track life changes.

Marketing Question

CVS/Caremart (CC) is the U.S.'s largest single buyer and dispenser of prescription drugs. What actions could CC take to help reduce national healthcare costs?

CONTROL OF, AND ACCESS TO, THE CUSTOMER DATABASE

Control of, and access to, the customer database are critical issues. A well-developed customer database is valuable to the firm and others. Many firms earn large revenues by selling customer data to non-competitors but these actions pose major consumer privacy issues.

ASSESSING THE VALUE OF CUSTOMERS AND DESIGNING FIRM ACTIONS

The firm implementing CRM well acts with significantly greater focus. The firm estimates profitability and CLV for each customer. The firm anticipates key customer events and initiates action. The more comprehensive the customer database, and the more creative the firm, the more valuable will be its initiative.

EVENT-DRIVEN MARKETING

Firms experienced in CRM identify events in their customers' lives that provide communication opportunities to enhance the relationship and/or make sales. Event types include those that:

- Do not require a customer decision but are often valuable for activating straightforward business processes, like credit card expiry.
- Provide the firm communication opportunities, like the end of a contract.
- Represent significant changes in customer life stage, like marriage.

CUSTOMER LOYALTY PROGRAMS

Loyalty programs are a central part of many CRM systems. Well-designed programs play a major role in retaining customers. All loyalty programs have a similar structure: customers earn rewards by purchasing goods and services. Program designers must consider value both for the customer and the firm to establish a successful program.

VALUE OF REWARDS PROGRAMS TO CUSTOMERS. There are several design considerations:

- **Rate of earning.** Should the customer earn the same points for each dollar spent? Or should she earn more points per dollar as she nears the goal?
- **Aspirational value of the reward.** Two rewards can have the same cash value, but different psychological value.
- **Cash value of the reward.** The reward should offer real economic value.
- **Deterministic or probabilistic rewards.** Many reward programs are *deterministic* — the customer accumulates *points*, then collects the reward. In *probabilistic* programs, the customer wins a large reward, or zero.
- **Ease of collecting the reward.** The customer must be able to redeem the reward.
- **Length of time to earn the reward.** Should the program have smaller rewards earned frequently or larger, delayed rewards?
- **Rewards based on the firm's product or services, or a broad variety.** Some programs reward customers with their own products and services. The alternative is to partner and offer many different rewards, like AmEx's Membership Rewards Program.
- **Soft versus hard rewards.** *Hard rewards*, just discussed, are denominated in dollars and cents or translatable points. *Soft rewards* include toll-free information numbers, restaurant seating, theater ticket availability, and hotel room and airline seat upgrades.
- **Type of reward.** Should it be *cash*? Or *products and services*?

Marketing Question

Many students have low incomes. But your educational investment may lead to high future income. Which firms understand that and actively seek your business with an eye to your future? How do they do so? Which firms seem oblivious?

VALUE OF THE REWARDS PROGRAM TO THE FIRM. A well-designed loyalty program decreases customer defection and increases customer retention, and enhances share of wallet. Specific benefits for the firm include:

- Creates barriers for competitors.
- Gains insight into customer behavior.
- Lowers costs to serve loyal customers.
- Makes loyal customers less price sensitive.
- Encourages loyal customers to spend more.
- Stimulates loyal customers to spread positive word of mouth.
- Increases sales via purchase acceleration as customers approach the goal.

TRUE / FALSE QUESTIONS

1. Retention is the inverse of defection or churn. ❏ **TRUE** ❏ **FALSE**

2. As retention rate increases, the firm's steady-state market share decreases. ❏ **TRUE** ❏ **FALSE**

3. The higher the retention rate, the greater the impact on market share for a given increase in retention rate. ❏ **TRUE** ❏ **FALSE**

4. The 80:20 rule means that 80 percent of the firm's revenues come from 20 percent of its customers. ❏ **TRUE** ❏ **FALSE**

5. The firm should continue selling to all customers since revenue generation and profitability are synonymous. ❏ **TRUE** ❏ **FALSE**

6. Many rewards are probabilistic. In these, the customer accumulates points, then collects the reward. ❏ **TRUE** ❏ **FALSE**

MULTIPLE CHOICE QUESTIONS

1. Which of the following is the correct formula for customer lifetime value?

   a. $CLV = m \times r / (1 + d - r)$
   b. $CLV = m - r / (1 \times d)$
   c. $CLV = m / r (1 - d)$
   d. $CLV = m + r / (1 + d + r)$

2. Which of the following is NOT one of the three options for current customers in enhancing customer lifetime value?

   a. increasing retention rate
   b. increasing profit margins
   c. decreasing discount rate
   d. increasing churn rate

3. All of the following are options for potential customers in enhancing customer lifetime value EXCEPT:

   a. retrieving customers
   b. acquiring customers
   c. ignoring customers
   d. growing customers

4. Which of the following is NOT one of the three major options for addressing low-profit or unprofitable customers?

   a. devising a new business model for low-profit or unprofitable customers
   b. investing in customer's future potential
   c. reducing resource investment
   d. firing customers

5. All of the following are reasons a firm may cease doing business with a current customer or forgo a relationship with the potential customer EXCEPT:

   a. customer standardization requirements
   b. non-payer
   c. foreclosing options
   d. impact on firm's reputation

6. Which of the following is NOT a critical issue for success in customer relationship management programs?

   a. objectives
   b. just-in-time inventory
   c. customer benefits
   d. technology

Answers on page 205

SECTION II
FUNDAMENTAL INSIGHTS
FOR STRATEGIC
MARKETING

Managing Marketing in the 21ˢᵗ Century

SECTION I: MARKETING AND THE FIRM

CHAPTER 1
Introduction to Managing Marketing

CHAPTER 2
The Value of Customers

SECTION II: FUNDAMENTAL INSIGHTS FOR STRATEGIC MARKETING

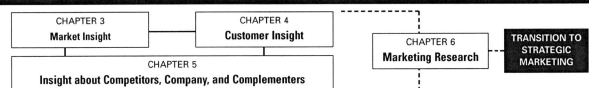

CHAPTER 3
Market Insight

CHAPTER 4
Customer Insight

CHAPTER 5
Insight about Competitors, Company, and Complementers

CHAPTER 6
Marketing Research

TRANSITION TO STRATEGIC MARKETING

SECTION III: STRATEGIC MARKETING

IMPERATIVE 1
Determine and Recommend Which Markets to Address

CHAPTER 7
Identifying and Choosing Opportunities

IMPERATIVE 2
Identify and Target Market Segments

CHAPTER 8
Market Segmentation and Targeting

IMPERATIVE 3
Set Strategic Direction and Positioning

CHAPTER 9
Market Strategy — Integrating Firm Efforts for Marketing Success

CHAPTER 10
Managing through the Life Cycle

CHAPTER 11
Managing Brands

SECTION IV: IMPLEMENTING THE MARKET STRATEGY

IMPERATIVE 4
Design the Market Offer

PART A: PROVIDING CUSTOMER VALUE

PART B: COMMUNICATING CUSTOMER VALUE

PART C: DELIVERING CUSTOMER VALUE

PART D: GETTING PAID FOR CUSTOMER VALUE

CHAPTER 12
Managing the Product Line

CHAPTER 15
Integrated Marketing Communications

CHAPTER 18
Distribution Decisions

CHAPTER 19
Critical Underpinnings of Pricing Decisions

CHAPTER 13
Managing Services and Customer Service

CHAPTER 16
Mass and Digital Communication

CHAPTER 20
Setting Prices

CHAPTER 14
Developing New Products

CHAPTER 17
Directing and Managing the Field Sales Effort

IMPERATIVE 5
Secure Support from Other Functions

CHAPTER 21
Ensuring the Firm Implements the Market Offer as Planned

IMPERATIVE 6
Monitor and Control

CHAPTER 22
Monitoring and Controlling Firm Functioning and Performance

SECTION V: SPECIAL MARKETING TOPICS

CHAPTER 23
International, Regional, and Global Marketing

CHAPTER 3
MARKET INSIGHT

DEFINING THE MARKET IS A FUNDAMENTAL BUT TRICKY MARKETING CHALLENGE. The four critical areas where the firm must seek market insight are: market structure, market and product evolution, industry forces, and environmental forces. The firm must be concerned with both the situation today, and any trends that will affect the future market.

THE CHANGING VIEW

OLD WAY	NEW WAY
Change as evolutionary	Change as revolutionary
Change is a problem	Change is an opportunity
Competitive advantages are long-lasting	Competitive advantages are quickly dissipated
Firms operate independently	Firms are networked
Focus on national and regional economies	Understand the integrated global economy
Future predictable — all that's needed is good forecasting	Future not completely predictable — need to be flexible
Imitation is common	Innovation is essential
Life cycles are fixed and constrained	Life cycles are dynamic and subject to firm influence
Reacting to environmental change is sufficient	Proactively influencing environmental change is a reasonable goal
The firm has ample time to recoup front-end investment	Peak profit-margin period arrives sooner, and disappears earlier

MARKET STRUCTURE

We use three separate concepts to describe **market structure**: the market, products/services serving the market, and the firm's own products.

....

THE MARKET

Markets comprise customers — people and organizations — who require goods and services to satisfy their needs. Basic customer needs like food, clothing, and shelter are enduring; many different offerings satisfy these needs. Other needs, like entertainment, tend to be more transitory.

Marketing Question

Select a product and industry with which you are familiar. Define the market at different levels. How much more broadly could you go (as Mark Cuban with the Mavs) and still maintain a focus? Illustrate your answer similarly to Figure 3.2 in the main text.

A broad approach to market definition ensures against **marketing myopia**, the risk of defining a *market* too narrowly at the onset because of biases or insufficient data. Defining the market broadly provides greater scope in the firm's opportunity search. More generally, a market definition that focuses on customer needs reinforces an external orientation and offsets tendencies toward internal orientations. But working with a broad market definition is not easy. The broader the market definition, the greater the challenge of gathering data.

PRODUCTS SERVING THE MARKET

A useful categorization of product offerings is *product class*, *product form*, *product line*, and *product item*.

- **Product class.** In any *market*, several *product classes* serve customer needs. Each product class provides distinct customer benefits. Several firms typically offer products in each product class. Example: computers.

- **Product form.** Several *product forms* comprise each product class. Competition is typically more intense among product forms than among product classes. Several firms typically offer products in each product form. Example: Laptop computers.

THE FIRM'S PRODUCTS

Product classes and product forms embrace products from all competitors. One firm may offer products in multiple product classes; another firm may specialize in just one or two product forms. IBM offers products/services in most (but not all) product forms in the information systems product class. By contrast, Gateway offers only PCs (IBM no longer offers PCs). When we consider the individual firm, we speak of product lines and product items.

- **Product line.** A group of related products that a single firm offers. Gateway offers a product line of desktop PCs and a product line of laptop PCs.

- **Product item.** A subset of the product line. A product item is uniquely identified, like having a specific size and color. The firm offers various product items to meet different customer needs. Gateway offers desktops and laptops, each with unique model numbers.

FACTORS AFFECTING MARKET SIZE

Current and potential market sizes are important data for evaluating firm opportunities. Before entering a market, the firm should know the numbers of current and potential customers and their purchasing power. For B2C markets, it should consider population size, population mix, geographic population shifts, income and income distribution, and age distribution.

- **Population size.** World population exceeds 7 billion. Increasing by 200,000 people daily, by 2030, population will exceed 8 billion. Population and population growth are unevenly distributed across nations.

- **Population mix.** In many developed countries, immigration drives population-mix changes. Most labor migration (legal and illegal) is from less-developed countries to more-developed countries. Frequently, provider and receiver countries are geographically close. Reduced mobility barriers in the European Union (EU) increase population shifts. In some ethnic and/or language groups, immigrants and their offspring represent significant marketing opportunities.

- **Geographic population shifts.** Generally, as national income grows, people leave rural areas for urban areas. Then urban areas become overcrowded. In developed countries, a more recent trend is *exurban* growth — return to rural communities. Desire for less crowding, a slower life pace, and advances in information technology are enabling this

Marketing Question

Suppose you had been a senior marketing executive at Kodak in the mid-1990s; how would you have defined Kodak's market? How would you change this definition today?

Marketing Question

Think about the firm and product you selected earlier (p. 23). What factors help determine market size — population (size, mix, geographic shift), income distribution, and/or age distribution? What other factors help determine market size in three to five years?

trend. Population shifts often follow the sun. In the U.S., the Northeast is losing population to the Southeast and Southwest.

- **Income and income distribution.** Around the world, income disparities are enormous. Several countries now surpass the U.S. in per capita income. The vast majority of countries have GNP per capita less than $1,000. Income disparities are also often large, especially within less developed countries, where small elite minorities control most national wealth.

- **Age distribution.** Median ages are increasing in both developed and developing countries. Major drivers are decreasing birth rates and family size and increasing life expectancy. These shifts have enormous implications for consumer marketers. Other important market-size drivers include marriage, marrying age, divorce and remarriage, family size, births, infant and adult mortality, and workforce composition. These variables can often help the firm make good market-size predictions.

MARKET AND PRODUCT EVOLUTION

Life cycles are the most common means for describing the evolution of markets and products — product classes, product forms, product lines, and product items. Understanding life-cycle phenomena helps the firm predict future market conditions and develop robust strategies. Typically, we partition life cycles into five phases or stages: introduction, early growth, growth, maturity, and decline.

THE FAMILY OF LIFE CYCLES

Life cycles fall into a simple hierarchy based on longevity and demand. *Market* life cycles last longest — generally, the firm has little impact on market life cycles. *Product-class* and *product-form* life cycles are each shorter than the market life cycle — understanding these two life cycles is helpful in developing market strategy. By investing in its product entries, the firm often affects these life cycles.

Product-item and *product-line* life cycles are critical for product and brand managers as they offer important performance data by product line and product item. The firm's actions greatly impact these life-cycles; they are shorter than product-class and product-form life cycles and come in many different shapes. But because they provide little insight into competitor activity, they are not helpful for drawing strategic implications.

PRODUCT-FORM LIFE CYCLES

The firm gains the greatest insight into market and product evolution by examining product forms. Although product classes compete with one another, competition both within and across product forms is typically more intense. We typically categorize product-form life cycles into five stages:

- **Introduction.** Sales volume is initially low.
- **Early growth.** Sales volume grows at an increasing rate.
- **Late growth.** Sales volume grows, but at a decreasing rate.
- **Maturity.** Sales volume averages about the same rate as GNP.
- **Decline.** Sales volume eventually declines.

STAGE 1: INTRODUCTION. Product introduction frequently follows many years of R&D and reflects the first market entry/entries by leading firms. Uncertainty characterizes introduction as suppliers struggle to build profitable volume. Introduction requires significant educational effort, and this stage may last many years. But fierce competition, increased innovation, and customer willingness to try new products are shortening this stage.

STAGE 2: EARLY GROWTH. Many products do not reach early growth, but survivor sales revenues grow at an increasing rate. As competitors struggle for market position, new distribution channels open up, and promotional effort remains high. The focus shifts to differentiation and selective demand based on features, functionality, and customer perceptions. In early growth, many firms increase sales volume and work at managing costs.

STAGE 3: LATE GROWTH. By late growth, many uncertainties that dominated introduction are largely resolved. Sales continue to increase, but the growth rate slows. Strong competitors initiate tough actions to maintain historic sales patterns, and force weaker entrants to withdraw. The distribution infrastructure is usually well developed, and price is a major competitive weapon, squeezing distributor margins.

STAGE 4: MATURITY. Slow growth or flat year-to-year sales characterize maturity. Most sales are to repeat and loyal users. Because competitive situations vary widely, the firm must secure deep market insight. Some markets are concentrated; others are fragmented.

- **Concentrated markets.** Market leaders often enjoy entry barriers like economies of scale, brand preference, and/or distribution-channel dominance. Market positions that firms achieve by early maturity often survive for many years. Leaders get into trouble when they fail to innovate new products and processes and do not reduce costs.

- **Fragmented markets.** No firm has large market share. Fragmentation generally occurs because of some combination of low entry barriers, high exit barriers, regulation, diverse market needs, and high transportation costs.

STAGE 5: DECLINE. Maturity may last many years, but eventually sales turn down. Firms often raise prices to cover costs as sales drop, but sales decline further, in a vicious cycle. Marketing efforts should target remaining customers. Firms with good cost management and a core of loyal price-insensitive buyers can be quite profitable.

The product-form life cycle is a useful framework, but two points are important:

- **Life-cycle shape.** A product's specific sales trajectory depends on several factors including underlying customer demand, product quality and consistency, and the overall commitment of resources by participating firms. In general, life cycles are shortening.

- **Profit curves.** Profit curves do not mirror sales curves. Margins are greatest in early growth — then drop in late growth and maturity. Do not confuse profit margin with gross profit. Gross profit may be greater later in the cycle — lower profit margins, but higher volume.

> ### Marketing Question
>
> Think about the firm and product you selected earlier (p. 23). In what life-cycle stage is the product form? How did you make this assessment? What are the implications for the firm's product strategy in the next three to five years?

INDUSTRY FORCES

The **five-forces model** used by marketing professionals identifies the pressures firms face: current direct competitors, new direct entrants, indirect competitors, suppliers, and buyers.

CURRENT DIRECT COMPETITORS

A firm's *current direct competitors* offer customers similar benefits with similar products, technology, and/or business models. Current direct competitors are the competitive *status quo*, the traditional rivalry between established players. Typically, managers in rival firms know their traditional competitors well. They observe their actions and performance, their successes and failures. They have good insight into their strengths and weaknesses and likely strategic moves.

Marketing Question

Suppose you were advising SABMiller, owner of the Miller brand. How would you react to the joining together of AmBev, Interbrew, and Anheuser-Busch to form Anheuser-Busch InBev (ABI)?

Current direct competitors may be traditional or may be created through acquisitions and divestitures, mergers, and leveraged buyouts that continually change the firm's competitive landscape.

- **Traditional direct competitors** fight according to *established rules of the game.* In mature markets, one firm rarely gains advantage quickly; rather, an improved position typically results from long-run sustained effort.
- **Acquisitions and divestitures.** Suppose one of your competitors or an outside firm acquires a second competitor. Your competitor has changed. Its objectives, strategy, action programs, and available resources will most likely all be different.
- **Merger.** In a merger, two entities combine as *equal* partners to create a stronger firm. By pooling strengths and mitigating weaknesses, the new entity is often a tougher competitor with capabilities that outstrip either former firm.
- **Leveraged buyouts (LBOs).** Sometimes firms rationalize their portfolios and *spin off* business units; typically, LBOs incur heavy debt as the price for independence. Lacking corporate resources, the now-independent unit may struggle. But it may also become a more nimble and tough competitor.

NEW DIRECT ENTRANTS

New direct entrants' products and services are similar to the firm's — but previously they did not compete. Entry barriers significantly affect market entry by new firms, but they may emerge from many sources.

- **Firm employees.** In some industries, firm employees pose a significant competitive threat. They may develop new business ideas and/or technologies the firm will not fund and leave to pursue them.
- **Geographic expansion.** New direct competitors are often profitable, well-capitalized firms from a different geography. They have solid strengths and cost advantages but may lack market knowledge and customer relationships. They may use superior cost positions to support low price strategies and aggressively seek market share.
- **Networks.** A network is a group of firms and/or individuals that collaborate using their combined talents and resources. Networks are very flexible and change composition as requirements evolve.
- **New sales and distribution channels.** Firms that develop new distribution channels can pose significant challenges to traditional players. Strong firms that add channels also heighten competition.
- **Start-up entry**. A startup is unencumbered by the *status quo;* flexibility can make it a potent competitor. By contrast, the incumbent firm may have old facilities, old technology, old processes, and/or an established organization and personnel set in their ways.
- **Strategic alliances.** When two firms pool resources, the strategic alliance may be stronger than either firm separately. Of course, partnerships often fail — partner objectives diverge, and/or one partner fails to provide agreed-upon resources.

INDIRECT COMPETITORS

Indirect competitors and the firm offer customers similar *benefits/values,* but *indirect competitors provide them in a significantly different way.* These *functional substitutes* often appear as different product forms or product classes. Indirect competitors often attack from different industry sectors; incumbents sometimes ignore them.

SUPPLIERS

Suppliers provide the firm's inputs. Typically, pressure increases as the supplier's importance increases — like providing a critical product or a large percentage of purchases. Pressure may also arise if the supplier's brand is attractive to firm customers. Supplier pressure may also lead to higher prices, poor service, and/or poor delivery. The most severe supplier threat is **forward integration** — the supplier becomes a new direct competitor by conducting operations the firm currently performs.

BUYERS

A firm with many small customers faces little buyer pressure but a small number of large customers can exert tremendous pressure. Buyer pressure typically increases as market share increases. Firm margins may shrink when powerful customers demand price discounts and expensive extra services. The most severe buyer threat is **backward integration** — the buyer becomes a new direct competitor by conducting operations the firm currently performs.

MULTIPLE INDUSTRY FORCES

Multi-business firms face multiple industry forces, but their individual businesses may also face multiple industry forces, notably when they participate in *two-sided markets* — the firm faces two or more distinct buyer groups, like viewers and advertisers for TV stations. Also, sometimes a firm can simultaneously be a direct competitor, indirect competitor, supplier, and buyer to another organization.

ENVIRONMENTAL FORCES

Environmental forces affect the firm and other industry participants. These **PESTLE** forces — *political, economic, sociocultural, technological, legal/regulatory* and *environmental (physical)* — and industry forces relate with one another. Some PESTLE forces affect individual businesses; others impact the firm as a whole.

POLITICAL

Governments set the frameworks for regulators to develop rules for business. Governments (federal, state, local) also participate as buyers and sometimes as sellers. Typically, governments intervene in economies to pursue political ends and enhance consumer welfare by creating a *level playing field.*

ECONOMIC

The country's economic well-being influences market demand. High inflation, high and rising interest rates, falling share prices, and a depreciating currency point to an unhealthy economy. High savings rates are generally positive, but too high rates lower consumption. Because *expectations* influence spending patterns, evaluating direction and rate of change are critical. Because of increased globalization, individual country economies are more closely linked than ever.

Marketing Question

Think about the firm and product you selected earlier, p. 23. Identify: (1) current direct competitors, (2) potential new direct entrants, (3) indirect competitors, (4) suppliers, and (5) buyers. In the next few years: (a) What changes do you expect in current direct competitors? (b) What positive and negative implications for the firm may occur from acquisitions, mergers, and leveraged buyouts? (c) How should relationships with the firm's suppliers and buyers affect its strategy?

Marketing Question

Suppose your firm transfers you to a marketing position in Brazil (France, Japan, Saudi Arabia, or your choice). What issues will you focus on to avoid professional and personal missteps?

SOCIOCULTURAL

Culture is "the distinctive customs, achievements, products, outlook, etc., of a society or a group; the way of life of a society or group." Culture is learned early in life, largely by influence from family, schools, and religious institutions; cultural norms are resistant to change.

CULTURAL GROUPS. A cultural group may inhabit a nation-state, a geographic region within a nation, or a multinational region, or may comprise a people, regardless of geographic location like the Armenian, Jewish, and Kurdish diasporas. A person may belong to several cultural groups that may comprise different subcultures, with each reflecting both group-culture and subcultural elements.

LOCALIZATION AND GLOBALIZATION. An important contemporary cultural issue is the tension between localization and globalization. Some groups seek identities based on factors like religion and ethnicity. Global and local trends have a profound impact on firms and the products they produce and sell.

TECHNOLOGICAL

The pace of technological change continues to accelerate. Some technological innovations are industry-specific; others, like the Internet, affect the entire economy. Moore's law says the transistor density on computer chips and microprocessor speed double every 18–24 months; improving price/performance ratios are transforming industry and commerce. Technological change can be either sustaining or disruptive.

- **Sustaining technologies** are often incremental. They improve performance for current products on dimensions that *existing* customers value.
- **Disruptive technologies** bring new and very different value propositions. They change customer behavior by finding new applications and initially a few new-to-the-market customers. Disruptive technologies spawn products that threaten and change entire industries.

Current suppliers tend to ignore disruptive technologies or at least underfund them. Two factors seem crucial:

- **Inferior performance.** Early on, the disruptive technology's performance is inferior to the current technology, and products lack critical attributes that current technology customers need.
- **Firm rewards.** Initial expectations of volume and profit margin in the disruptive technology are less attractive than continued investment to serve current customers.

LEGAL/REGULATORY

The legal framework (LF) is the rules for business. It aims to protect societal interests, regulate market power, hinder collusion, and stop deceptive practices. LFs differ across countries, but generally govern mergers and acquisitions, capital movements, consumer protection, and employment conditions.

ENVIRONMENTAL (PHYSICAL)

Natural and man-made forces coexist in an uneasy equilibrium. Firms face increasing pressure from governments, environmentalists, single-issue advocacy groups, and the public at large to assume greater environmental responsibility for their products, packaging, and production systems.

The Internet

The Internet has changed the way society works and functions. The Internet is an efficient distribution channel, interactive communications tool, marketplace, and information system. The Internet reduces transactions costs; Adwords and Facebook ensure that contextually appropriate ads reach targeted customers. Sellers reach more buyers on the Internet; buyers access more suppliers. Perhaps the Internet's greatest impact will be in industries where products can be digitized. The most important recent trends are the growth of Facebook, LinkedIn, Twitter, and others, and the Internet's interface with mobile devices like cell phones and tablet computers.

INTERACTIONS AMONG PESTLE FORCES

Each PESTLE force — political, economic, sociocultural, technological, legal, and environmental (physical) — interacts with its sister forces. These interconnected forces form the firm's environmental panorama and in turn interact with industry forces. The Internet, a technological force, has major implications for sociocultural and political forces, especially in countries with little political freedom, and has major implications for industry forces.

THE MANAGERIAL PROCESS ENVIRONMENT

Executives use *intellectual capital* (IC) — concepts, frameworks, ideas, and tools — to lead and manage their firms. IC evolves via research efforts at business schools, the culling of consulting experience, and learning by practicing managers. IC spreads through the business environment rapidly; in recent years, firms have adopted benchmarking, best practice sharing, branding, customer relationship management (CRM), experience curves, market share/profitability relationships, outsourcing, policy matrices, portfolio models, positioning, strategic objectives, re-engineering, shareholder value, and total quality management (TQM).

Marketing Question

Consider the firm/product you selected earlier, p. 23. How does each PESTLE force — political, economic, sociocultural, technological, legal/regulatory, and environmental (physical) — affect the product or market? What changes do you expect in the next three to five years? Will these be positive or negative for the firm?

TRUE / FALSE QUESTIONS

1. Market life cycles are the longest in the family of life cycles. ❏ **TRUE** ❏ **FALSE**

2. Most new products reach early growth and level off in the maturity stage of the product life cycle.
   ❏ **TRUE** ❏ **FALSE**

3. Indirect competitors often attack from different industry sectors, and incumbents sometimes ignore them. ❏ **TRUE** ❏ **FALSE**

4. The most severe supplier threat is backward integration. ❏ **TRUE** ❏ **FALSE**

5. Disruptive technologies spawn products that threaten and change entire industries. ❏ **TRUE** ❏ **FALSE**

MULTIPLE CHOICE QUESTIONS

1. A firm has the least amount of impact on which of the following families of life cycle?

   a. product-form
   b. market life cycle
   c. product-class
   d. product item

2. Which of the following stages of the product life cycle is most characterized by uncertainty?

   a. introduction
   b. early growth
   c. maturity
   d. decline

3. In which of the following stages of the product life cycle are sales mostly to repeat and loyal customers?

   a. introduction
   b. early growth
   c. maturity
   d. decline

4. In a(n) _____, two entities combine as equal partners to create a stronger firm.

   a. acquisition
   b. merger
   c. leveraged buyout
   d. backward integration

5. Which of the following is NOT one of the PESTLE forces?

   a. political
   b. sociocultural
   c. technological
   d. economic
   e. localization

Answers on page 205

CHAPTER 4
CUSTOMER
INSIGHT

THE FIRM CAN ONLY ATTRACT, RETAIN, AND GROW CUSTOMERS if it provides them with value. To deliver value the firm must focus on three elements of securing good customer insight. Who are the customers? What do customers need and want? How do customers buy?

THE CHANGING VIEW

OLD WAY	NEW WAY
Basic customer understanding is sufficient	Sophisticated and timely customer insight is critical
Cognitive bias regarding customer insight	Broader view of customer behavior
Customer insight mainly applied in consumer packaged goods	Customer insight applied in many domains: product and service, public and nonprofit, nation states, politics, and personal careers
Customers passive	Customers pro-active and interactive; want to be informed and engaged
Customers uninformed and accepting	Customers well-informed and demanding
Domestic view of customers is sufficient	Global view of customers essential
Focus on customers only	Focus also on organizational stakeholders and other influencers
Marketing concepts apply to consumers as buyers	Marketing concepts apply both to consumers and organizations as buyers
Narrow view of customers — like direct customers only, or consumers only	Multi-tiered, more complex view of customers
Supplier power dominates	Customer power dominates

WHO ARE THE CUSTOMERS?

Identifying customers is the crucial first step in securing **customer insight**. *A customer is any person or organization, in the channel of distribution or decision (excluding competitors), whose*

Marketing Question

UPS makes offers to mail-room personnel; shipping, customer service, and logistics managers; CFOs; and CEOs. If you were developing a message for the CFO, what needs would you highlight? If you focused on the shipping manager, how might your message differ?

actions can affect the purchase of the firm's products and services. This definition reflects the fact that:

- Both organizations — *macro level*, and individuals — *micro level*, are called customers.
- **Customer** roles in purchase decisions include influencers and decision-makers.
- The firm should consider both *current customers* and *potential customers*.
- *Direct customers* pay the firm for its products and services, but *indirect customers* — customers of direct customers (and of other indirect customers) — frequently influence purchases.
- Some *two-sided markets* comprise customers that *pay* for products, and customers that receive *free* products.

MACRO-LEVEL CUSTOMERS AND MICRO-LEVEL CUSTOMERS

To gain customer insight, the firm must understand how customers fit into the buying process. *Macro-level customers* are the organizational units — manufacturers, wholesalers, retailers, government entities (B2B) — and families (B2C) that purchase products and services. *Micro-level customers* are individuals within the macro-level customer that influence purchase or have decision-making authority. When micro-level customers jointly make a purchase decision, they act as a **decision-making unit (DMU)**.

ROLES IN THE PURCHASE DECISION

Both macro-level and micro-level customers may play several different roles in purchase decisions. *Macro-level customers* like distributors and retailers *purchase* firm products; they also *sell*, *deliver*, *store*, and/or *service* them. Micro-level customers play similar roles in both B2C and B2B purchase decisions:

- **Buyer.** Has formal power to make the purchase, like company purchasing agents.
- **Coach.** Helps the firm navigate the customer's organization and advises how to address influencers and decision-makers.
- **Decision-maker.** Has the formal power to make the purchase decision.
- **Gatekeeper.** Has the power to impede access to decision-makers and influencers.
- **Influencer.** The decision-maker values the influencer's opinion. Two special types of influencer are spoilers and champions.
  - **Champions/Sponsors** are the opposite of spoilers. They promote the firm's interests, based on positive experiences with the supplier or personal relationships.
  - **Spoilers**, like disgruntled former employees, try to prevent the customer from purchasing firm product.
- **Information provider.** Provides the firm with important information about the customer.
- **Initiator.** Recognizes a problem and sets the purchas process in motion.
- **Specifier.** Exercises influence indirectly by providing expertise like setting specifications.
- **User.** Has little direct role in the purchase decision, but often has veto power.

VARIETY AND EVOLUTION OF PURCHASE DECISION ROLES. Because macro-level customers make many different types of purchases, DMU composition typically varies markedly from one decision to another.

CURRENT CUSTOMERS AND POTENTIAL CUSTOMERS

Current customers provide revenues and profits today; customer retention has enormous value for the firm. But the firm must also identify potential customers.

DIRECT CUSTOMERS AND INDIRECT CUSTOMERS

Typically, the firm's direct customers exchange money for its products and services. Many indirect customers buy the firm's products from these direct customers or from other indirect customers. Sometimes direct customers are distributors or retailers, or end users that buy and use the firm's finished products. Sometimes the firm *may not know* its indirect customers and hence have little insight into the values and benefits they seek.

WHAT DO CUSTOMERS NEED AND WANT?

The firm attracts and retains customers by delivering value to satisfy their needs. **Customer value** equates to the value in the firm's offer, less the customer's cost and/or efforts expended to secure the offer, less the customer's monetary, time, effort, and emotional costs. Two sorts of firm action are important:

- Make offers of value to satisfy customers' needs
- Communicate the value of those offers to customers.

RECOGNIZED NEEDS VERSUS LATENT NEEDS

Sometimes customers understand their needs — *recognized needs* — and sometimes they don't — *latent needs*. Recognized needs may be expressed or non-expressed:

- **Expressed needs.** Customers often ask for advice on how to satisfy their needs.
- **Non-expressed needs.** Customers do not express their needs.

Customers are not consciously aware of *latent needs*. These needs may surface as technological innovation raises awareness and customers require benefits/values they could not previously express.

ATTRIBUTES AND FEATURES VERSUS BENEFITS AND VALUES

Many firms define their products and services in terms of **attributes** and **features**. But customers *do not care about your products or services* — they are not interested in the attributes and features. Customers do *care* about satisfying *their needs* and the *benefits/values* your products and services provide.

- **Attributes and features.** Design elements or functions the firm builds into its products and services.
- **Benefits.** Something the product/service delivers that satisfies a customer need.
- **Values.** Something the product/service provides that has broader scope than a benefit.

HIERARCHIES OF NEEDS, FEATURES, BENEFITS, AND VALUES

Psychologists have studied individual needs extensively. We explore a popular need framework developed by the psychologist Abraham Maslow that marketers often use. Maslow's ideas from the basis of the feature/benefit/value ladder.

MASLOW'S HIERARCHY OF NEEDS. Maslow's classic framework identifies five major groups of needs — *physiological, safety and security, social, ego,* and *self-actualization* — ordered low to high. Generally, we expect individuals to satisfy lower-level *physiological, safety,* and *security* needs before high-level needs like *ego* and *self-actualization.*

Marketing Question

What product did a firm target to you that did not satisfy your needs? What needs did the product not satisfy? Why do you think this occurred?

LADDERING FEATURES, BENEFITS, AND VALUES. Many marketers meld Maslow's hierarchical approach to individual needs with the feature/benefit/value distinction to form a **feature/benefit/value ladder**. This ladder has three main characteristics:

- **Focuses attention on customer value.** Firms typically design attributes/features into their products/services. The feature/benefit/value ladder forces a translation into benefits and values.
- **Provides alternatives for communicating with customers.** The variety of benefits/values broadens firm options for communicating with customers.
- **Broadens the view of competition.** When the firm focuses on attributes/features, its scope is direct competitors. A focus on customer benefits and values broadens this scope.

FUNCTIONAL, PSYCHOLOGICAL, AND ECONOMIC BENEFITS AND VALUES

Customers base purchase decisions on a need hierarchy. The firm must translate the attributes/features of its offer into a hierarchy of benefits and values that align with these needs. But we must go one step further to explore the three types of benefits and values.

FUNCTIONAL BENEFITS AND VALUES. Firms design products and services to provide functional benefits and values that satisfy customer needs.

PSYCHOLOGICAL BENEFITS AND VALUES. Psychological values typically satisfy status, affiliation, reassurance, risk, and security needs. Firms often offer psychological and functional benefits together.

ECONOMIC BENEFITS AND VALUES. Economic benefits and values concern financial aspects like price and credit terms.

- **Economic value for the customer (EVC)** is the competitive product's price, plus the net added value from the firm's product.

The firm's challenge is to deliver the right combination of functional, psychological, and economic benefits and values to those customers it wants to attract, retain, and grow.

CHARACTERISTICS OF BENEFITS AND VALUES

ACTUAL VALUE VERSUS POTENTIAL VALUE. The critical value the firm offers may lie not in the product itself, but in the customer's ability to secure additional value, if and when needed.

FUTURE VALUE. Generally, customers purchase products and services for benefits and values they expect to receive directly. But they may also purchase for expected future benefits and values.

PRESENCE VALUE. A firm can provide considerable customer *value* just by being a supplier, so long as its products are acceptable and prices are reasonable. When a customer has one strong and one weak supplier, the weak supplier's presence keeps the strong supplier *honest* and inhibits the exercise of monopoly power.

SCARCITY VALUE. Some firms deliberately make small product volumes to provide scarcity value.

VALUE FOR WHOM. Consumers (B2C) typically make purchases for themselves, a friend or colleague, a family member, or a group like the family. B2B purchases may satisfy either organizational or individual needs.

Marketing Question

The three major overnight shipping firms offer various benefits and values. Do you agree with these category assignments, based on their slogans?

Functional Provider:
UPS – "Moving at the speed of business" and "See what Brown can do for you."

Psychological Provider:
FedEx – "Be absolutely sure" (that is, don't get fired).

Economic Provider:
United States Postal Service (USPS) – "We deliver." USPS's prices are lower than UPS and FedEx.

WHEN CUSTOMERS RECOGNIZE VALUE. The categories of *search*, *use*, and *credence* benefits capture customer uncertainty and can offer important insight:

- **Search benefits.** Significant product/service data from the firm and/or independent sources.
- **Use benefits.** Relatively little data on customer value before purchase. Value is revealed when the customer consumes the product/service.
- **Credence benefits.** Impossible to assess value until long after purchase.

Marketing Question

Choose one product each that offers mainly *search*, *use*, and *credence* benefits and values. How would your communications to customers differ?

BEYOND CUSTOMER BENEFITS AND VALUES – CUSTOMER EXPERIENCES

As competition increases, growing numbers of firms focus on providing **customer experiences** (brand, consumption, product, shopping, and service) — conditions, events, or states that consciously affect buying behavior. We may categorize these experiences as *real* (experienced directly), *anticipatory* (looking forward to), or *vicarious* (experienced through someone else).

Five modes of customer experience are:

- **Sense.** Creates sensory experiences through sight, sound, touch, taste, and smell.
- **Feel.** Appeals to inner feelings and emotions.
- **Think.** Appeals to the intellect.
- **Act.** Enriches by showing alternative ways of doing things, alternative lifestyles and interactions.
- **Relate.** Contains aspects of the first four experience modes, but reaches beyond individual personal, private feelings to something outside his/her private state.

HOW DO CUSTOMERS BUY?

The purchase **decision-making process (DMP)** ranges from relatively simple to highly complex. The DMP can be as quick as an impulse purchase or take months/years. Marketers must understand how customers move through the process and the various options for influence.

PURCHASE-DECISION STAGES

A robust purchase model has five distinct stages:

STAGE 1 – RECOGNIZING PROBLEMS. Some customer needs are critical to system functioning like food and drink for individuals, and raw materials and capital equipment for firms. Other needs are discretionary.

STAGE 2 – ACQUIRING INFORMATION. After recognizing a problem, customers generally seek information to help identify:

- The *feature* set — attributes/features that may satisfy the need.
- Criteria for evaluating satisfactory performance by the attributes/features.
- The *awareness* set — alternatives that may satisfy the need.
- The degree to which each alternative meets the attribute/feature criteria.

STAGES 3 AND 4 – EVALUATING ALTERNATIVES AND MAKING A CHOICE. Customers evaluate alternatives based on information they acquire in Stage 2. Frequently, customers exclude several alternatives in the *awareness* set with little evaluation by forming a short list — *consideration set* — based on the purchase criteria. Membership in the *consideration set* is crucial because customers choose among this restricted number of alternatives. Customer choices from the consideration set may be rational, or may deviate from rationality.

A. Rational approach. The firm can take several actions to improve the value it offers customers:

- Improve perceived performance on important attributes.
- Add new valued attributes, especially important ones.
- Show customers that it performs better than competitors on important attributes.
- Show that the attributes where it performs really well are highly important.

Marketing Question

Do you always act rationally in your purchase decisions? Identify situations where you have behaved less than rationally.

B. Deviations from rationality. *Behavioral decision theory* and *behavioral economics* researchers have identified many purchase processes that seem *irrational*. In both B2C and B2B markets, customers seem to base their choices on irrelevant factors. Deviations from rationality include:

- ***Compromise* effect.** Customers tend to avoid extreme price/value options in favor of intermediates.
- ***Decoy (asymmetric dominance)* effect.** Customer choice among alternatives is affected by adding another option acting as a *decoy*.
- **Describing alternatives.** The way alternatives are described.
- **Features of alternatives.** Adding an irrelevant option to an alternative affects the purchase decision.
- **How customers evaluate the alternatives.** Many factors affect how people evaluate alternatives. Just focusing attention on alternatives plays a role.
- **When customers evaluate the alternatives.** Time of purchase may be rational, but researchers find that consumers pay different prices on different days.

STAGE 5 – POST-PURCHASE PROCESSES. Customers typically engage in several post-purchase processes. These can affect future purchases — for customers and others they influence.

- **Use.** For some products the firm may only be concerned with sales; for others, like credit cards, use is important.
- **Use experience.** The customer may be satisfied/dissatisfied with the product/service.
- **Dissonance reduction.** If the product/service does not meet expectations, reduce dissonance by seeking information and/or recalibrating product performance.
- **Communications with customers/potential customers.** Word of mouth (WOM) has always been an important post-purchase process; many firms hire people to stimulate WOM. Social networking on the Internet has increased its importance.
- **Comparison with others.** Consumers modify consumption when they learn that neighbors' behavior is more socially acceptable.
- **Product and packaging disposal.** Environmental advocates pay increasing attention to disposal.
- **Repurchase.** Repurchase drives customer lifetime value. All things equal, high customer satisfaction increases customer loyalty and repurchase.

PURCHASE-DECISION CATEGORIES

We can usefully categorize purchases into three categories: routinized-response behavior, limited problem-solving, and extended problem-solving.

ROUTINIZED-RESPONSE BEHAVIOR. The customer has well-defined purchase criteria and frequently makes similar purchases.

LIMITED PROBLEM-SOLVING. The customer has well-defined purchase criteria, but one (or more) purchase alternatives is novel, and performance is uncertain.

EXTENDED PROBLEM-SOLVING. The purchase is novel, and the alternative(s) and potential supplier(s) are often new to the customer; purchase criteria are not well-developed.

These three purchase categories have important implications:

- **DMU varies by type of purchase.** *Extended problem-solving* typically involves more individuals and more senior individuals.
- **Purchase categories depend on the customer, not on the product.** Different customers use different purchase criteria and purchase processes for identical products.
- **Suppliers should consider shifting decision-making from simple to complex.** *Routinized-response behavior* often favors established suppliers. For *limited problem-solving* and *extended problem-solving*, customers must reframe the decision.

INFLUENCES ON CONSUMER PURCHASE PROCESSES

Deep understanding of *environmental* and *individual* factors can help the firm be proactive in strategy development.

ENVIRONMENTAL FACTORS

Environmental influences range from broad to narrow: culture, social class, other people, family, and the situation.

- **Culture.** Consumer purchasing behavior and product preferences are conditioned by cultural and subcultural norms.
- **Social class.** All societies have hierarchically ordered groupings — social classes. Wealth and income are key discriminators, but occupation, residential location, and education also matter.
- **Other people.** Other people and groups influence consumers. Individuals have frequent face-to-face contact with *primary reference groups*, *secondary reference groups*, and *aspirational groups*.
- **Family.** The *nuclear family* and/or the *extended family* may exert considerable influence.
- **Situation.** Consumers face situational influences daily — presentations and displays, and time constraints. *Purchase location aesthetics* are also important.

INDIVIDUAL FACTORS

Several individual factors also influence purchase decisions. We commence with resources:

- **Cognitive.** Consumers need cognitive resources to process information.
- **Economic.** Economic resources are necessary for purchase.
- **Technological competence.** Internet websites offer consumers immediate access to many options — and are changing shopping patterns.
- **Time.** In many societies, time is an increasingly scarce resource.

Other individual factors are:

- **Physical and mental health.** The ability of individuals to present themselves and function as desired has a major impact on many purchasing decisions.
- **Should/want conflicts.** Individuals often face want/should conflicts in their purchasing decisions — choosing between an option that brings short-term pleasure — want, and an option in their long-term best interest — should.

> *Marketing Question*
>
> The last time you purchased a ticket for long-distance air travel, what critical resource most influenced your decision?

Marketing Question

Take the VALS survey. What VALS type are you? Do you agree with this assessment? How does your VALS type compare with the VALS types for your friends and family members? Can you identify a person for each of VALS' eight lifestyles? Can the VALS types explain differential preferences for breakfast cereal, cars, leisure activities, or vacation preferences? How?

- **Life-cycle stage.** Age, family size, and marital status are critical elements in the consumer life cycle. Life-cycle stage often influences purchasing behavior.
- **Lifestyle.** Lifestyle embraces the way people live their lives and spend their time. The VALS lifestyle framework integrates several of the foregoing factors and is the most influential approach to categorizing lifestyles. VALS recognizes two major lifestyle dimensions — *self-orientation* and *resources*:
  - **Self-orientation** comprises three ways that consumers pursue and acquire products/ services and experiences to give their identities "shape, substance, and character":
    - **Action-orientation** — guided by a desire for social/physical activity and risk-taking.
    - **Principle-orientation** — guided by abstract idealized criteria.
    - **Status-orientation** — guided by a desire for approval and the opinions of others.
  - **Resources** encompasses the full range of psychological, physical, demographic, and material assets, including education, income, health, eagerness to buy, and energy.

INFLUENCES ON ORGANIZATIONAL PURCHASE PROCESSES

Organizational buying generally concerns larger sums of money than consumer purchases, is often more protracted and complex, engages more people, and may involve company politics. Processes and/or rules often govern organizational purchasing, and interfacing with suppliers.

CHANGES IN THE PROCUREMENT PROCESS

Important changes include:

- **Broader scope of procurement responsibilities.** Historically, purchasing departments focused on buying factory inputs. Today, procurement is often also responsible for spending categories like auto rental, consulting services, and travel.
- **Centralization.** Technological advances in telecommunications, computers, and the Internet provide corporate buyers with greater leverage.
- **Globalization.** The centralizing trend is expanding globally, as multinational firms broaden their supplier searches.
- **Internet.** Using *reverse auctions*, Internet-based B2B exchanges significantly affect the purchase of standard products.
- **Procurement expertise.** Skilled procurement staffs introduce new strategies like strategic sourcing to reduce costs, improve quality, and increase efficiency.

EVOLUTION IN BUYER-SELLER RELATIONSHIPS

Some firms evolve relationships with selected customers from vendor to quality supplier and even to partner:

- **Vendor.** Customer and supplier operate at *arm's length* in this traditional adversarial relationship. Contracts are typically short-term with frequent re-bidding.
- **Quality supplier.** Both supplier and customer believe they receive value from a close long-term relationship.
- **Partner.** Both firms share (or jointly develop) future strategies, technologies, and resources.

INCREASED CORPORATE ATTENTION TO PROCUREMENT

At many firms, the *procurement spend/company revenue ratio* has increased dramatically. Several factors are responsible:

- **Branding.** The rising importance of branding allows many firms to resell products made by others.

- **Organizational downsizing.** Many firms are downsizing by replacing labor with capital.

- **Outsourcing.** Outsourcing allows firms to reduce balance-sheet assets and fixed costs while increasing productivity, functional expertise, and flexibility.

REDUCING THE NUMBER OF SUPPLIERS

Traditional purchasing departments sent specifications to many potential suppliers, then chose on criteria like price and delivery. Factors driving the trend of closer relationships with fewer suppliers include attempts to:

- Address increased purchase complexity involving multiple technologies.

- Improve product quality by securing tighter control over raw material inputs.

- Move closer to suppliers and enjoy better communications, greater transparency, improved operational excellence like just-in-time (JIT) inventory systems, and greater control.

- Reduce input costs via
  - Increased procurement effectiveness.
  - Purchase assemblies versus parts: auto firms buy complete dashboards; Boeing buys complete wings.
  - Secure lower prices by letting selected suppliers gain economies of scale.

- Secure better and more consistent service in multiple geographies.

TRUE / FALSE QUESTIONS

1. Identifying customers is the crucial first step in securing customer insight. ❏ **TRUE** ❏ **FALSE**

2. Users of a product/service often have a direct role in the purchase decision process.
   ❏ **TRUE** ❏ **FALSE**

3. Typically, the firm's direct customers buy the firm's products from intermediaries like manufacturers or distributors. ❏ **TRUE** ❏ **FALSE**

4. Economic value for the customer (EVC) is the competitive product's price, plus the net added value from the firm's product. ❏ **TRUE** ❏ **FALSE**

5. Membership in the awareness set is more important than membership in the consideration set as customers choose among the alternatives in the awareness set. ❏ **TRUE** ❏ **FALSE**

MULTIPLE CHOICE QUESTIONS

1. Which of the following is NOT a major group of needs according to Maslow's Hierarchy of Needs?

   a. psychological
   b. safety
   c. ego
   d. self-actualization

2. Which of the following best describes customer benefits/values that are NOT known until long after purchase?

   a. search benefits
   b. use benefits
   c. credence benefits
   d. virtual benefits

3. All of the following are modes of customer experiences EXCEPT:

   a. sense
   b. feel
   c. think
   d. All of the selections represent a mode of customer experience.

4. Which of the following types of problem-solving is described as a novel purchase where the alternative(s) and potential supplier(s) are often new to the customer?

   a. routinized-response behavior
   b. limited problem-solving
   c. extended problem-solving
   d. perceptual problem-solving

5. According to the VALS framework, which of the following orientations comprises three ways that consumers pursue and acquire products/services and experiences to give their identities "shape, substance, and character"?

   a. self-orientation
   b. principle-orientation
   c. status-orientation
   d. action-orientation

Answers on page 205

CHAPTER 5

INSIGHT ABOUT COMPETITORS, COMPANY, AND COMPLEMENTERS

IN THIS CHAPTER, WE BUILD ON THE FIVE-FORCES MODEL from Chapter 3 to secure competitive insight. We also gain insight into the firm and its complementers.

THE CHANGING VIEW

OLD WAY	NEW WAY
Competitive analysis concerns sales and marketing	Multifunctional involvement
Competitive consolidation nationally	Competitive consolidation globally
Competitive focus local/regional/national	Competitive focus regional/multinational/global
Competitive strategy a low priority	Competitive strategy a high priority
Competitor description only	Competitor evaluation and projection widespread
Conflict-based views of competition	Collaborative arrangements more common
Customers purchase the firm's products	Customers as potential competitors — backward integration
Ethical considerations often ignored	Ethical considerations becoming more salient
Examine competition at the firm level	Examine competition by brand and market segment
Focus only on direct competitors	Focus on a broad competitor set — indirect and supply-chain competitors, current and potential competitors, and competitive networks
Industry structure fixed	Industry structure evolves
Limited attention to gaining competitor insight	Increased emphasis on gaining competitor insight
Passive and reactive competitive strategy	Active and proactive competitive strategy
Suppliers supply raw materials	Suppliers as potential competitors — forward integration
The firm operates independently	The firm operates interdependently

Competitors

DEVELOPING COMPETITIVE INSIGHT

Competitive intensity is increasing across the board in virtually all industries. But many firms put too little emphasis on gaining competitive insight. Good competitor insight can reduce the uncertainty in your decision-making. The firm should always know who their competitors are today and who they will be tomorrow; what they are doing now and what they may do in the future. Firms often face internal challenges in securing, and acting on, competitive insight. The firm:

- Bases insight on out-of-date data from tired sources.
- Claims that the cost of securing good competitive data is too high.
- Fails to go beyond a basic description of competitors.
- Focuses on current competitors but ignores potential competitors.
- Gains good insight but will not take action.
- Will not commit the necessary resources.

A commonly used five-step framework for securing competitive insight is: **identify**, **describe**, **evaluate**, **project**, and **manage**.

IDENTIFYING COMPETITORS

A **competitor** is any organization whose products/services provide similar or superior benefits and values to the same customers the firm seeks to attract, retain, and grow. Today the firm faces *current competitors*; tomorrow it may face *potential competitors*. We argue for a broad view of competitors; by viewing competition too narrowly, the firm fails to identify many serious medium- and long-term threats. The firm should consider three areas: the structure of competition, competitive dynamics, and the firm itself as a competitor.

> **Marketing Question**
>
> Use the five-forces model to chart out competitive forces facing McDonald's.

STRUCTURE OF COMPETITION

Of the five forces the firm faces, three are competition: *current direct competitors*, *new direct competitors*, and *indirect competitors*. The two other forces are *suppliers* and *buyers*. Two identifying dimensions that help evaluate competitors and gain deep insight are:

DIRECT VERSUS INDIRECT COMPETITORS. *Direct competitors* target similar customers by offering similar benefits/values with similar products, technology, and/or business models. *Indirect competitors* target the same customers with similar benefits and values, but have different products, technology, and/or business models.

CURRENT VERSUS POTENTIAL COMPETITORS. Today the firm faces *current competitors*; tomorrow it may face *potential competitors* — some may not even be around today.

These dimensions identify four types of competitive threat. The framework helps the firm decide which threats are most serious and where it should deploy resources.

- **Current direct competitors.** The competitive *status quo* — the traditional rivalry between established firms.
- **Current indirect competitors.** More difficult to identify. They act differently and develop customer benefits and values differently.
- **Potential direct competitors.** May emerge from a different industry and/or geography.
- **Potential indirect competitors.** The most difficult competitors to identify. They do not compete today, and it is unclear when and where they will emerge.

COMPETITIVE DYNAMICS

The firm must understand how competition is likely to evolve. Dramatic changes may occur, as when new competitors enter the market or when local or regional competitors become national or multinational. There are eight possible transitions:

- **Transition I** — from *potential direct* competitor to *current* direct competitor
- **Transition II** — from *potential indirect* competitor to *current* indirect competitor
- **Transition III** — from *potential direct* competitor to *withdrawal*, no longer a threat
- **Transition IV** — from *potential indirect* competitor to *withdrawal*, no longer a threat
- **Transition V** — from *current direct* competitor to *withdrawal*, no longer a threat
- **Transition VI** — from *current indirect* competitor to *withdrawal*, no longer a threat
- **Transition VII** — from *current direct* competitor to *current indirect* competitor; direct competitor has developed some new approach to satisfy customer needs
- **Transition VIII** — from *current indirect* competitor to *current direct competitor* — indirect competitor has decided to compete on an *apples-to-apples* basis

THE FIRM AS A COMPETITOR

For product and brand managers, the toughest competition may be internal. The firm may encourage **intra-firm** competition, or it may occur by happenstance.

DELIBERATELY INDUCED INTERNAL COMPETITION. Some firms foster Darwinian *internal* competition so as to improve effectiveness against *external* competitors. These firms believe increased competitiveness more than compensates for resource duplication, especially if customers tend to switch products or brands.

INTERNAL COMPETITION BY HAPPENSTANCE. Internal competition often evolves. Over time, market segments may merge, and/or firm products/services become more similar. Two originally independent approaches to the market now become competitive.

DESCRIBING COMPETITORS

Typically, it is not practical to seek insight into all the firm's competitors; managers must carefully select those on which to focus. Describing competitors concerns four key areas:

- What *competitor data* should the firm collect?
- What *sources* of competitor data are available?
- What *processes* should the firm use for competitive data-gathering?
- What *frameworks* can the firm use to describe competitors?

COLLECTING COMPETITOR DATA

To describe competitors effectively, the firm must decide what it wants to know based on the sort of decisions it has to make. We consider *level of data* and *type of data*.

LEVEL OF DATA. The firm should consider several organizational levels like corporate, business unit, market, and market segment. We illustrate with a competitive focus on GE's refrigerator business:

- **Corporate.** How does GE allocate resources across its major businesses like financial services, healthcare, home appliances, and jet engines?

> ### *Marketing Exercise*
>
> Suppose you were brand manager for leading U.S. bottled-water firm Poland Spring. Identify a direct or indirect competitor. On a single sheet of paper, sketch out a data-gathering plan. For each data item, note why you want to collect it.

Marketing Question

Returning from an industry conference, the attractive young woman took her seat on the plane. The middle-aged man in the next seat glanced at her reading material, noting they had both attended the same conference. He introduced himself as marketing VP of a major pharmaceutical firm. She introduced herself as a product manager for its chief competitor. Trying to impress, the VP discussed, at length, his firm's marketing plans. The young woman listened attentively!

Did the young woman behave ethically? Would your answer change if she had not indicated her employment status? What do you think of the VP's behavior?

- **Business unit.** How does GE allocate resources across its home appliance portfolio: refrigerators, dishwashers, washers and driers, and ranges?
- **Market.** What is GE's strategy in the refrigerator market? How does it segment the market? Where is GE focusing its efforts?
- **Market segment.** For segments where the firm competes with GE: What brand(s) does GE offer? How does GE position these brands? What are GE's models? What are GE's prices? What aer GE's credit terms?

TYPE OF DATA. The firm should collect both quantitative and qualitative data. *Quantitative* data include measures like market share and profitability. *Qualitative* data include competitor manager expertise and anticipated strategic moves. In addition to marketing data, the firm should also seek data on costing systems, financial strength, logistics, operations, R&D, speed of action, and business philosophy.

SOURCES OF COMPETITIVE DATA

The firm probably already has some competitive data internally: it should also seek competitor data externally. For both internal and external data, there are two approaches. *Secondary data* are available in various reports, publications and/or the Internet; the firm must collect, sort, and give them meaning. *Primary data* requires a focused acquisition effort like customer interviews and surveys.

INTERNAL PROCESSES FOR SECURING COMPETITIVE DATA

Many competitive data-gathering efforts fail because of poor processes. Competitive data-gathering options differ by focus and required resources:

- **Competing.** Sometimes the best way to learn about competitors is just to observe them, by operating in the marketplace day-by-day.
- **Competitive intelligence system.** The firm builds a culture where all employees are responsible for competitive intelligence. They come across competitive data daily; the critical step is to share these data with a competitor intelligence group.
- **Competitive intelligence department (CID).** The CID is responsible for collecting, analyzing, and distributing competitive information. The CID can be highly focused but is expensive.
- **Formal development of strategic plans.** When the firm has few major competitors, it can develop strategic plans as though it were the competitor. This highly focused approach is usually only practical for one or two competitors.
- **Gaming with multifunctional teams.** In these *war games*, executive teams play one of two roles: the *firm* or the *competitor*. Each team develops and presents its strategy and action plans; the firm and competitor then develop counter-strategies and action plans.
- **Review of business lost and business gained.** When the firm wins or loses a sale, it should find out why it won or lost. In well-managed firms, this process is standard operating procedure.
- **Shadow system.** Individual executives or teams *shadow* specific competitors, either as a full- or part-time job. When shadowing is an extra responsibility, it can be an effective way of focusing attention on individual competitors, at relatively low cost.

Counter-intelligence is also vital. The firm should take affirmative steps to protect its data:

- Classify information according to the degree of secrecy warranted.
- Execute employee **noncompete agreements** to prohibit former employees from working for competitors for a defined time period.

- Train employees on the danger of loose tongues, especially when attending industry meetings and social events. Teach them to be good listeners — ears open, mouths shut!
- Use **nondisclosure agreements (NDAs)** that prohibit revealing information to third parties.

FRAMEWORKS TO DESCRIBE COMPETITORS

To gain insight, the firm must organize competitive data into a useful framework. Good competitive insight often results from a *differential diagnosis* of the firm versus competitors. We use four basic building blocks: *competitor's organization, strengths and vulnerabilities, firm in the environment*, and *mind-set*.

COMPETITOR'S ORGANIZATION. How the organization functions:

- **Culture.** The behaviors, norms, beliefs, and values that together describe what the competitor stands for and how its members operate and behave.
- **Infrastructure.** The line organization — basic responsibilities and reporting relationships.
- **Processes.** Accounting, information, control and reward systems, and processes.

STRENGTHS AND VULNERABILITIES. Assets, capabilities, and competences:

- **Assets.** Financial, human, knowledge, organizational, perceptual, physical, and political assets that embrace the competitor's brand equity and customer loyalty — proprietary and non-proprietary. The firm should also evaluate competitor liabilities.
- **Capabilities and competences.** Activities the competitor does well, including *local* expertise and broad-scale abilities, and areas where it does poorly.

FIRM IN THE ENVIRONMENT. Embraces relationships with other organizations:

- **Value chain.** Major work activities the competitor conducts and how they connect to external entities like suppliers and customers. The firm asks four core questions:
  - Where does the competitor have a cost advantage?
  - Where is the competitor at a cost disadvantage?
  - Where does the competitor have a value advantage?
  - Where is the competitor at a value disadvantage?
- **Alliances and special relationships. Alliances** are formal economic relationships between the competitor and other entities (partners) — customers, distributors, and suppliers. **Special relationships** are informal and may embrace government agencies, political parties, and public interest groups — as well as suppliers and customers.
- **Networks.** Interconnected sets of alliances and relationships.

MIND-SET. How the competitor thinks and the bases for its decisions. What are its *assumptions*? Assumptions are the outcomes of analyst judgments, inferred from competitive data.

CURRENT STRATEGY AND PERFORMANCE. How the competitor behaves and its results:

- **Market strategy.** The firm observes the competitor actions and infers its strategy.
- **Other major resource commitments.** The competitor may build new factories, expand existing plants, and/or spend extensively on a particular type of R&D.
- **Performance.** Most performance measures are market-oriented or financially based.

PULLING IT ALL TOGETHER

The firm can secure data on competitor advertising, distribution, price, product, service, and other factors — but does not see what was behind them. The firm must make inferences about

Marketing Question

If you are a full-time student, select the firm you want to work for. If you are a part-time student, select your firm's major competitor. Use the Internet and other resources to complete the competitive analysis framework for the firm you chose.

competitor strategy from these data. Finally, competitors *do not make* decisions: People working for competitors make decisions. The firm should identify competitor decision-makers and influencers.

EVALUATING COMPETITORS

The reason for *evaluating* competitors is to generate their strategic options. Knowing these options allows the firm to *project* competitor actions. **Competitor assessment analysis** and **game theory** help answer three competitive evaluation questions:

- What options does the competitor have to be successful in the market?
- What would the competitor have to do to pursue each of these options?
- Is the competitor capable? (Does it have the resources to implement a particular option?)

COMPETITOR ASSESSMENT ANALYSIS

This powerful tool focuses on an individual competitor or group of similar competitors in a market segment and maps customer perspectives into required resources. From the analysis, the firm identifies where it has a **differential advantage** over competitors and where competitors have a **differential advantage**. Identifying differential advantage has five stages:

- **Stage 1 – Identify customer requirements in terms of needs, benefits, and values.** Brainstorm or use marketing research.
- **Stage 2 – Rank in order of importance.** Reduce the items from stage 1 to a manageable number, typically six to ten. Rank items in order of importance to customers — columns A and B.

Customer Requirements: Needs, Benefits, Values **A**	Customer Importance Rank **B**	Necessary Capabilities / Resources **C**				
		Efficient Manufacturing	**Good Distribution**	**Just-in-Time Delivery**	**Well-Funded R&D**	**Access to Low-Cost Materials**
Easy product availability	1	* YN	* YYY			
Low prices	2	* YN				* YYN
Low inventories	3			* N		
Access to cutting-edge technology	4				* YYN	
Etc.						

- **Stage 3 – Determine necessary capabilities and resources.** Any firm would require these capabilities/resources to satisfy the customer requirements in column A; they map directly. To satisfy the most important item, *easy product availability*, requires *efficient manufacturing and good distribution*.
- **Stage 4 – Identify the matches.** Place an asterisk (*) in each matrix cell where a customer need/benefit or value — column A, intersects with a firm capability/resource — column C.
- **Stage 5 – Examine the matches.** Ask up to three questions of each asterisked matrix cell. Asking a subsequent question depends on the answer to a previous question.
  a. **Relevance.** Does the firm have the capabilities/resources necessary to address the customer need/benefit or value? If yes, enter **Y**; if no, enter **N**, and stop.

Marketing Question

Huawei is a major Chinese technology firm that frequently competes with Cisco. Write a short memorandum identifying the type and level of threat that Huawei poses for Cisco.

b. **Superiority.** For each cell where the firm entered **Y**: Are the firm's capabilities/resources superior to the competitor? If yes, enter **Y**; if no, enter **N**, and stop.

c. **Sustainability.** For each cell where the firm entered **YY**: Would it be difficult for the competitor to match the firm's capabilities/resources? If yes, enter **Y**; if no, enter **N**.

The meaning of the entries is:

- **YYY.** The firm has a sustainable differential advantage.
- **YYN.** The firm has an advantage, but the competitor could match it fairly easily.
- **YN.** Firm capabilities/resources match customer needs/benefits or values, but are no better than the competitor.
- **N.** The firm has a significant weakness or gap. The competitor probably has a differential advantage.

GAME THEORY

Game theory is a structured way of identifying options and evaluating consequences. Game theory helps marketers think through the impact of firm actions on competitors — and vice versa. Game theory helps assess the consequences for the firm and competitor from pursuing each option.

PROJECTING COMPETITOR ACTIONS

The evaluation step generates a set of options for the competitor; the firm must assess which the competitor will choose. To start: What is the competitor trying to achieve? Specific questions include:

- What are the competitor's objectives in the market?
- What market segments will the competitor address? How will the competitor try to achieve its objectives — price leadership, operational excellence, product leadership, or distribution strength?
- What is the competitor's staying power? Is the competitor committed for the long run?

Scenarios are a particularly effective way of evaluating competitor options; they help the firm understand and predict competitor actions. The scenario for a plausible option is a descriptive narrative of how the future may evolve; the firm should develop a scenario for each option. Three major scenario types are:

- **Emergent scenarios.** Start with the current strategy and consider what might emerge.
- **Unconstrained scenarios.** Based on open-ended *what-if* questions that suggest possible end states.
- **Constrained scenarios.** *What-if* scenarios that ask how the competitor may act under different market and/or industry conditions.

Effective scenarios have several important attributes:

- **Articulated plot and logic.** The *story* comprises a set of events and cohesive logic.
- **Internally consistent logic.** The *story* hangs together.
- **Specific time frame.** The *story* specifies a time element for key actions, events, and results.
- **Decision/action-oriented.** The firm can derive and demonstrate implications for its current and future decisions.

As the firm builds scenarios, it must incorporate:

- **An end state.** An outcome at some specific future point.
- **A plot.** What the competitor must do to get to the end state.

> *Marketing Exercise*
>
> Abu Dhabi, Dubai, and Qatar are investing substantially in new airports. Flagship carriers, respectively, Etihad Airways, Emirates, and Qatar Airways, are each growing at double-digit rates. As an airline industry analyst, identify three likely scenarios and implications for Lufthansa.

- **Driving forces.** The circumstances, conditions, events, and trends that shape or drive the story described in a particular plot.
- **Logics.** The evidence and rationale for the end state and plot.

MANAGING COMPETITORS

Identifying competitor options and projecting its strategies put the firm in good position. But shaping (managing) competitor actions is even better! Before trying to get competitors to behave in beneficial ways, the firm must answer two questions:

- What actions does the firm want its competitor(s) to take?
- What actions does the firm prefer that its competitor(s) not take?

SIGNALING

Sometimes firms send signals to competitors, hoping they will process the information and act accordingly. The firm should ensure its signals do not violate antitrust laws.

- **Pre-emptive signals.** The firm sends *pre-emptive* signals so that competitors will take decisions favorable to the firm.

Sometimes, the firm must decide whether, and how, to *respond* to competitors. Many competitor moves do not require direct action, but the responding firm must make several decisions:

- Where should the firm respond? In the same market or in a different market?
- How fast should the firm respond — immediately, or wait to assess the market reaction?
- How large should the response be? Match or outdo the competitor?

Two types of response signals are:

- *Tit-for-tat* **signals.** The firm designs tit-for-tat signals to bring competitors into line and stop them from making unilateral gains. The firm encourages the competitor to behave by matching (but not overreacting to) competitor actions.
- **Warning signals.** Warning signals tell competitors that if their actions reach certain thresholds, the firm will take serious steps. The firm makes sure that competitors can predict its responses.

MISINFORMATION

Misinformation is a signal designed to mislead competitors. Misinformation may buy time for a developing strategy, but overuse can cause credibility problems.

The Company

Two approaches help the firm gain self-insight — *company description* and *company assessment analysis*.

COMPANY DESCRIPTION

The four building blocks are *the firm's organization, strengths and vulnerabilities, firm in the environment*, and *mind-set* — just as previously used for describing competitors. These elements help show how the firm settled on its *current strategy* and achieved its *current performance*. To apply this framework, simply substitute *the firm* wherever *competitor* appears.

COMPANY ASSESSMENT ANALYSIS

The company assessment analysis identifies where the firm possesses a differential advantage and where it might place resources to *secure* a differential advantage. The analysis is identical to the competitor assessment analysis just discussed.

Complementers

A **complementer** is any organization whose actions affect the firm's sales. Both independent organizations and competitors can be complementers.

INDEPENDENT ORGANIZATIONS AS COMPLEMENTERS

Because complementers can help each other generate sales they should develop mutually beneficial strategies.

CUSTOMERS AS COMPLEMENTERS. Customers act as complementers when they enhance the firm's offer.

SUPPLIERS AS COMPLEMENTERS. Suppliers often complement the firm's actions to increase sales — like conducting joint R&D and/or helping with market development.

COMPETITORS AS COMPLEMENTERS

As a general rule, competitors are the firm's nemesis. They try to attract, retain, and grow the same customers as the firm. But competitors can act as complementers, without getting into antitrust problems.

STRONG COMPLEMENTARITY: MARKETPLACE OR FRONT-OFFICE. Sometimes competitors work together to better satisfy customer needs, like agreeing on technological standards.

STRONG COMPLEMENTARITY: BACK OFFICE. Competitors may *compete* fiercely in the market, but their back offices *collaborate* extensively. Back-office collaboration occurs in non-customer-facing activities, reduces costs and improves efficiency for all firms.

WEAK COMPLEMENTARITY. Marketplace and back-office complementarity generally require formal agreements. Other types of complementarity are weaker but may contribute positively:

- **Cost reduction.** When several competitors have common suppliers, one competitor's actions may affect the others, like increasing volume and reducing costs.
- **Greater customer calue.** A firm's product may provide greater customer benefit when combined with a rival's product.
- **Increasing demand.** Competitors engage in joint advertising and other promotions so all firms benefit.
- **Keeping the firm sharp.** Tough competition keeps a firm on its toes. Some firms deliberately seek out tough competitors.
- **Market development.** Competitor market-development actions may assist the firm.
- **Political action.** Competitors join trade associations to lobby governments for favorable decisions.

UNWELCOME COMPLEMENTARITY. Sometimes firms do not want their products associated with other firms — unwelcome complementers — like unauthorized parts manufacturers for OEMs.

> *Marketing Question*
>
> What organizations are complementers for NBC (U.S. television network)?

TRUE / FALSE QUESTIONS

1. Direct competitors target the same customers as the firm with similar benefits but have different products, technology, and/or business models. ❏ **TRUE** ❏ **FALSE**

2. Quantitative data include measures like market share and profitability. ❏ **TRUE** ❏ **FALSE**

3. Secondary data are available in various publications and on the Internet. ❏ **TRUE** ❏ **FALSE**

4. Game theory helps marketers think through the impact of the firm's actions on competitors — and of the competitors' actions on the firm. ❏ **TRUE** ❏ **FALSE**

5. Tit-for-tat signals tell competitors that if their actions reach certain thresholds, the firm will take serious steps to create a disadvantage for the competitor. ❏ **TRUE** ❏ **FALSE**

MULTIPLE CHOICE QUESTIONS

1. Which of the following types of competitive threats is the competitive *status quo*?

    a. current direct competitors
    b. current indirect competitors
    c. potential direct competitors
    d. potential indirect competitors

2. Which of the following is NOT one of the key areas for describing competitors?

    a. type of competitor data the firm should collect
    b. available sources of competitive data
    c. processes the firm should use for gathering competitive data
    d. All selections represent key areas for describing competitors.

3. Which of the following describes the internal process for securing competitive data in which executive teams play one of two roles: the firm or the competitor?

    a. shadow system
    b. competitive intelligence system
    c. formal development of strategic plans
    d. gaming with multifunctional teams

4. A _____ prohibits former employees from working for competitors for a defined time period.

    a. nondisclosure agreement
    b. noncompete agreement
    c. value chain
    d. shadow system

5. As a firm builds scenarios, it must incorporate all of the following EXCEPT:

    a. an end state
    b. a plot
    c. a beginning state
    d. logics

Answers on page 205

CHAPTER 6

MARKETING
RESEARCH

MARKETING RESEARCH IS ANY PROCESS OF DATA COLLECTION, analysis, and interpretation the firm adopts to improve the quality of its marketing efforts. Astute marketers need not become marketing research experts, but they should become *intelligent customers* of marketing research.

THE CHANGING VIEW

OLD WAY	NEW WAY
Basic analysis (tabs, X-tabs, regression)	Sophisticated analysis (complex methods, choice models)
Customer market focus only	Research on multiple constituencies
Data scarce	Data plentiful
Descriptive orientation	Causal orientation
Direct elicitation techniques	Projective techniques
Focus groups and one-on-one interviews	Eclectic methodologies
Identify trends	Build trends into market strategy
Loose measurement technology	Careful measurement technology
Market research is unfamiliar to much of the public	Market research is familiar to much of the public but many people are unhappy with intrusive phone calls
Observational methods rare	Observational methods often employed
One major market research approach used	Combination of multiple research methodologies
Pencil and paper surveys	Web panels and online surveys
Quantitative results	Actionable results
Sometimes cavalier attitude to confidentiality	Much stricter observance of privacy rights
Strive to increase sample sizes	Strive to improve management of large databases
Typically instrumental	Purely investigative more common

THE MARKETING RESEARCH PROCESS

A critical element of success rests with the relationship between the manager and the researcher; the manager must provide guidance to the researcher. To ensure that marketing research is tightly aligned with marketing decision-making, the marketing research process must follow a consistent methodology.

DEFINE THE BUSINESS ISSUE

A primary responsibility for marketing managers is defining the business issue. Sometimes the *presenting* (immediate) problem may actually be a symptom and not the real problem; you may have to dig deeper.

IDENTIFY A RESEARCHABLE PROBLEM

Marketing research may be unable to solve all your problems, but a good marketing researcher will help frame the issues and problems so that research can be useful. Good marketing research can highlight the facts, point the firm in the right direction, and help reduce uncertainty.

FORMULATE OBJECTIVES AND HYPOTHESES

Together with the marketing researchers, you should agree upon research objectives and hypotheses you will test. Objectives and hypotheses are usually related, but hypotheses are always more specific. Examples of insightful questions include:

- **What:** What do consumers think about our product versus competitor products?
- **Why:** Why do some consumers switch among brands?
- **How and how much:** How frequently do consumers purchase our product?
- **Who:** Who makes the purchase decision for these products?
- **When:** When do consumers consume these products?

CONDUCT A PRELIMINARY INVESTIGATION

Before conducting *primary* research directly with respondents, the researcher should always evaluate *secondary* data. Secondary data (existing sources) may be inside the firm, but are often outside from publicly available sources. Secondary data may provide partial (or even complete) answers to your research questions more quickly and less expensively than primary research.

DEVELOP THE RESEARCH PLAN

As your research blueprint, the more detailed research plan should include data-collection methodologies, embracing data-collection instruments like questionnaires, and a sampling plan identifying who will provide data.

COLLECT AND ANALYZE DATA

There are many ways to collect data. If you plan to collect survey data, make sure your subjects are representative of the target population. Also pay careful attention to response rates and implement procedures for dealing with non-responders; they may be systematically different from responders.

Marketing Question

Your firm collects confidential consumer data via face-to-face interviews. You suspect one of your interviewers is lazy and is faking the data, yet he denies your accusations. How would you proceed?

PREPARE THE REPORT

As a marketing manager, you will often review marketing research reports that others prepare. They present findings, but your goal and responsibility is always to seek insight. Many firms are rich in *data and information* but lack *knowledge* and may have little *insight*.

CRITICAL DISTINCTIONS IN MARKETING RESEARCH

Marketing Exercise

It's the first day at your new job and your boss calls you into her office. "I want you to design a marketing research study to determine the reasons for customer loyalty." Prepare a response for your boss.

PRIMARY AND SECONDARY RESEARCH

The researcher should assess available secondary data, then fill information *gaps* with primary data.

SECONDARY RESEARCH. Some person or organization has already collected secondary data for another purpose. Three basic types of secondary data are:

- **Company data.** Comprises routinely generated data from transactions with customers and suppliers; information from internal databases on costs, production, and capacity; customer lists; delivery, maintenance, and servicing reports; customer purchases (what, when, how many, prices paid), complaints, information requests, payment history, and service calls; salesperson call reports; and previously completed marketing research reports.
- **Public data.** Includes information about competitors, customers, and suppliers; industry trends; and technologies.
- **Technical analysis.** Includes objective, repeatable descriptions of product and services or production capacity collected by internal engineers or developers.

PRIMARY RESEARCH. Typically this type of research is more expensive than secondary research. The firm usually collects primary data for a specific purpose, often to close gaps between data required to make decisions and data already available from secondary research.

QUALITATIVE AND QUANTITATIVE RESEARCH

QUALITATIVE RESEARCH. Qualitative research (QualR) is typically not concerned with numbers. QualR is generally flexible and versatile but is rarely conclusive and does not project to a larger population.

QUANTITATIVE RESEARCH. Quantitative research (QuanR) uses numerical data and mathematical analyses, often from large representative samples. Marketing researchers use QuanR to test hypotheses formulated earlier in the research process.

The researcher should ask three types of question about QuanR:

- **Internal validity.** Do these data measure what I want to be measuring?
- **Reliability.** If I repeat the data collection, will I get the same results?
- **External validity.** Will the results I secure generalize to other populations?

SECURING QUALITATIVE RESEARCH DATA

Focus groups, one-on-one interviews, Internet and social networks, projective techniques, observation, and ethnographic research are the most popular primary data-gathering methods for securing insight into customers' needs and motivations.

FOCUS GROUPS

Focus groups are one of the most popular qualitative data-collection methods. Typically, focus groups comprise eight to 12 members (often paid for participation and selected for their interest, knowledge, and/or experience with the topic) moderated by a skilled facilitator.

ONE-ON-ONE INTERVIEWS (OOOs)

OOOs combine direct and indirect questions asked of individuals to probe needs and underlying purchase motivations. Mostly, researchers conduct OOOs in person or on the telephone.

INTERNET: BLOGS, FORUMS, SOCIAL NETWORKS, TWITTER, WIKIS, YOUTUBE

In the online world, customers are increasingly willing to post complimentary and/or critical comments about products, brands, and firms. By offering its own forum, the firm may receive valuable customer feedback. The firm must also be vigilant about other Internet postings; many bloggers develop significant followings and become very influential.

PROJECTIVE TECHNIQUES

Researchers use projective techniques (aka motivation research) mainly to uncover latent customer needs. Developed by psychologists, projective techniques have a long history in marketing:

- **Constructing a collage.** The respondent collects pictures from newspapers and magazines that express his feelings about the topic.
- **Imagery.** The respondent draws a picture showing herself interacting with the product, then interprets the picture.
- **Role-playing.** Respondents pretend they are a brand's friend and write it a letter, or they explain why a neighbor/work colleague may like/dislike a particular product.
- **Storytelling.** The respondent receives a picture or description of a situation relevant to the topic. The respondent makes up a story about one or more characters in the stimulus.
- **Word associations.** The researcher supplies a stimulus word. The respondent offers the first word that comes to mind.

OBSERVATION

Observation can assess a respondent's behavior, including emotional responses, body language, person-to-person interactions, and the environment where people live. Conducted correctly, observational data are objective, accurate, and unbiased by researcher intervention. Broadly speaking, observational research falls into two categories — planned and unplanned:

PLANNED OBSERVATION. The firm does not ask questions, but secures insight by watching (sometimes using one-way mirrors) and recording behavior (often by video) in naturalistic settings.

UNPLANNED OBSERVATION. Individuals may gain significant insight about markets, customers, and/or competitors without planning to do so. Simple observation may trigger an idea with tremendous payoff.

ETHNOGRAPHIC RESEARCH

Derived from anthropology, **ethnographic research** is an observational method where researchers spend *a day in the life of (DILO)* their customers, corresponding to the anthropologist *living with the tribe.*

SECURING QUANTITATIVE RESEARCH DATA

Alternative ways of securing data for quantitative analysis are:

SURVEYS

Sample surveys of the target population are the most common way to secure primary data for quantitative analysis. Selecting a sample that reflects the underlying population is critical. So is assessing the required sample size for estimating parameter(s) of interest at the desired accuracy level. Questionnaire design is critical to survey success and should involve both researcher and manager.

PANELS

A panel allows the firm to follow up on individual responses. In a **tracking study** (aka longitudinal study), the firm forms a panel of individuals who agree to provide responses periodically.

OBJECTIVE SALES DATA

The firm's sales reporting system can provide valuable quantitative data. Sales data to end-user customers may be difficult to secure when products move through distribution channels. In supermarkets, the widespread use of barcodes and retail scanners makes it easy to collect and store sales data by sku (stock-keeping unit).

BEHAVIORAL MEASUREMENT

Increasingly, firms use technology for marketing research. *Infrared sensors, video cameras,* and *digital voice recorders* monitor supermarket aisle-traffic patterns; *checkout scanners* measure consumer purchases. Electronic metering systems capture radio listenership and TV viewing by channel; GPS-enabled *cell phones* identify consumers' locations.

EXPERIMENTS

Experiments allow researchers to definitively establish causal relationships like A → B. The researcher manipulates independent variables, like advertising and price levels, and measures results, like awareness and sales.

PREDICTION MARKETS

In prediction markets, buyers and sellers trade assets whose cash value is tied to a particular event. Prediction markets have successfully predicted Oscar nominations and various economic events.

Marketing Question

Go to your local supermarket and observe consumer behavior in the cereal aisle. What can you learn? What hypotheses can you develop that you could test by quantitative methods?

Marketing Question

How would you design an experiment to measure the impact of advertising spending and price on sales of your product? (Choose your own product.)

ANALYZING QUANTITATIVE RESEARCH DATA

Quantitative research data are amenable to a broad variety of statistical analyses. If the underlying assumptions are valid, quantitative methods can have a significant predictive power and be very helpful to the firm in making marketing decisions.

MARKET AND SALES POTENTIALS, MARKET AND SALES FORECASTS

Two related concepts — **potentials** and **forecasts** — are important for understanding market demand and the firm's performance. *Potential* embraces having a *capability* or *future* state; *forecast* concerns *expectations.*

ASSESSING MARKET POTENTIAL

Market potential is the *maximum market-level sales* from all suppliers the firm believes could occur in a future time period. Market potential is an upper bound to actual sales, based on a set of assumptions about future market conditions. Market potential is especially important when contemplating entry in a new market. To assess market potential, the firm should estimate the number of likely customers and the amounts they are likely to buy. The three steps are:

- **Identify likely market segments.** Most markets comprise several segments. The firm must understand these segments, even though some may not buy at each time period.
- **Estimate numbers of customers in each segment.** The firm estimates the number of customers likely to buy in the time period for which it seeks market potential.
- **Estimate the number of products to be purchased.** The firm estimates the number of products customers in each segment are likely to buy during the relevant time period.

The firm secures market potential by multiplying number of customers by purchase amount per segment, then aggregating across segments.

ASSESSING SALES POTENTIAL

Sales potential is the maximum sales the firm could achieve in a given time period. Sales potential is conditioned on assumptions about market potential, the firm's likely efforts, and future market conditions, like number and strength of competitors. The firm can calculate sales potential directly from market potential by assessing its potential market share. The firm's potential share depends both on the resources it could commit to the market and the actions it believes competitors will take.

FORECASTING MARKET SIZE

Market forecasts often focus on the short run, like the upcoming year, where the firm can assess market conditions with a fair degree of accuracy. To forecast market size, the firm may focus either on the overall market or on individual segments that it later aggregates. Generally, a segmented approach provides better forecasts if data are available. Three broad approaches to assessing market size are judgmental:

JUDGMENTAL METHODS. These are the simplest methods for forecasting market size:

- **Executive judgment.** The responsible manager has a deep familiarity with key variables.
- **Delphi method.** A valuable approach when several people have opinions about the market. Each person makes a forecast and specifies the rationale. Each person then receives all forecasts and rationales, and revises their forecast — often for several rounds.

Marketing Question

In 1999, Airbus predicted demand for its superjumbo A380 jet aircraft at 1,440 planes and forecast that 10 U.S. airlines would buy 281. In spring 2007, with Airbus expected to deliver its first plane in October, Airbus had orders for 156 aircraft from 14 airlines, yet none were U.S.-based. How do you explain the discrepancies?

TIME-BASED METHODS. These methods use past sales to predict future sales directly:

- **Judgmental extrapolation.** A special case of executive judgment using history to predict a percentage change from the previous year.
- **Linear extrapolation.** Two-variable regression analysis estimates year-by-year change in sales.
- **Moving average.** The manager uses sales data from previous years to calculate an average; this average is the forecast.
- **Exponential smoothing.** This method uses previous sales data in a slightly unusual way. Rather than forecasting based only on actual sales data from previous years, exponential smoothing uses both last year's actual sales and last year's forecast sales.

CAUSAL-FACTOR METHODS. The most common causal-factor method for predicting market size is *multiple regression analysis*. The researcher selects several independent (predictor) variables that she believes could be related to market size, the dependent (criterion) variable. She uses historical data to determine the relationships, if any, between these predictor variables and market size. She then uses these relationships to predict future sales.

MARKETING EXERCISE

Form a group of five or six students. Each person in the group forecasts the Dow Jones average (or some other event) for the last day of class and provides a rationale. Team members exchange forecasts and rationales and repeat the process one or more times. On the last day of class, compare the forecast with the actual Dow Jones average.

MAKING THE SALES FORECAST

The sales forecast is the firm's expected sales in a future time period, often the upcoming year. The sales forecast is central to many day-by-day operating processes like financial budgeting and production planning. Three broad approaches to sales forecasting are *top-down*, *bottom-up*, and *synthetic*:

- **Top-down sales forecasting.** Top-down sales forecasts follow directly from analyses of market potential, market size forecasts, and the firm's market share estimates.
- **Bottom-up sales forecasting.** Bottom-up forecasts embrace the granularity (and reality) of sales by customer that is absent in top-down forecasts. The firm aggregates forecasts from individual salespeople to develop the bottom-upl sales forecast.
- **Synthetic sales forecasts.** Synthetic sales forecasts combine the best features of top-down and bottom-up forecasting. The top-down forecast comes from the marketing planning process; the sales department independently prepares a bottom-up forecast. Marketing and sales negotiate an agreement.

CATEGORY AND BRAND DEVELOPMENT INDICES

The **category development index (CDI)** and **brand development index (BDI)** are useful devices for assessing market and sales, potentials and forecasts:

- CDI — the percentage of category sales divided by the percentage of U.S. population, converted to a percentage.
- BDI — the percentage of brand sales divided by the percentage of U.S. population, converted to a percentage.

TRUE / FALSE QUESTIONS

1. Before conducting secondary research, a marketing researcher should always check on available primary data. ❑ **TRUE** ❑ **FALSE**

2. Qualitative research is generally flexible and versatile, but is rarely conclusive and does not project to a larger population. ❑ **TRUE** ❑ **FALSE**

3. Marketing researchers conduct most focus groups on the telephone. ❑ **TRUE** ❑ **FALSE**

4. Sales potential is conditioned on assumptions about the firm's likely efforts and future market conditions, like the number and strength of competitors. ❑ **TRUE** ❑ **FALSE**

5. Synthetic sales forecasts combine the best features of top-down and bottom-up forecasting. ❑ **TRUE** ❑ **FALSE**

MULTIPLE CHOICE QUESTIONS

1. Which of the following is NOT one of the three types of questions a researcher should ask when collecting and evaluating quantitative data?

   a. internal validity
   b. reliability
   c. flexibility
   d. external validity

2. In which of the following projective techniques does the research ask the respondent to draw a picture that shows the respondent interacting with the product, and then asked the respondent to interpret the picture?

   a. word association
   b. storytelling
   c. role-playing
   d. imagery

3. Which of the following techniques for collecting research data is the most common way to secure primary data for quantitative analysis?

   a. surveys
   b. focus groups
   c. objective sales force data
   d. experiments

4. Rather than forecasting based only on actual sales data from previous years, _____ uses both last year's actual sales and last year's forecasted sales.

   a. judgmental extrapolation
   b. exponential smoothing
   c. linear extrapolation
   d. moving average

5. The most common causal-factor method for predicting market size is _____.

   a. exponential smoothing
   b. moving average
   c. linear extrapolation
   d. multiple regression analysis

Answers on page 205

TRANSITION
TO STRATEGIC
MARKETING

CHAPTERS 3 THROUGH 6 FOCUS ON SECURING market, customer, competitor, company, and complementer insight. The material in these chapters forms the basis for the *situation analysis* — the foundation for the market plan. The best way to build a solid superstructure for market strategy and implementation is to transition from *insight* in the situation analysis to *assumptions* about the future. Planning assumptions are critical supporting elements in the market plan. Drawing from the various insight elements, marketers should identify candidate planning assumptions on which to build market strategy and implementation.

Of course, planning assumptions vary on several dimensions; two of the most important are *magnitude of effect* and *probability of occurrence*. Core assumptions for market plans are those with *high* magnitude of effect and *high* probability of occurrence. To complete the process, the marketer should identify implications for the firm of each high magnitude-of-effect and high-probability-of-occurrence assumption, then turn these assumptions into "We believe..." statements.

SECTION III
STRATEGIC
MARKETING

Managing Marketing in the 21ˢᵗ Century

Determine and Recommend
Which Markets to Address

CHAPTER 7

IDENTIFYING AND CHOOSING OPPORTUNITIES

MARKETING'S FIRST, AND ARGUABLY MOST IMPORTANT, IMPERATIVE is to influence firm decisions about which markets to address. A systematic approach to developing, selecting, and implementing growth opportunities embraces strategy for growth, screening criteria, and implementation.

THE CHANGING VIEW

OLD WAY	NEW WAY
Competencies are fixed	Competencies are variable
Conglomeration is good	Conglomeration is bad
Firm goes it alone	Firm considers strategic alliances and other inter-organizational relationships
Growth is always desirable	*Right* and *timely* growth is desirable
Insourcing as a growth strategy	Insourcing and outsourcing as growth strategies
Organic growth by developing new products internally	Organic growth by expanding into global markets
Reinvest in historically profitable businesses	Prudent selection of appropriate growth ventures
Swift implementation of new opportunities desirable	Swift implementation of new opportunities critical

STRATEGY FOR GROWTH

A **strategy for growth** uses a set of frameworks to help the firm evaluate current businesses, decide which businesses *to be in*, and which businesses *not to be in*. Firms can generate attractive opportunities using four components: **vision**, **mission**, **growth path**, and **timing of entry**.

VISION

Vision is a description of the firm's ideal future state — an impressionistic picture of what the future should be. *Corporate vision* concerns the firm as a whole; *business-unit vision* focuses on an individual business. Good visions set a broad direction, and should inspire employees for the long run.

MISSION

Mission guides the firm's search for market opportunities more directly than vision. A well-developed mission keeps the firm focused in a limited arena where success is likely. Mission avoids dispersing firm energy and resources in multiple directions.

ARTICULATING THE MISSION. In articulating its mission, the firm should consider three internal resource (IR) dimensions and two externally focused (EF) dimensions:

- **IR – Core ingredient or natural resource.** The firm maximizes value from a core ingredient or natural resource — *We are a forest products company.*
- **IR – Technology.** The firm focuses on a core technology — *We are an electronics firm.*
- **IR – Product or service.** This firm's mission focuses on a product/service — *We are an automobile company.*
- **EF – Customer needs.** This mission directs the firm to serve customers having a specific set of needs, with any product, using any technology — *We satisfy people's transportation needs.*
- **EF – Market or market segment.** A firm with this type of mission could make many products using various raw materials and technologies — *Our markets are families with young children.*

EVOLVING THE MISSION. Typically, successful firms evolve their missions. If opportunities are scarce with the current mission or a target of opportunity appears, the firm should consider *broadening* the mission. Sometimes a firm is spread too thin and should consider *narrowing* the mission.

> *Marketing Question*
>
> Based on your knowledge and/or Internet research, write one-sentence missions for AXA, Citigroup, Comcast, Disney, ExxonMobil, Facebook, Ford, GE, Groupon, Hitachi, IP, Morgan Stanley, Novartis, Siemens, Toyota, Twitter, Verizon, Yahoo!, and/or Xerox.

GROWTH PATH

Growth path is more focused than mission. Growth path is specifically concerned with the trade-off between expected financial return and risk. The firm should consider three factors:

- Revenue and profit potential of opportunities relative to the required investment
- Core competencies from its portfolio of businesses, technologies, products, and markets
- Assessment of risk

Four broad approaches to growth are:

- **Market penetration.** Focus on current products and current markets.
- **Product growth.** Bring related and new products to existing markets.
- **Market growth.** Sell existing products to related and new markets.
- **Product and market diversification.** Sell related and new products to related and new markets.

CHOOSING THE *RIGHT* GROWTH PATH. To identify and separate worthwhile opportunities from the others typically requires significant marketing research and analysis. The firm should identify the scope of the opportunity, competition, and assess its ability to deliver the necessary customer value to secure differential advantage. More generally, the firm should evaluate its ability to be successful in various growth paths.

> *Marketing Question*
>
> Use the growth-path matrix to identify the growth trajectory of your favorite firm, or a firm for which you would like to work.

Marketing Question

For the firm you chose on p. 64, identify the timing-of-entry strategy for its various growth initiatives.

TIMING OF ENTRY

Along with identifying the *right* growth path, when to seize an opportunity — **timing of entry** — is also crucial. Four broad options are *pioneer, follow-the-leader, segmenter,* and *me-too*:

- **Pioneer.** *Pioneer* firms blaze trails and create new markets via consistent and extensive R&D. They accept risk and understand that failure often accompanies success.
- **Follow-the-leader.** *Follow-the-leader* firms enter rapidly growing markets on the heels of pioneers. Pioneers make large research investments to develop innovative new products/services; follow-the leader firms focus on development. A successful follow-the-leader strategy should have:
  - Vision of serving a mass market
  - Good competitive intelligence to develop products/services as soon as possible
  - Good developmental engineers to leverage/enhance the pioneer's successful research
  - Proactive patent lawyers to identify weak spots in the pioneer's patents
  - Financial strength and commitment to outspend the pioneer
  - Ability to differentiate offers and deliver superior customer value
  - Will and persistence to succeed
- **Segmenter.** *Segmenters* enter established markets in late growth by adding value for specific segments. Segmenter strategies can be very effective in maturing markets.
- **Me-Too.** *Me-too-ers* enter mature markets with limited product lines. They base low-price/low-cost strategies on value engineering, efficient high-volume production (often in low-cost countries), low overhead, aggressive procurement, and great attention to detail.

CHOOSING THE *RIGHT* TIMING OF ENTRY STRATEGY. Similar to growth-path decisions, the firm should identify which *timing-of-entry* strategy best fits its capabilities, then match this strategy to market opportunities.

SCREENING CRITERIA: EVALUATING OPPORTUNITIES

Four **screening criteria** — *objectives, compatibility (fit), core competence,* and *synergy* — help the firm evaluate opportunities and decide where to invest.

OBJECTIVES

An investment opportunity must satisfy firm objectives. Revenue and profit growth are critical for creating shareholder value, but unmitigated growth can be a real problem. The firm must temper its desire for growth with concern for risk, stability, and flexibility.

REVENUE AND PROFIT GROWTH. To assess revenue and profit potential, the firm should consider both non-financial and financial measures. Leading indicators include market potential, current market size and expected growth rates, forces driving market growth, number and strength of competitors, and market-share forecasts.

RISK. The firm must weigh forecast revenues and profits against the risk and required investment. The firm should consider each opportunity's return-risk profile and the impact of each opportunity on other opportunities.

TIMING. In addition to financial return and risk, when evaluating an opportunity the firm must consider the timing of contribution to profits. Depending on the firm's financial circumstances, a moderate return opportunity that delivers profits in the medium term may be more attractive than a higher return opportunity promising profits much later.

STABILITY. A related criterion is *stability*. Suppose the firm must choose between two opportunities: A — high growth, significant variability; B — lower growth, low variability. The firm may prefer the lower growth option.

FLEXIBILITY. All firms face increasing environmental change and complexity. No matter how good the firm's forecasting, it may be blindsided by unexpected events. Alternative ways to gain flexibility are:

- **Acquisitions.** Intel, Microsoft, and Cisco acquire firms with positions in adjacent markets.
- **Joint technology agreements.** Oil companies often form partnerships for oil-drilling platforms and their operations, like Texaco and Shell in the Gulf of Mexico.
- **Partial ownership.** Major drug companies often invest in biotechnology firms.
- **Research and development (R&D).** The firm hedges its bets by investing in competing technologies.
- **Venture capital.** The firm provides venture capital to startup companies but retains options to increase ownership later.

COMPATIBILITY (FIT)

Can the firm be successful in the opportunity? The firm should examine three types of compatibility (fit): product-market fit, product-company fit, and company-market fit.

PRODUCT-MARKET FIT. Is the product appropriate for the market? Restated: Does the product satisfy customer needs in the target market segments better than competitors?

PRODUCT-COMPANY FIT. Does the firm possess the financial, human, and other abilities/resources to succeed? Can the firm successfully upgrade its efforts as the market evolves?

COMPANY-MARKET FIT. Can the firm compete effectively in the market? Does it have sufficient customer insight, reputation, and capabilities/resources to defeat competitors?

RELATIONSHIPS AMONG THE THREE FORMS OF FIT. All three compatibility criteria are important for evaluating individual growth opportunities, but product-market fit is different from the others. If product-market fit is poor — the product does not satisfy customer needs — the firm should dismiss the opportunity. If product-market fit is good, but other fits are poor, then:

- **Poor product-company fit.** Divest the product/technology to a firm better suited to make and sell the product.
- **Poor company-market fit.** Form a strategic alliance with a better-positioned firm.

Marketing Question

Can you identify three examples of successful product-market fit? Can you identify three examples of failed product-market fit? What are the risks of unsuccessful product-market fit?

CORE COMPETENCE

Core competences are knowledge, skills, and other capabilities/resources that the firm possesses. Generally, the firm is better off pursuing opportunities that use its core competencies. But lack of competencies should not necessarily deter the firm from pursuing an attractive opportunity if it can secure what is necessary for success.

SYNERGY

Synergy explores how an opportunity relates to existing firm capabilities/resources. *Positive synergy* reflects the notion that 2+2 can be greater than 4! Synergy kicks in when the firm uses existing resources for an opportunity, like selling a new product through existing distributors. When 2+2 is less than 4, *negative synergy* is at work; pursuing a new opportunity may erode revenues and profits from existing products.

CONTRIBUTION TO THE VENTURE PORTFOLIO

In addition to considering opportunities individually, the firm should consider all opportunities as elements in its venture portfolio. A firm with good cash flow but few growth businesses may heavy-up on longer-term, higher-risk options. A firm with little cash may focus on short-term, low/moderate-risk opportunities.

IMPLEMENTING GROWTH STRATEGIES

The firm has several options for implementing its growth strategy:

INTERNAL DEVELOPMENT

Most firms put significant effort into internal development of new products/services. This approach is appropriate in all cells of the growth-path matrix and for all timing-of-entry options. Internal development has several advantages over alternative growth modes:

- **Control.** The firm has control over the entire development process. It purchases (or leases) required resources and makes all decisions about suppliers and distributors.
- **Cost.** Internal development is typically less expensive than securing new products by acquisitions and other means.

Disadvantages of internal development are:

- **Expertise.** The firm must successfully direct the R&D effort, or the resulting products may require commercialization skills the firm does not possess.
- **Resources.** Some resources may be unavailable or too expensive to develop/acquire.
- **Time.** Market windows are increasingly short; internal development takes time.

INSOURCING

The firm captures more value-added in the supply chain by undertaking additional activities in developing, producing, marketing, distributing, and promoting. The firm can expand upstream by conducting supplier activities — *backward integration*, or downstream by conducting customer activities — *forward integration*.

Marketing Exercise

Develop a table in which you assess the pros and cons of each method of implementing a strategy for growth.

OUTSOURCING

Outsourcing is the opposite of insourcing — the firm engages other firms to undertake activities it previously conducted in-house. The firm can better focus its resources on delivering customer value and securing differential advantage.

ACQUISITION

Generally, growth by acquisition has a speed advantage — the firm gains immediate access to new products and/or new markets. The firm also gains the supporting infrastructure — human resources, operational capabilities, and systems and processes. But acquisitions are no panacea. Acquiring successful firms/business units can be expensive; marrying the cultures of acquired and acquiring firms may also be difficult.

Some acquisitions add value; some do not. We can usefully distinguish between two very different types:

- **Major acquisitions.** Multi-million-dollar acquisitions can cause major realignments of products and markets. Many of these are unsuccessful.
- **Small *fill-in* acquisitions.** These acquisitions complement an existing strategy. These acquisitions have a better success record than major acquisitions.

STRATEGIC ALLIANCE

Generally, strategic alliances address poor product-company fit and/or poor company-market fit without the capital investment and risks inherent in acquisitions. A good alliance partner complements firm strengths and/or compensates for firm weakness. The combined entity is stronger than either firm acting alone.

LICENSING AND TECHNOLOGY PURCHASE

Licensing and technology purchase are alternative ways to access technology developed by others. In licensing, the licensor owns the technology; the licensee typically pays a minimum royalty (fixed payment regardless of use) and an earned royalty rate based on volume (units/dollars) or profits. Technology purchasers typically pay a fixed price to own the technology. In both cases the acquiring firm avoids the risks and expenses of R&D, but may pay highly to secure successful new technology.

EQUITY INVESTMENT

Many firms augment internal development efforts by making equity investments — taking partial ownership in startups. Sometimes they form or *incubate* startups by spinning off their own successful product development efforts.

IMPLEMENTING GROWTH STRATEGIES IN THE MODERN CORPORATION

We learned that the components of a strategy for growth are *vision, mission, growth path*, and *timing of entry*. Together, these elements form a set of lenses the firm can use to approach markets and identify, generate, and decide to invest (or not) in opportunities. Each entry strategy demands quite different capabilities/resources for success. Today, leading firms use multiple approaches to implement growth strategies, often built on *repeatability*. These firms leverage skills in internal development, in/outsourcing, acquisitions, strategic alliances, and/or equity investment; hence, they are better able to address challenges and results are more predictable.

> *Marketing Question*
>
> A startup biotech firm has a single R&D project that promises to produce a product that will significantly reduce the incidence of skin cancer. How would you advise this firm to proceed in drug development and marketing?

TRUE / FALSE QUESTIONS

1. Typically, successful firms evolve their missions over time. ❏ **TRUE** ❏ **FALSE**

2. Segmenter firms enter rapidly growing markets on the heels of pioneers. ❏ **TRUE** ❏ **FALSE**

3. Me-too-ers enter mature markets with limited product lines. They base their low-price/low-cost strategies on value engineering, efficient high-volume production, low overhead, aggressive procurement, and great attention to detail. ❏ **TRUE** ❏ **FALSE**

4. Core competences are skills, knowledge, and other capabilities/resources that the firm possesses.
    ❏ **TRUE** ❏ **FALSE**

5. Positive synergy reflects the notion that 2 + 2 is equal to 4. ❏ **TRUE** ❏ **FALSE**

MULTIPLE CHOICE QUESTIONS

1. A successful follow-the-leader strategy must have all of the following criteria EXCEPT:

    a. a vision of serving a narrow market segment
    b. the ability to differentiate its offer by delivering superior customer value
    c. the will and persistence to succeed
    d. financial strength and commitment to outspend the pioneer

2. _____ enter established markets in late growth by adding value for specific segments.

    a. pioneers
    b. follow-the-leader
    c. segmenter
    d. me-too-ers

3. With _____, the firm captures more value-added in the supply chain by undertaking additional activities in developing, producing, marketing, distributing, and promoting.

    a. insourcing
    b. off shoring
    c. outsourcing
    d. downsizing

4. Which of the following is NOT a disadvantage of internal development as an option for implementing a firm's growth strategy?

    a. control
    b. expertise
    c. resources
    d. time

Answers on page 205

*Identify and Target
Market Segments*

CHAPTER 8

MARKET SEGMENTATION AND TARGETING

MARKET SEGMENTATION IS A FUNDAMENTAL MARKETING CONCEPT that embraces three separate, but related, strategic tasks. First, the firm conducts a market segmentation process to identify market segments. Second, the firm selects which segments to target. Third, the firm develops a market-segment strategy for each target segment (Chapter 9).

THE CHANGING VIEW

OLD WAY	NEW WAY
Crude segmentation	Precise segmentation
Databases poorly developed	Databases central to segmentation
Few large segments	Many small segments — tend to segments-of-one
Intuition-driven segmentation	Analytically driven segmentation
Low levels of analytic expertise	Increasingly sophisticated analyses
Market segments based mainly on demographics	Market segments based on many types of variables
Segmentation applied mainly in consumer packaged goods	Segmentation in B2B and B2C, public and non-profit, nation-states, politics, personal careers
Segmentation focused primarily on consumers	Segmentation extends to multiple customer levels and other company stakeholders

THE MARKET SEGMENTATION PROCESS

Market segmentation is a conceptual and analytic process critical for developing and implementing effective market strategies. In this process, the firm groups actual and potential customers in a market into various *market segments*. The firm then chooses which segments to **target** for effort. The firm must *position* itself in each target segment (segmentation, targeting, positioning [STP]) and develop a *market segment strategy*. When the segment strategy is set, the firm designs a suitable market offer. By executing the process well, the firm:

- Secures better insight into the market, customers, competitors, the company, and complementers — in particular, customer needs.
- Develops a clearer focus on market strategy.
- Identifies opportunities to customization for target segments.
- Designs better offers comprising product, promotion, distribution, and price.
- Secures superior differential advantage and greater customer satisfaction and loyalty.
- Uses resources more efficiently and earns higher profitability.

LEVELS OF SEGMENTATION

Segmentation forms smaller, more discrete groups out of a whole. The firm chooses a broad market to address (Marketing Imperative 1) then identifies several market segments. Within any single market segment, the firm may segment further, forming subsegments as it zeros in on target customers.

DEVELOPING MARKET SEGMENTS

The firm can approach the market segmentation process from two different directions: **customer needs** first or **candidate descriptor (segmentation) variables** first. The firm can also use *qualitative* or *quantitative* approaches.

CUSTOMER NEEDS FIRST. The firm identifies differing customer need profiles, then uses them to form groups. Customers within each group have relatively homogeneous (similar) need profiles, but the various groups have heterogeneous (different) need profiles. The firm must select descriptor variables that identify these groups.

CANDIDATE DESCRIPTOR (SEGMENTATION) VARIABLES FIRST. The firm uses candidate descriptor variables to construct customer groups. Then it searches for homogeneous (similar) need profiles within each group and heterogeneous (different) need profiles across groups. Descriptor variable types are:

- **Geography** — forms different geographical units like country, region, county size, city or Standard Metropolitan Statistical Area (SMSA) size, population density, and climate.
- **Demography** — forms groups based on demographic variables. B2C variables include age, education, family size, gender, income, and life cycle. B2B variables include balance sheet items, firm size, growth, industry, and profitability.
- **Behavioral** — forms groups based on uses of (and responses to) the product, decision-making practice, and decision-making unit.
- **Socio-psychological** — forms groups based on knowledge and attitudes, social class, lifestyle, life stage, and personality characteristics.

METHODOLOGICAL APPROACHES TO FORMING SEGMENTS

Methodological approaches to forming market segments fall into two main categories.

QUALITATIVE (JUDGMENTAL). The segmentation task is highly judgmental, requiring significant conceptual skill. The firm's raw material is creative insight (Chapters 3, 4, 5) typically gained from field marketing research (Chapter 6) and/or customer relationship management (CRM) systems.

> ## *Marketing Question*
>
> What firms demonstrate the *warm-tea* syndrome — address markets generally, even though customer groups have different need profiles?

QUANTITATIVE (DATA-CRUNCHING). Large-scale market segmentation studies use extensive customer survey data and sophisticated multivariate statistical techniques. Cluster analysis approaches include the following steps:

- Develop many statements (variables) about customer needs.
- Develop a set of questions (variables) that identify customers.
- Administer the statements and questions to a random sample of current and potential customers.
- Analyze customer need responses by cluster analysis. Choose the number of clusters (segments) that form the *best* groupings of customer needs.
- Examine each customer cluster (segment) for identifying characteristics.

GOOD SEGMENTATION PRACTICE. The fundamental segmentation task is to link each segment's need profile to appropriate *descriptor* (*segmentation*) variables. If segmentation is done well, each segment has a well-defined need profile and is easily described by segmentation variables.

> **Marketing Question**
>
> How would you segment the market for dog food? Two possible approaches are:
>
> 1. Descriptors of dogs.
> 2. Need profiles of dog owners.
>
> Which approach is easier? Which approach provides greater insight into the dog food market?

MARKET SEGMENTS

Sometimes the market segmentation process develops *good* segments; other times the segments are not that useful. **Good segments** are those the firm could target for marketing effort with a reasonable chance of success. So far, we focused on two important segmentation criteria.

- **Differentiated.** Customers in different segments have different need profiles. Accordingly, they should respond differently to market offers.
- **Identifiable.** The firm can identify customers by using descriptor (segmentation) variables and hence reach them with market offers.

Good market segments satisfy four additional criteria:

- **Accessible.** The firm can reach the segment via communications and distribution channels using appropriate and cost-effective approaches.
- **Appropriate size.** Different firms like different-sized segments. Generally, large firms want large segments to justify their efforts and costs. By contrast, small firms like small segments so they avoid large and powerful competitors.
- **Measurable.** The firm can measure important characteristics like size and growth.
- **Stable.** Customers stay in the segment for a reasonable period of time.

STANDARDIZED MARKET SEGMENTS

Some B2C firms competing in mature markets use **standardized segments** are based on established buying trends, habits, and customer needs. The best-known approach is *PRIZM* (Nielsen Claritas), a U.S. segmentation system. The PRIZM scheme, based largely on income, urbanity, and lifestage, comprises 66 clusters organized as 14 social groups: Affluentials, City Centers, Country Comfort, Elite Suburbs, Inner Suburbs, Landed Gentry, Micro-City Blues, Middle America, Middleburbs, Midtown Mix, Rustic Living, Second City Society, Urban Uptown, and Urban Cores.

KEY QUESTIONS ABOUT MARKET SEGMENTS

Managers often raise questions regarding their own approaches to market segments and the market segmentation process. Here are the most common:

HOW MANY MARKET SEGMENTS ARE ENOUGH? How should the firm trade off enhancing customer satisfaction by defining large numbers of segments in a market, and cost efficiency via few segments? The core options are:

- **Large number of segments.** As the firm develops increased numbers of segments, the similarity of customer need profiles within each segment increases. Hence the firm can earn high customer satisfaction by targeting specialized groups. But product development and marketing costs are high, and economies of scale are few.

- **Small number of segments.** When the firm develops fewer segments, customer needs are less granular and more diffuse. Customer satisfaction from addressing individual segments is necessarily lower, but costs are also lower and segment management is less difficult.

CAN AN INDIVIDUAL CUSTOMER BE A MARKET SEGMENT? Firms that address B2B markets, or sell customer goods through large retail chains, often focus their efforts on individual customers — **segments-of-one**. The firm treats an individual strategic (key) account as a market segment in its own right.

DO MARKET SEGMENTS EVOLVE? If two firms are equally accomplished in designing market offers, the firm with better market segmentation will win. The firm's offers will be more precisely tailored to customer needs than those of competitors. But customer need profiles are constantly evolving, so the firm's segmentation must also evolve, based on good market, customer, competitor, and complementer insight. When markets are young, early entrants are often successful providing basic functional benefits. Then, as the product life cycle evolves, competitors enter, and basic functional benefits become the *cost of entry.*

HOW DO CUSTOMER LIFE CYCLES AFFECT MARKET SEGMENTS? Generally, promoting and selling products to current customers is less expensive than focusing on new customers. Firms increasingly recognize the lifetime value of current customers (CLV) and continually refocus their efforts to increase long-term customer loyalty (Chapter 2). B2B customers may continue indefinitely, but the B2C firm has two polar options:

- **Focus on a fixed age group.** The firm targets an age-defined segment, continually adding new consumers as current customers age and no longer want its products.

- **Retain consumers as they age.** The firm evolves its offer to match changing consumer need profiles and reaps the benefits of consumer loyalty.

DOES A *SEGMENT* OF CUSTOMERS DIFFER FROM A *GROUP* OF CUSTOMERS? Within a segment, customers have similar need profiles; these profiles differ from customers in other segments. By contrast, the firm can form groups in many ways: by degree of use, propensity to buy innovative products, and customer loyalty. Groups may be very important for understanding buyer behavior, but they may not be segments. To illustrate, many markets have *heavy users* and *light users* (groups); but heavy user customers may have many different need profiles (segments).

CAN WE DEVELOP SEGMENTS BASED ON JUST OUR CURRENT CUSTOMERS? Most firms segment the entire market, both current and potential customers. But when the firm has many current customers, it may use customer relationship management (CRM) approaches to place purchase transactions in a **data warehouse**. The firm can then use **data-mining** techniques to identify groups based on purchasing patterns and tailor offers to individual customers based on those patterns.

TARGETING MARKET SEGMENTS

The firm never has sufficient resources and/or abilities to address all segments in a market; hence, it must decide where to target its efforts. Some segments receive greater effort and resources; some segments receive little or no effort. By effective targeting, the firm can better address customer needs and minimizes direct competition. The firm should make targeting decisions conscious of the Principle of Selectivity and Concentration — Chapter 1.

- Marketing must carefully choose targets for firm efforts.
- The firm should concentrate resources against those targets.

Two separate approaches can help the firm decide which segments to target.

THE MULTIFACTOR MATRIX APPROACH TO TARGETING (STRATEGIC POSITION ANALYSIS)

The **multifactor matrix** (*strategic position analysis*) helps the firm decide which market segments to target. For each candidate segment, the firm must answer two questions:

- How attractive is this segment?
- Does the firm have the business strengths to win in this segment?

MARKET SEGMENT ATTRACTIVENESS. The firm should identify useful factors for evaluating many segment choices. Sometimes it considers corporate-level attractiveness factors; other times, it focuses on an individual business. A business with growth and market share objectives typically has different attractiveness factors than one focused on improving cash flow.

BUSINESS STRENGTHS. Required business strengths are specific to each market segment being evaluated. First, the firm must identify those strengths (capabilities/resources) that *any* competitor would require to be successful. Second, it must assess the firm's possession of those strengths.

WHICH MARKET SEGMENTS TO TARGET? The multifactor matrix produces two index numbers per market segment: *attractiveness* and *business strengths*. The firm can use these index numbers to develop a simple diagram that is very helpful in segment selection.

PERCEPTUAL MAP APPROACH TO TARGETING

The perceptual map complements the multifactor matrix approach. The targeting process has four stages:

- **Stage 1 — Customer need dimensions.** Identify two key customer need dimensions for the perceptual map.
- **Stage 2 — Product perceptions.** Plot customer product perceptions on the map.
- **Stage 3 — Market segments.** Plot market segment ideal points on the map.
- **Stage 4 — Targeting decisions.** Use product data (stage 2) and segment data (stage 3) to target market segments.

TARGETING MARKET SEGMENTS AND COMPANY SIZE

Large firms generally have greater resources than small firms, so a large firm that segments and targets well is difficult to beat. But market segmentation and targeting can even the odds for smaller firms. Many large firms cannot achieve a specialized focus on market segments. Large firms may also spread themselves too thin over many segments, allowing smaller, more-focused competitors to gain advantage. Smaller firms face three problems:

- **Demand shortage.** Of necessity, the small firm targets few market segments. If demand drops, other segments cannot cushion the impact.
- **High costs.** Narrow focus implies high costs that cannot be offset by high prices.
- **Too successful.** The small firm is too successful and attracts the attention of major players.

SEGMENT INTERRELATIONSHIPS IN TARGETING

Generally, the firm targets segments individually but sometimes it must target segment A to reach segment B. In many markets, like pharmaceuticals and medical diagnostics, the firm must successfully target a segment of influentials before addressing other segments.

In the British plumbing market, consumers typically rely on plumbers to advise on shower choice. Aquilisa developed the revolutionary, easy-to-install, electronic Quartz shower providing significant consumer value via consistent water pressure and temperature. But plumbers distrusted electronics and were very conservative; hence they did not recommend Quartz. Aquilisa achieved success by targeting showrooms where consumers selected showers and forced plumbers to install their choices. Plumbers learned Quartz's value and started recommending it to customers. Similarly, target customers for *Managing Marketing in the 21st Century* are students in marketing courses, yet Wessex directs marketing effort at instructors.

Marketing Question

Think of a small firm that failed. What role did segmentation and targeting play in its failure? Which pitfall(s) contributed to its failure? What could the firm have done better to understand the limitations of its market strategy?

TRUE / FALSE QUESTIONS

1. Candidate descriptor variables include geography, demography, behavioral, and socio-psychological.
❑ **TRUE** ❑ **FALSE**

2. Large-scale market segmentation studies use extensive customer survey data and sophisticated multivariate statistical techniques. ❑ **TRUE** ❑ **FALSE**

3. *Good* market segments should always be large in size. ❑ **TRUE** ❑ **FALSE**

4. If two firms are equally accomplished in designing market offers, the firm with better market segmentation will win. ❑ **TRUE** ❑ **FALSE**

5. The multifactor matrix produces two index numbers for each market segment: one for market segment attractiveness and one for firm business strength. ❑ **TRUE** ❑ **FALSE**

MULTIPLE CHOICE QUESTIONS

1. Attitudes, life stage, personality, and life-style characteristics are examples of which of the following categories of candidate descriptor variables?

   a. geography
   b. demography
   c. behavioral
   d. socio-psychological

2. *Good* market segments should satisfy all of the following criteria EXCEPT:

   a. stable
   b. measurable
   c. undifferentiated
   d. accessible

3. Firms that address B2B markets, or sell to consumer goods through large retail chains, often focus their efforts on individual customers, known as _____.

   a. segments-of-one
   b. the modularity approach
   c. data mining
   d. factor analysis

4. When a firm has many current customers, it can use _____ approaches to place purchase transactions in a data warehouse. The firm can then use data mining techniques to identify groups based on purchasing patterns and tailor offers to individual customers based on those patterns.

   a. perceptual mapping
   b. factor analysis
   c. linear extrapolation
   d. customer relationship management

5. All of the following are problems smaller firms face regarding targeting market segments EXCEPT:

   a. demand shortage
   b. being too successful
   c. high costs
   d. backward integration

Answers on page 205

CHAPTER 9

MARKET STRATEGY— INTEGRATING FIRM EFFORTS FOR MARKETING SUCCESS

THE FIRM DEVELOPS MARKET STRATEGY with the goal of attracting, retaining, and growing customers. Each market strategy comprises one or more market-segment strategies.

THE CHANGING VIEW

OLD WAY	NEW WAY
Competitor considerations ignored or demeaned	Competitor considerations play a major role
Compromise is common — fuzzy value propositions	Clarity is critical — value propositions are clear and differentiated
Functional programs are poorly coordinated	Market strategy links together functional programs
Integration is limited to the marketing mix	Integration spans all functions
Internal and budgetary focus to market strategy	External and strategic focus to market strategy
Market strategy is the marketing mix	Market strategy drives the marketing mix
Market strategy development done by marketing and general management	Cross-functional teamwork crucial in market strategy development
Marketers focus on volume and share	Marketers concerned with creating shareholder value
Objectives uniform across products and markets	Objectives differ across products and markets
Positioning is poorly understood	Positioning is a crucial strategic element

THE PURPOSE OF MARKET AND MARKET-SEGMENT STRATEGIES

The market **strategy** specifies what the firm is trying to achieve, which segments it will target for effort, and how it will position itself in those market segments. The firm must make three types of decisions:

- **Results.** What the firm wants to achieve from addressing the market.
- **Resources.** Broadly speaking, how the firm will deploy its resources to achieve these results.
- **Actions.** Which actions the firm intends to take to be successful.

PROVIDING STRATEGIC DIRECTION IN THE MARKET

Market and market-segment strategies provide strategic direction on how to attract, retain, and grow customers, in the face of competitors trying to do the same thing.

SECURING DIFFERENTIAL ADVANTAGE

Well-developed market and market-segment strategies must clarify why customers should buy from the firm rather than competitors. They also identify how the firm will gain differential advantage.

GUIDING THE EFFECTIVE ALLOCATION OF SCARCE RESOURCES

A *good* market strategy considers resource limitations. It must define, generally yet clearly, effective allocations to support the firm's strategic direction. The firm must make two types of allocations. *Externally*, the firm allocates resources among target market segments, selecting the resources for securing differential advantage by segment. *Internally*, the firm allocates resources among activities like product development, advertising, and selling.

ACHIEVING CROSS-FUNCTIONAL INTEGRATION

Achieving integration across different parts of the firm and/or business units is critical, yet often elusive. The market strategy must coordinate the actions of various parts of the firm, so they all pull together to secure differential advantage. Without effective integration, significant internal conflict can arise.

ELEMENTS OF THE MARKET-SEGMENT STRATEGY

The market-segment strategy is the basic unit of the market strategy. A market strategy frequently combines several interrelated market-segment strategies. The four pillars of a market-segment strategy are:

- **Performance objectives.** Stated as results the firm seeks; includes strategic objectives and operational objectives.
- **Strategic focus.** The broad direction of the strategy.
- **Positioning.** How the firm wants customers to view its offer; comprises customer targets, competitor targets, value proposition, and *reasons to believe.*
- **Implementation programs.** How the firm should implement the strategy; includes the marketing mix and supporting functional programs.

Marketing Question

What is *your* career strategy? What will you do when you graduate? Describe your objectives, the job market segment you intend to enter, and your strategy for managing your career and achieving your goals.

Marketing Question

In rural areas of emerging countries, the farmer uses a yoke on his team of oxen. Is *yoke* a good metaphor for the market strategy?

Marketing Question

The market strategy is not visible, but we can *reverse engineer* a strategy by observing firm actions. Suppose you compete with McDonald's. What implementation programs can you identify? Then ask these questions: What core segment does McDonald's address? How do you assess McDonald's performance objectives? What is McDonald's strategic focus? What is McDonald's positioning? Is McDonald's positioning *good* for the future?

PERFORMANCE OBJECTIVES

Performance objectives articulate firm goals for the market segment. Two components state clearly and simply what the firm is trying to achieve: strategic objectives and operational objectives.

STRATEGIC OBJECTIVES

Strategic objectives establish the type of results the firm requires; they are qualitative and directional. Strategic objectives are not concerned with numbers, but declare, in general terms, how the firm will measure its success. The three broad categories of strategic objectives are growth and market share, profitability, and cash flow.

GUIDELINES FOR CHOOSING AMONG STRATEGIC OBJECTIVES

In the introduction and early growth stages of the product life cycle, firms often set priorities on growth and/or market share. Priorities often shift to profit in late growth and for much of the maturity stage. Late in the maturity stage, especially if decline is imminent, cash flow predominates.

OPERATIONAL OBJECTIVES

Operational objectives are quantitative and time-bound. Operational objectives provide the numbers and time-frame to attach to strategic objectives. Operational objectives answer the following questions: How much is required, and by when? Operational objectives should specify how much growth, market share, profit, or cash flow the firm should earn during a specific time frame. The firm uses operational objectives to evaluate performance. Operational objectives should be SMART — specific, measurable, achievable, realistic, and timely.

SETTING PERFORMANCE OBJECTIVES

Sometimes managers fail to distinguish between strategic and operational objectives. Far too often, they state objectives in terms of profits. "Our profit target for 20XY is $45 million." In principle, setting a $45 million target is not wrong, but the problem is in not asking (yet alone answering) two basic questions: *How will achieving this profit objective affect the firm's overall objectives? and How shall we get there?*

STRATEGIC FOCUS

Once the firm has established performance objectives for its target market segment, it must decide where to allocate resources. The **strategic focus** does exactly that. The two main branches for improving profits and return on investments (ROI) are: Branch A — increase unit sales volume and Branch B — improve margins and investment returns. The firm must select among the branches and sub-branches to create a focus that best helps achieve its strategic and operational performance objectives.

INCREASE UNIT SALES VOLUME (BRANCH A)

Branch A has two sub-branches, C and D, for increasing unit sales volume. Sub-branch C focuses on the firm's current revenue base; sub-branch D focuses on securing new revenues. Each sub-branch provides two alternatives. In sub-branch C, the firm enhances current revenues by *increasing customer retention* and *increasing customer use*. In sub-branch D, the firm secures new revenues by *attracting customers from competitors* and *securing new business* by identifying opportunities.

IMPROVE MARGINS AND INVESTMENT RETURNS (BRANCH B)

Branch B has two sub-branches, E and F, for improving margins and investment returns, holding unit sales constant. Sub-branch E focuses on increasing firm revenues — sub-branch F focuses on reducing costs and assets. Each sub-branch provides two alternatives. In sub-branch E, the firm increases revenues by *raising prices* and *improving the sales mix*. In sub-branch F, the firm lowers costs and assets by *reducing operating costs* and *improving asset utilization*.

POSITIONING

Positioning is the heart of the market segment strategy. The firm must make four key decisions *within* the segment:

1. Select customer targets.
2. Frame competitor targets.
3. Design the value proposition.
4. Articulate reasons to believe.

SELECTING CUSTOMER TARGETS

Customer targets are where the firm places the bulk of its marketing efforts. Three issues are important when targeting customers:

- **Choosing the distribution system.** The firm must identify the appropriate distribution system — possibly comprising multiple levels — so its products reach end-user customers.
- **Targeting levels within the distribution system.** The firm must decide which level(s) in the distribution system should receive the most marketing effort. The broad options are:
  - **Push strategy.** The firm places most marketing effort *upstream* on direct customers like manufacturers and distributors.
  - **Pull strategy.** The firm places most marketing effort *downstream* on indirect customers — consumers/end users.
- **Targeting specific person types/roles.** The firm must identify what specific person types/roles it should target for effort at the chosen distribution levels.

Creativity is important in customer targeting. The firm should consider:

- **Reachability.** Target customers should be easy to reach — but gaining access may be difficult.
- **Obvious versus creative targets.** Some customers are easy to identify and reach, but targeting them can be ineffective because they are obvious — they may also be competitors' customer targets! Deep customer insight, creativity, and a contrarian position can pay great dividends.
- **Influencers.** Customer targets may not be decision-makers, but they should influence the buying decision.
- **Personally benefits but does not pay.** The ideal customer target has significant influence, personally benefits from the purchase, but does not pay.

> **Marketing Question**
>
> State-owned Russian airplane manufacturer Sukhoi seeks to expand its customer base beyond Russia, Cuba, Iran, and a few African countries with its 75–95-seat, short-haul, single-aisle Superjet 100. Develop a strategy for entering the U.S. and/or Western European markets.

FRAMING COMPETITOR TARGETS

The firm decides which competitors to compete against. **Competitor targets** can be current and/or potential competitors, direct and/or indirect competitors, and/or supply-chain competitors. Choice of competitor target depends on firm strength in the market segment. Key issues are:

- **Categories of competitors.** Competitors fall into one of two categories: competitors to avoid and competitors the firm is quite happy (and chooses) to face.
- **Customer perceptions.** Competitive targeting shapes customer perceptions of the firm's offer.
- **Subtlety in competitor targeting.** The most effective competitor targeting may not be obvious. When Avis *tries harder*, what is the competitor target? Maybe Hertz, but more likely smaller players like National and Budget.

DESIGNING THE VALUE PROPOSITION

A well-designed **value proposition** provides a convincing answer to a deceptively simple question: "Why should target customers prefer the firm's offer to those of competitors?" *Positioning is the heart of the strategy* — the *value proposition* is the heart of positioning. The firm bases its value proposition on functional, psychological, and economic value and related benefits it offers customers. The firm should base its value proposition on the principles of customer value and differential advantage:

- Focus on satisfying important customer needs,
- Attempt to meet these needs better than competitors and, where possible,
- Offer values and benefits that are difficult for competitors to imitate.

In particular, the value proposition should follow the BUSCH system — **b**elievable, **u**nique, **s**ustainable, **c**ompelling, and **h**onest. The *value proposition* plays two separate but related roles:

- **Externally** — is the firm's major competitive weapon for attracting, retaining, and growing customers. *Value proposition* defines why the firm's benefits and values are superior to competition.
- **Internally** — defines the firm's implementation task; provides the organizing framework for implementing all firm activities.

The firm must develop a value proposition for each target customer type.

ARTICULATING REASONS TO BELIEVE

Declaring the firm's intentions in the *value proposition* is one thing; convincing target customers that the firm will deliver on its promises is quite another. The *reasons-to-believe* statement supports the firm's value proposition with compelling facts to make its claims believable.

DEVELOPING POSITIONING STATEMENTS

"Positioning is not what you do to a product — positioning is what you do to the mind of the prospect."

A compelling positioning statement is vital for guiding and coordinating the firm's marketing efforts. But developing the positioning statement is complex, difficult, and time-consuming.

Marketing Question

Google is the market leader in Internet search; Microsoft's search entry is Bing. How would you advise Microsoft to increase market share? How would you advise Google to resist Microsoft's efforts?

Many people may be involved. The positioning statement must clearly distinguish the firm's offer from competitors' offers. Positioning should:

Convince	[customer target]
In the context of other alternatives	[competitor target]
That they will receive these benefits	[value proposition]
Because we have these capabilities/features	[reasons to believe]

Positioning statements should be **d**istinct, **c**ompelling, **a**uthentic, **p**ersuasive, and **s**ustainable (DCAPS).

IMPLEMENTATION PROGRAMS

Strategic focus and positioning specify the firm's approach to achieve its performance objectives. Two types of implementation programs describe specific actions the firm must take to execute its approach. Top executive support is crucial for superb implementation.

IMPLEMENTING THE MARKETING MIX

Each element in the marketing mix must support the value proposition, and each must also support the others. Marketing-mix elements include product, promotion, distribution, price, and service. Three issues are important for implementing the marketing mix:

SUPPORTS THE VALUE PROPOSITION AND EACH OTHER. Each marketing-mix element should support the value proposition. Chapters 12 through 20 focus on individual marketing-mix elements.

BUDGET SIZE AND ALLOCATION. Budgetary issues are critical in designing the marketing mix. The firm must set an overall budget but be prepared for modifications based on corporate priorities, competitor actions, and/or difficult economic times. The firm must allocate the budget across different marketing-mix areas.

ALIGNING CROSS-FUNCTIONAL SUPPORT

Competition is so intense that the entire firm must work together as a competitive weapon by aligning all functional areas like finance, human resources, legal, operations, and R&D — to support the value proposition.

MANAGING MULTI-SEGMENT STRATEGIES

When the firm targets multiple segments, it faces three possible implementation situations:

- **Independence.** Individual segment strategies and implementation programs are unrelated.
- **Positive synergies.** The firm enjoys positive synergies from implementation programs across segments. The firm may secure cost efficiencies from using the same sales force, distribution channels, and/or sharing brand equity.
- **Negative synergies.** The firm suffers negative synergy from implementation programs across segments. Multiple products confuse the sales force; brand extensions confuse customers.

Marketing Question

Select your favorite (or least favorite) politician. In his/her most recent political campaign, what segments did s/he target? How did the positioning — customer target, competitive target, value proposition, reasons to believe — differ from segment to segment? How did segment strategies mutually interface?

Marketing Question

What is the iPhone's value proposition? What is its marketing mix? Do the marketing-mix elements support the value proposition and one another?

TRUE / FALSE QUESTIONS

1. The basic market-strategy unit is the market-segment strategy. ❏ TRUE ❏ FALSE

2. The three broad categories of strategic objectives are growth and market share, profitability, and cash flow. ❏ TRUE ❏ FALSE

3. A firm implementing a pull strategy places most marketing effort upstream on direct customers — manufacturing and distributors. ❏ TRUE ❏ FALSE

4. A compelling positioning statement is vital for guiding and coordinating the firm's marketing efforts. ❏ TRUE ❏ FALSE

5. The firm enjoys positive synergies by targeting an additional segment, although new products may confuse the sales force. ❏ TRUE ❏ FALSE

MULTIPLE CHOICE QUESTIONS

1. The firm must make all of the following types of decisions when determining which segments it will target for effort and how it will position itself in those market segments EXCEPT:

   a. results
   b. resources
   c. actions
   d. retraction

2. Which of the following is NOT one of the four pillars of a market-segment strategy?

   a. performance objectives
   b. cultural identities
   c. strategic focus
   d. positioning

3. Positioning requires the firm to take each of the following actions within segments EXCEPT:

   a. Screen new product ideas.
   b. Frame competitor targets.
   c. Design the value proposition.
   d. Articulate the reasons to believe.

4. Which of the following is NOT one of the three important issues when targeting customers?

   a. Identify the appropriate distribution system for its products/services to reach end-user customers.
   b. Select the distributor that uses a focus strategy to target its customers.
   c. Decide at which level(s) in its distribution system organizations should receive the most marketing effort.
   d. Identify what specific persons or types of person at the chosen distribution levels it should target for effort.

5. The firm _____ from implementation programs for individual segments. The firm may gain cost efficiencies from using the same sales force and similar distribution channels and/or sharing brand equity.

   a. experiences independence
   b. suffers negative synergy
   c. experiences interdependence
   d. enjoys positive synergy

Answers on page 205

CHAPTER 10

MANAGING THROUGH THE LIFE CYCLE

THE FIRM CAN MORE EFFECTIVELY DEVELOP ITS MARKET STRATEGY by anticipating competitor actions and then acting pre-emptively. The life-cycle framework can be very helpful for anticipating likely competitive scenarios.

THE CHANGING VIEW

OLD WAY	NEW WAY
Accept low returns and cross-subsidize products	Shareholder value discipline applied rigorously
Commoditization is viewed as inevitable	Innovation is a major strategic weapon
Competition to the death	Merger and consolidation viewed as legitimate strategies in shareholders' interest
Evolutionary change of management approach	Proactively planned change of management approach
Firms cut costs when times are bad	Firms monitor cost efficiency and cut costs continually
Firms hide behind regulatory barriers, often supported by government	Governments work aggressively to increase competition
Firms maximize cash flow by minimizing investment in mature markets	Innovation rejuvenates market growth
Industry structure viewed as fixed	Industry structure viewed as variable
Pre-emptive strategies are rare	Pre-emptive strategies are commonplace
Sequential product development	Concurrent product development
Slow market development with sequential product introductions worldwide	Rapid market development with simultaneous new product launches in multiple countries
Tied to traditional distribution systems and business models	New business models, distribution methods, and technologies to increase efficiencies and add value
Uninformed entry strategies	Entry strategies driven by sophisticated understanding of market development

DEVELOPING COMPETITIVE STRATEGIC OPTIONS

Marketing Question

Can you identify firms and products corresponding to the nine scenarios in Figure 10.1 (main text)?

The firm generates **strategic options** by developing scenarios that let it anticipate future competitor actions. The main building block is the classic life cycle — introduction, early growth, late growth, maturity, and decline — typically at the product form level. The *life-cycle approach* is very powerful because market conditions tend to be similar at the same life-cycle stage across many product types and technologies. Each scenario has a limited number of strategic options. Although the scenarios and strategic options are valid for many product cycles, generally life cycles are shortening. Implications are:

- When life cycles were longer, firms could enter a market, fail, redevelop products, and re-enter with a reasonable chance of success. Today, re-entry windows are closing.
- Shortening life cycles reduce the time — in early growth — to earn the highest unit margins.
- Good strategic thinking early in the life cycle is more important than ever.
- Faster cycles require proactive management of strategy over the life cycle; evolutionary approaches may be too slow.

BUILDING PRODUCT LIFE-CYCLE SCENARIOS

We identify nine product life-cycle-based scenarios.

SCENARIO 1: INTRODUCTION STAGE: PIONEERS

Pioneering firms typically incur significant R&D and market launch expenditures; they must invest in plant, equipment, and systems before launch. Marketing expenses are high, and revenues may not cover the firm's ongoing operating costs, much less its fixed costs. Early on, cash flows are often negative. The pioneer should lay the foundation for achieving market leadership and profitability, at least in the short and medium run. The pioneer must develop an appropriate strategy as the life cycle moves toward early growth, often slowing/forestalling competitive entry by creating (or exploiting) entry barriers — government-imposed, product-specific, and firm-driven.

GOVERNMENT-IMPOSED BARRIERS. Patents are the most common government-imposed barrier. Patents provide owners with legal monopolies for several years.

PRODUCT-SPECIFIC BARRIERS. Product-specific barriers relate directly to the product and include access to capital, raw materials, human resources, and a minimum scale of operations. Sometimes these barriers relate to the product itself so the firm can exploit them; other times the firm can actively raise barriers.

FIRM-DRIVEN BARRIERS. The firm can build *low-cost* barriers via **penetration pricing.** The firm may also develop and exploit **first-mover advantages:**

- **Low-cost barriers and penetration pricing.** With penetration pricing (PP), the firm plans on low profit margins for a substantial time period. PP is risky and takes significant resolve. PP requires substantial resources as the firm continually reduces costs and prices, builds capacity, and grows quickly.
- **First-mover advantage.** The pioneer may earn advantages because it was first. The pioneer may be able to sustain technological advantage by improving products and/or developing new applications. A firm with first-mover advantages may maintain high prices — **price skimming (PS).** PS works if entry barriers are high, customers willingness to try is strong, and customers are relatively price-insensitive.

SCENARIO 2: EARLY-GROWTH LEADERS

Customers have accepted the product form, and market demand is growing rapidly. Generally, the market leader has a strong position. The leader has worked out its market-entry problems, and unit costs are under control. The firm should be profitable, but cash flow may be negative as the firm invests to grow the market and adds new capacity. The leader has four strategic options — two each based on *continuing* and *surrendering* leadership:

- Continue to be leader — enhance position
- Continue to be leader — maintain position
- Surrender leadership — retreat to a market segment or segments
- Surrender leadership — exit the market

CONTINUE TO BE LEADER: ENHANCE POSITION. The firm leverages its success to seek market dominance. The firm grows and broadens the market by continually investing in R&D to produce new products, extensive advertising, and personal selling. The firm increases production capacity ahead of market demand and aggressively reduces costs. As competitors enter, firm communications shift from market development to emphasizing superiority over competitors.

CONTINUE TO BE LEADER: MAINTAIN POSITION. The firm may prefer a more conservative approach and merely try to maintain market position. The firm may enjoy monopoly-like status and be concerned about potential political, legal, and regulatory difficulties. The firm requires good up-to-date competitive intelligence, and must carefully select customer and competitor targets. The firm must have a clear strategy, sufficient resolve to stick to the strategy despite temporary hiccups, and thoughtful contingency and/or scenario planning.

SURRENDER LEADERSHIP: RETREAT TO A MARKET SEGMENT OR SEGMENTS. The firm makes a deliberate choice to surrender leadership. The firm may lack resources for fully developing the market and/or for funding an ongoing stream of new products. Or a financially stronger competitor sets a market-leadership goal, and the firm knows it cannot win a head-to-head battle. The firm decides to target one or more market segments as a specialized competitor.

SURRENDER LEADERSHIP: EXIT THE MARKET. Leaving a market after being the pioneering leader can seem defeatist, but may be prudent. If the value of its market position, based on the projected discounted profit stream, is less than the current sale value, the firm should consider selling, especially if the product is not central to its mission.

> *Marketing Question*
>
> Suppose you have the following information about a market:
> - Market growth rate — 15 percent annually
> - Leader's market share — 40 percent
> - Follower's market share — 10 percent
> - Leader's growth rate — 15 percent annually.
>
> Question: How fast must the follower grow annually, to overtake the leader in six years?
>
> Answer: 45 percent.

SCENARIO 3: EARLY-GROWTH FOLLOWERS

Some firms prefer to be **followers**, entering markets in the early-growth stage. By pursuing a *wait-and-see* strategy, they can better assess market potential, and learn from the leader's mistakes. Followers in early growth have similar strategic options to the leader. But because they start from inferior positions, choosing among them has a different cadence. The options are:

- Seek market leadership.
- Settle for second place.
- Focus on gaining leadership in a market segment or segments.
- Exit the market.

SEEK MARKET LEADERSHIP. The follower can pursue leadership by *imitating* or *leapfrogging* the market leader:

- **Imitation.** The follower copies the leader but executes more effectively. Successful imitators spend heavily to play *catch-up* on product development and outspend the leader in promotion.

- **Leapfrog.** The follower improves on the leader. The follower offers enhanced value by developing innovative and superior products, and/or it enters emerging market segments before the leader. Generally, the leapfrogger avoids head-to-head price competition.

SETTLE FOR SECOND PLACE. Settling for second place may be a reasonable and profitable option. Perhaps the leader is content with current market share. Customers may demand a second supplier, multiple competitors may simplify product standards, and/or the political/legal/regulatory environment may be favorable.

FOCUS ON A MARKET SEGMENT OR SEGMENTS. This option may be attractive if the follower has fewer resources than the leader and other followers and if the segment (or segments) is attractive.

EXIT THE MARKET. If the business' sale value is greater than the projected discounted profit stream, the firm should consider exiting the market. The product may have high value for a potential acquirer eager to enter the product's market (market segment).

SCENARIO 4: LATE-GROWTH STAGE

The firm receives minimal value from early market leadership, or being a fast follower. Although the customer benefits that drove purchase in introduction and early growth are still important, they may not enter the customer choice decision. More likely, these elements have become *qualifiers* or *antes*, and the customer decides on other values. The firm requires considerable marketing research skills to conduct market segmentation, decide which segment(s) to target, satisfy customer needs in the target segment(s), and monitor evolving segments for new opportunities. Successful firms address target segments with *rifle-shot marketing* and then build defensible positions against competitors.

SCENARIO 5: GROWTH IN A MATURE MARKET

When assessing if the life cycle is really in maturity, the firm must analyze the barriers to growth:
- **Behavioral barriers.** Requiring significant behavioral change by customers is often a barrier.
- **Economic barriers.** Economic barriers are often linked to technology.
- **Government-imposed barriers.** When the government removes regulations, competitors often enter, and growth explodes.
- **Technological barriers.** Innovation may obliterate technological barriers to growth.

Generally, if the market is not *really* mature, the firm's key strategic objective should be growth. The most serious barrier to growth may be lack of creativity. Creatively generating and analyzing opportunities and approaching seemingly mature markets can spur growth in several ways:

INCREASE PRODUCT USE. The firm may increase product use via reminder and reinforcement communications; promoting different use applications, occasions, and/or locations; providing incentives and bundling opportunities; and reducing undesirable consequences of frequency. There are many specific techniques.

IMPROVE THE PRODUCT/SERVICE. Firms should expect sales to slow if products do not satisfy customer needs. The remedy is simple: *Improve the product/service!*

IMPROVE PHYSICAL DISTRIBUTION. Sophisticated package delivery and tracking systems have helped grow electronic commerce.

REDUCE PRICE. Generally, price reductions increase sales.

REPOSITION THE BRAND. The firm offers the same product but with new benefits/values for new customers.

Marketing Question

Assume you work for Ford or GM. What barriers to growth exist in the automobile market? Are these barriers different for foreign manufacturers?

ENTER NEW MARKETS. When fax capability threatened overnight document delivery, FedEx refocused efforts on shipping physical goods for direct marketers. New markets can often be in new geographic areas.

SCENARIO 6: LEADERS IN CONCENTRATED MATURE MARKETS

Generally, **concentrated markets** support a few substantial competitors whose aggregate market share often exceeds 60 percent; several small players may target market niches. Profit margins should be high for low-cost leaders. The market leader has two strategic options:

- Maintain leadership over the long run.
- Harvest the business.

MAINTAIN LEADERSHIP OVER THE LONG RUN. The core decision for maintaining market leadership is choosing the *right* investment level. *Overinvestment* to gain market share from entrenched competitors often wastes resources. Pressures for overinvestment are:

- **Few alternative opportunities.** The firm fails to develop other growth opportunities like new products or strategic alliances.
- **Internally focused funding criteria.** The firm bases funding on current financial performance and underfunds unprofitable new products.
- **Political power of mature-product champions.** Senior executives directing the firm's large product lines are typically powerful — their products are today's profit-makers and they lobby successfully for large budgets.

Conversely, *underinvestment* can leave the firm vulnerable to aggressive competitors, and the firm loses market share. Reasons for underinvestment are:

- **Fear of cannibalization.** The firm could maintain leadership by introducing a lower-profit version(s). The firm fails to act because it fears losing sales of higher profit product(s).
- **Inertia.** Performance is acceptable and the firm sees no reason to change.
- **Limited view of the competition.** The firm does not think broadly enough.
- **Misunderstanding the challenger's strategy.** The firm's competitive data-gathering and analysis is weak; it fails to act gain good competitive insight.

HARVEST. The firm is market leader, but a harvest strategy may be more important than maintaining sales and market share. Reasons include:

- **Change in firm strategy.** The product becomes less central to the firm.
- **Desire to avoid specific competitors.** If the firm forecasts tougher competition, harvesting may be the best option.
- **Government regulations.** The government may restrict the industry or eliminate product use.
- **Investment requirements are too high.** Necessary investment for continued competitiveness, like new product or new process technology, may be too high.
- **New technology.** The product will soon become obsolete.

Once the firm decides to harvest, the critical question is *fast* or *slow?* For fast harvesting — divest the product and gain immediate cash. Slow harvesting — the firm should focus on three issues:

- **Cut costs.** Simplify the product line; streamline distribution; reduce advertising, promotion, and services; and eliminate small and unprofitable customers.
- **Minimize investment.** Make little or no further product investment.
- **Raise prices.** Raise prices or eliminate extras like free delivery or extended warranties.

> ### Marketing Question
> Suppose you managed the Gillette brand for P&G. What actions would you take to secure long-run profits?

SCENARIO 7: FOLLOWERS IN CONCENTRATED MATURE MARKETS

Followers have three broad strategic options, each with several sub-options:

IMPROVE MARKET POSITION. Careful and creative market segmentation, kenneling, and direct attack are three primary alternatives to grow and, perhaps, ultimately dethrone the market leader:

- **Market segmentation.** Creative segmentation is the dominant option for counteracting the market leader's advantages. The follower should conduct careful research to identify and target emerging segments.
- **Kenneling.** Kenneling is a metaphor for bringing several *dog* (seemingly worthless) products together. A follower may acquire several unprofitable (or marginally profitable) low-market-share products and then do a *roll-up* into a single offer.
- **Direct attack.** If the leader has been lazy, underinvested, set prices too high, and/or served customers poorly, direct attack may be the follower's best option. Good market intelligence helps find the leader's weak spots, so the follower can invest and exploit them.

KEEP ON TRUCKIN'. This adage describes maintaining or rationalizing the firm's current position:

- **Maintain position.** Holding market share roughly constant over the long run can be viable if the firm has a profitable market position and strengths in one or more segments.
- **Rationalize position.** If profits are marginal or negative, rationalizing operations may be a way to go. The firm should examine all aspects of operations, distribution, and sales with a *fine-tooth comb*, and make tough cost-cutting decisions.

EXIT. Followers should choose *exit* if profitability is unlikely or if the product's future is doubtful, perhaps due to negative brand image or slowing market demand. Choices are divest or liquidate:

- **Divest.** The firm can secure cash quickly by selling the business.
- **Liquidate.** If no buyers appear, the only reasonable action may be liquidation — closing down the business and selling the assets.

> *Marketing Question*
>
> For decades, P&G and Unilever competed fiercely in laundry detergents; P&G has been the market leader for many years. In 2008, Unilever divested its U.S. detergent business to a private equity firm. Why? What five-year strategies would you suggest for P&G and the new private equity owner?

SCENARIO 8: FRAGMENTED MATURE MARKETS

Fragmented markets have many players, but no firm is dominant. Hence, leader/follower distinctions have little relevance. An important objective is increasing market share. Two strategic options for restructuring or repositioning offers are acquisition, and standardization and branding.

ACQUISITION. Acquisition is similar to kenneling; it can be very successful when geography drives fragmentation.

STANDARDIZATION AND BRANDING. In fragmented industries, many players typically offer a wide range of products/services. Standardization is a way to reduce variation and improve consistency across various suppliers; branding assures customers that each provider supplies the same value.

SCENARIO 9: MARKETS IN DECLINE

We assess declining products in two dimensions: market hospitality and the firm's business strengths.

MARKET HOSPITALITY. A declining market is **inhospitable** if:

- Decline is rapid and/or uncertain.
- The market is commodity-based; there are no price-insensitive segments.

- Competitors:
  - are viable and credible.
  - are evenly balanced and view the market as strategically important.
  - have high fixed costs and are very sensitive to sales declines.
- Customer switching costs are low.

Declining markets are *especially* inhospitable if, in addition:

- Bankruptcy laws allow failing competitors to return with lower costs, like U.S. airlines.
- Competitor exit barriers are high.
- Competitors are emotionally committed to their products.
- The product is part of a vertically integrated supply system.
- The government or the community pressures (or subsidizes) some firms to remain.

BUSINESS STRENGTHS. Firms with good **business strengths** should have low costs, good raw material contracts, and/or be able to keep productive assets running without major investment.

Strategic options boil down to three groups:

LEADERSHIP

Pursuing leadership is a viable option when the market is hospitable and the firm has high business strengths. The firm should publicly recognize the decline, but also demonstrate its commitment.

HARVEST, DIVEST, SEGMENT

For other market hospitality/business strength combinations, harvest or divest are the most likely reasonable options. However, medium-run viability may be an option if the firm is well-positioned in price-insensitive segments.

LEVERAGE THE BRAND

The firm may be able to leverage a strong brand in other markets. By diversifying away from its original business, the firm may yet survive and grow.

> ### Marketing Question
>
> Suppose you were a full-service travel agent. What actions would you take to ensure your survival?

TRUE / FALSE QUESTIONS

1. A firm generates strategic options by developing scenarios that let it anticipate future competitor actions. ❑ **TRUE** ❑ **FALSE**

2. The follower's strategic objective is to lay the foundation for achieving market leadership and profitability, at least in the short and medium run. ❑ **TRUE** ❑ **FALSE**

3. Patents are the most common government-imposed barriers that firms can exploit. ❑ **TRUE** ❑ **FALSE**

4. In a leapfrog situation, the follower improves on the leader and offers enhanced value by developing innovative and superior products, and/or it enters emerging market segments before the leader. ❑ **TRUE** ❑ **FALSE**

5. During the late-growth stage, the value to the firm from early market leadership, or being a fast follower, is still growing rapidly. ❑ **TRUE** ❑ **FALSE**

MULTIPLE CHOICE QUESTIONS

1. The options for a follower in the early growth stage of the product life cycle include all of the following EXCEPT:

   a. seeking market leadership
   b. exiting the market
   c. settling for third place
   d. focusing on gaining leadership in a particular market segment or segments

2. Which of the following is NOT a method of generating growth in a mature market?

   a. increasing product use
   b. increasing price
   c. repositioning the brand
   d. improving physical distribution

3. All of the following are reasons that firms underinvest in mature products EXCEPT:

   a. limited view of the competition
   b. internally focused funding criteria
   c. fear of cannibalization
   d. inertia

4. Which of the following is NOT an issue of focus for a firm that is considering harvesting its product line slowly?

   a. cutting costs
   b. minimizing investment
   c. raising prices
   d. decreasing prices

5. Which of the following is NOT a broad strategic option for a follower in a concentrated mature market?

   a. improving market position by growing sales
   b. keep on truckin'
   c. exiting
   d. developing a new product

Answers on page 205

Set Strategic Direction and Positioning

CHAPTER 11

MANAGING BRANDS

IN RECENT YEARS, BRANDING HAS SHIFTED from being a relatively low-level tactical issue concerned with naming products/services, to being a critical driver of contemporary marketing practice. Branding is now a major decision area for both senior managers and marketing executives alike.

THE CHANGING VIEW

OLD WAY	NEW WAY
Brand management is a junior executive responsibility	Brand management is an important senior management responsibility
Brand owners desire total control over their own brands — co-branding is rare	Brand owners are willing to engage in cooperative strategies — co-branding is increasingly used
Brand proliferation common	Brand rationalization common
Branding is a name	Branding is a multi-sensory memorable experience
Brands help customers reduce purchase risk	Brands provide customers with many values
Brands tied to products and stock-keeping units (skus)	Brands assets to be managed in their own right
Firms add brands haphazardly	Firms carefully consider brand architecture
Local and regional brands are dominant	Global brands increasingly pre-eminent
Only brand owners use brands	Brand licensing increasingly common

WHAT IS A BRAND?

Brands are different from products. A brand is a symbol around which the firm and its customers construct a relationship. We define a brand as: *A collection of perceptions and associations that customers hold about a product, a service, or a company. This collection embodies values that create meaning for customers that represent a promise of the experience customers expect when they have contact with a brand.* Important implications are:

- The primary meaning of any brand is carried in customers' minds.
- The brand makes an implicit or explicit promise of a customer experience. This promise provides value to customers over and above the basic product/service.
- *Brand* applies widely to an individual product, product line, or group of product lines.

Marketing Question

What is your favorite brand? What promise does this brand offer over and above the generic product/service?

Features of brands are:

- Anything can be branded — a product, service, country, or even yourselves!
- Brands can provide psychological value: safety and security.
- Some brands may become generic — synonymous with the product class.
- Customer judgments and expectations about brands drive purchase decisions.
- Customers often form communities to demonstrate their commitments to brands.

The firm must choose a **brand identity** for each of its brands — associations like personal, lifestyle, or type of customer it *wants* people to hold. By contrast, **brand image** is the actual associations customers hold about the brand.

BRAND ASSOCIATIONS

The firm should strive for **brand associations** that reinforce the desired brand identity and align these associations with brand image. Brand associations are thoughts the customer generates when faced with a stimulus like brand name, logo, message, or spokesperson. These associations combine to form **brand personality**.

Effective brand associations are:

- **Strong.** Personally relevant for customers and presented consistently over time.
- **Favorable.** Desired by customers and successfully delivered by the brand.
- **Unique.** Perceived by customers as unique, different from other brands.

BRANDING IS NOT JUST FOR CONSUMERS ...

Branding is very important for B2C marketing but is also important in B2B markets, especially for firms with many customers like banking, capital goods, computing, consulting, office equipment, and shipping. B2C and B2B branding use different languages. B2C firms focus on brand image or associations; B2B firms want customers to view them as experienced, risk-free, and trustworthy suppliers, preferably with a solid track record and stellar market reputation.

... AND IS NOT JUST ABOUT ADVERTISING

Another common misunderstanding is that advertising is the only approach to branding. Not so! Reaching a broad audience for its communications is as important for corporate brands as for many product brands. But the firm can build and reinforce its brand identity via other communications forms like brochures, direct mail, managerial actions and speeches, products and packaging, promotions, publicity and public relations, stationery, physical facilities, telephone interactions, and websites.

THE BASIS FOR BRANDING

Historically, the brander and producer were synonymous. Today, there is no necessary relationship between the brand owner and the producer of the branded product. The brand/production relationship may take many forms:

- **Totally integrated production operations.** Ford's old Rouge River plant is the prototypical example. Ford received iron ore and coal at one end; Model Ts rolled off at the other end.
- **Subcomponent assembly.** The brand owner assembles components produced by other firms. Examples include contemporary automobile production and Dell's model for building PCs.

- **No production responsibility.** The brand owner may design the product, set quality control standards, and distribute and market products. It does not manufacture but does own the customer experience.

BRAND EQUITY AND THE VALUE OF BRANDS

The most widely accepted definition of **brand equity** is "a set of brand assets and liabilities linked to a brand, its name, and symbol that add to (or subtract from) the value provided by a product or service to a firm and/or that firm's customers." From this definition we see that brand value accrues to both the *firm* and its *customers*. It follows that there are two types of brand equity: *customer brand equity (CBE)* — the value customers receive, and *firm brand equity (FBE)* — the value the firm receives.

CUSTOMER BRAND EQUITY

The brand provides customers two types of value: *pre-purchase equity* and *post-purchase equity*.

PRE-PURCHASE EQUITY reduces search costs and purchase risks because of what customers believe before purchase.

POST-PURCHASE EQUITY enhances the consumption experience. After purchase, brands provide *functional* value — doing the job they were designed to do — and *economic* value — like low cost of ownership. They also provide *psychological* value, like feelings of security from insurance, and the assurance of continued functional value.

CBE, either pre- or post-purchase, is generally greater when:
- Comparing alternative products is difficult.
- Customers do not realize value until some time after purchase.
- Customers are inexperienced or unfamiliar with the product class.
- Product quality from some suppliers is variable.
- The product is socially visible.
- There is mental flexibility in portraying the brand.

FIRM BRAND EQUITY

FBE results from customer responses to firm actions and links directly to CBE. High brand awareness, positive attitudes, high perceived quality, positive word of mouth, intention to purchase, purchase, brand loyalty, positive brand image and associations, and satisfaction all enhance FBE. CBE and FBE reflect the trust between the brand and its customers.

High FBE has many positives. Firms with high FBE:
- Can set higher prices and earn better profit margins.
- More easily introduce similarly branded items in different product classes and markets.
- Use cross-selling to encourage existing customers to purchase in different product classes.
- Generate leverage in distribution channels by securing more and better shelf space and more favorable transaction terms.
- Raise entry barriers for competitors.
- Exploit licensing opportunities.

Marketing Question

You, the reader, are a brand! What is your *brand identity*? What *brand image* and *brand associations* do people hold about you? Do these associations conform to your desired brand identity? Are the image and associations consistent, or do they differ across people — friends, parents, professors, and prospective employers? Are you satisfied with these associations? If so, how will you sustain and enhance them? If not, how will you change them? How do your postings on Facebook support your brand identity?

Marketing Question

Some individuals build brands; others reap the fruits of successful brand building; still others attempt to recover brand equity following well-publicized missteps. What can you learn about branding from Paris Hilton, Michael Jordan, Sarah Palin, Martha Stewart, Maria Sharapova, Donald Trump, and Tiger Woods? Feel free to substitute your own selections.

MONETIZING BRAND EQUITY

Brands have monetary value for both customers and firms.

CUSTOMER BRAND EQUITY

Customers receive value from a generic product; typically they receive greater value from a *branded* product. The **dollarmetric** method assesses the monetary value of CBE. The firm asks a customer how much extra she would pay for the *branded* product versus an unbranded product; this amount is CBE's monetary value.

FIRM BRAND EQUITY

FBE relates directly to the brand's current and future ability to attract paying customers and increase shareholder value. We assess FBE's monetary value at the firm level. Valuation components are:

- **Revenue.** The price difference between the branded product and an identical generic product, multiplied by the branded product's forecast sales volume.
- **Cost.** The costs of supporting the brand.

BASIC APPROACH. FBE's monetary value is the sum of the year-by-year differences between revenues and costs discounted to the present.

MARKET VALUE METHOD. The market provides the best FBE measure. FBE equals market value less book value, plus non-brand intangibles like human resources, know-how, and patents. When market value does not exist, as for most product brands, the firm must use internal methods.

INTERNAL METHODS. Two internal methods for assessing FBE are:

- **Replacement cost.** The firm multiplies the anticipated brand-replacement cost by the probability of success.
- **Cash flow.** These approaches are intuitively more appealing, but estimating future cash flows is difficult. Interbrand (brand consultant) uses a proprietary method to estimate FBE based on future cash flows.

RELATIONSHIP BETWEEN CUSTOMER BRAND EQUITY AND FIRM BRAND EQUITY

We just showed how to assess individual-customer CBE and firm-level FBE. We now develop a brand typology based on the relationship between CBE and FBE.

CBE and FBE allow us to develop a brand typology. CBE is either high or low; FBE is also high or low depending on sales volume:

- **CBE-low, FBE-low: Commodity brand.** Like store-brand canned goods.
- **CBE-low, FBE-high: Mass-market brand.** High-volume, low-price brands like Almaden wine and Dell PCs.
- **CBE-high, FBE-low: Specialty brand.** Low-volume, high-price brands like Lafite-Rothschild wine, Steubenware glassware, and Rolex watches.
- **CBE-high, FBE-high: Iconic brand.** Customers enjoy high brand equity; the firm sells high volume at high prices. Includes brands like Sony and Nike.

BUILDING AND SUSTAINING A STRONG BRAND

An important goal of developing and implementing a market strategy is to build and sustain a strong brand. Strong brands induce positive responses from customers.

BUILDING A STRONG BRAND

The firm builds a strong brand by making good brand decisions during the branding process.

BRAND IDENTITY. Brand identity is what the firm wants the brand to mean. *Brand identity* is the blueprint for many marketing decisions.

BRAND AWARENESS. Typically, the firm must invest significantly to achieve brand awareness at target customers. When the brand is first entrant in a new product form, the pioneer must educate potential customers about the product form, as well as about the brand.

BRAND ASSOCIATIONS AND BRAND IMAGE. Brand associations are the meanings the brand has for individual customers — *brand image* is the overall sum of brand associations. A critical firm task is to secure congruence between brand image and brand identity.

BRAND QUALITY AND VALUE PERCEPTIONS. Consistency in communications and customer brand experiences are crucial for developing positive brand quality and value perceptions. Achieving consistency is always difficult, but organizational practices like short tenure of brand managers can make it impossible.

BRAND LOYALTY. Consistency in brand quality and value perceptions lead to brand loyalty. The firm earns high brand loyalty by:

- Selecting the *right* brand identity for target customers and consistently executing on that identity.
- Ensuring that firm employees and third-party organizations, like advertising agencies, are motivated to deliver on the brand identity.
- Continuously measuring customer satisfaction with the brand and making the necessary course corrections.

BRAND BROADENING. The firm may broaden (leverage) a strong brand to other product forms (and classes).

SUSTAINING A STRONG BRAND

The key to sustaining a strong brand for the long run is continual assessment of *brand health*. **Brand health checks** use metrics indicating FBE changes and *balanced-scorecard* approaches. Four popular types of measures and sources are:

- **Purchasing and sales** — firm accounting and CRM systems and industry-focused research suppliers.
- **Perceptual** — survey research.
- **Marketing support** — firm accounting and business intelligence systems and industry-focused suppliers.
- **Profitability** — firm accounting system.

Marketing Question

Barcelona and Manchester United are the world's leading soccer clubs. How would you suggest they monetize their brand equities? (Or substitute your favorite sports team.)

Marketing Question

How do you assess the branding strategy for your college, school, or university? Does your institution pursue a multi-branding strategy or an umbrella branding strategy? How could your college, school, or university improve its branding?

MANAGING BRAND ARCHITECTURE

Many firms maintain multiple brands — brand portfolio — each with its own brand identity. The firm's **brand architecture** — organizing structure for multiple brands — is an important decision area. Because firm brands have a major impact on shareholder value, branding decisions should have high priority. The firm should carefully consider what to brand, brand identities, and desired brand associations. The firm should also carefully plan brand additions and deletions.

MULTI-BRANDING VERSUS UMBRELLA BRANDING

In **multi-branding** — aka *House of Brands* strategy — the firm uses multiple brands for its various products. The firm seeks target-customer loyalty to individual brands but not necessarily to the parent-company brand. By contrast, a firm using **umbrella branding** emphasizes a monolithic brand for several products (or product lines).

Pros for umbrella branding are:

- **Company culture.** Enhances the firm's ability to deliver a consistent message.
- **Intra-firm competition.** Reduces the likelihood of intra-firm competition.
- **Scale economies.** By promoting a single brand, the firm secures advertising economies.
- **Transfer of positive associations.** Customers may transfer positive associations across product forms/classes.

Pros for multi-branding are:

- **Transfer of negative associations from an umbrella brand.** Customers may transfer negative associations across products. Does not occur with multi-branding.
- **Intra-firm competition.** Some firms favor enhanced intra-firm competition
- **Targeting and positioning.** Allows the firm to better target and position products in multiple market segments.

BRAND BROADENING (LEVERAGING)

Brand broadening (**leveraging**) occurs when the firm undertakes a brand extension — attaching an existing brand to a different product form (class) to address a new opportunity. Before leveraging, the firm must consider potential opportunities and obstacles, and several branding issues.

OPPORTUNITIES AND OBSTACLES. The firm must address the following sorts of questions:

- Is there sufficient demand for the new venture?
- Is the firm sufficiently strong to succeed in the face of competition?
- Can the firm access the new market through current distribution channels?
- Is the firm capable of satisfying potential demand?
- Does the firm have access to raw materials and other production inputs?
- Does the firm possess other competencies necessary to be successful?

BRANDING ISSUES. These concern brand associations held by customers and their fit with the extension:

- Do customers perceive a fit between the original product form (class) and the new product form (class) in terms of product features and concepts?
- What are customer brand image and associations for the core product? Will these associations *transfer* to the new product?

- What is the reverse relationship? How will customer associations for the new product *back transfer* to associations for the core product?
- How does the corporate brand, and/or monolithic brand, relate these various associations?

Once the firm has addressed opportunities, obstacles, and several issues, the brand must meet two baseline conditions for an extension to be viable:

- The brand must have strong positive associations.
- Brand associations and the product extension should not be incongruous.

Brand extensions tend to fail when:

- Associations between the brand and the extension are not obvious.
- The brand has a unique image and associations that do not transfer.
- The new product form (class) has a dominant competitor.
- The positioning is confusing and/or inconsistent.
- The extension's quality does not match customer expectations for the brand.

HOW BRAND BROADENING (LEVERAGING) FITS IN. Brand broadening is one of a family of strategies relating brands and product forms (classes). Other options are line extensions, **flanker brands**, and new products:

- **Line extension.** The firm adds a new but similar product to its product line and uses the same brand name.
- **Flanker brand.** The firm adds a new yet similar product, but develops a new brand, or a distinguishing sub-brand.
- **New product.** The firm adds a new product form (class) and develops a new brand.

BRAND MIGRATION

Firms sometimes retire individual brands. The challenge is to retain the brand equity being retired by transferring it to another brand — **brand migration**. Most approaches have two main stages:

- Associate the brand to be retired with the surviving brand;
- Drop the retired brand.

STRATEGIC ALLIANCES

Strategic alliances can extend the firm's brand into new market segments. Strategic alliances have important **co-branding** implications when the co-branding partner can transfer positive customer attitudes. Co-branding between customers and suppliers is increasingly common. When firms co-brand with themselves, they must ensure that the brand associations are appropriate for the product and target segment.

AGING AND DEFUNCT BRANDS

Some aging brands have loyal customers and survive for many years. One option for improving sales in mature markets is *repositioning the brand*. Key approaches to repositioning are:

- Target new market segments.
- Change brand associations.
- Alter the competitive target.

Marketing Question

In 1984, Bulgari sold Bulgari brand luxury products in five Bulgari stores. By 2003, Bulgari had 180 stores; 600 outlets also sold Bulgari watches, and 14,000 outlets sold Bulgari perfumes. Bulgari formed Bulgari Hotels and Resorts in a joint venture with Marriott. Do you think Bulgari hotels will succeed? Why or why not? Do you think Bulgari's acquisition by LVMH will affect its hotel venture?

TRUE / FALSE QUESTIONS

1. The brand gives customers two types of value: pre-purchase equity and post-purchase equity.
   ❏ TRUE ❏ FALSE

2. In the dollarmetric method of monetizing brand equity, the firm asks a customer how much extra he or she would pay for the branded product versus an unbranded product. This extra amount is the customer brand equity monetary value. ❏ TRUE ❏ FALSE

3. Firm brand equity equals market value times book value and non-brand intangibles like patents, know-how, and human resources. ❏ TRUE ❏ FALSE

4. In multi-branding, a firm emphasizes a monolithic brand for several products. ❏ TRUE ❏ FALSE

5. Brand leveraging occurs when the firm undertakes a brand extension — it uses an existing brand to address a new opportunity, typically in a different product form or product class. ❏ TRUE ❏ FALSE

MULTIPLE CHOICE QUESTIONS

1. All of the following are characteristics of effective brand associations EXCEPT:

   a. strong
   b. favorable
   c. unique
   d. common

2. Which of the following is NOT a form in which the brand/production relationship may take?

   a. totally integrated production operations
   b. subcomponent assembly
   c. no production responsibility
   d. All selections represent viable forms the relationship may take.

3. _____ reduces customers' search costs and purchase risks because of what customer believe before purchase.

   a. Pre-purchase equity
   b. Post-purchase equity
   c. Cross-sectional purchase equity
   d. Virtual equity

4. Which of the following brand typologies best describes a commodity brand like store-brand canned goods?

   a. low consumer brand equity and low firm brand equity
   b. low consumer brand equity and high firm brand equity
   c. high consumer brand equity and low firm brand equity
   d. high consumer brand equity and high firm brand equity

5. Which of the following is NOT one of the types of measures that are part of a balanced scorecard?

   a. purchasing and sales data
   b. perceptual data
   c. profitability
   d. depreciation data

Answers on page 205

SECTION IV
IMPLEMENTING THE MARKET STRATEGY

Managing Marketing in the 21ˢᵗ Century

Design the Market Offer

PART A – PROVIDING CUSTOMER VALUE

CHAPTER 12

MANAGING THE PRODUCT LINE

PRODUCTS AND SERVICES ARE CENTRAL TO THE FIRM'S MARKETING MIX. Since decisions about products and services cross functional lines, they have a broader impact on firm operations than many other marketing-mix decisions. Managing the product line is a critical aspect of increasing shareholder value.

THE CHANGING VIEW

OLD WAY	NEW WAY
Caveat emptor (buyer beware)	*Caveat venditor* (seller beware)
Ethical considerations relatively rare	Ethical considerations recognized as vital
Focus on profits	Focus on shareholder value
Judgments made exclusively with financial criteria	Judgments based on market and financial criteria
Product managers on pedestals	Product managers subject to executive control
Product profitability data rare	Product profitability data becoming ubiquitous
Product proliferation common, rationalization rare	Product line breadth carefully managed, rationalization common
Products and brands often treated similarly	Products and brands carefully discriminated
Products viewed independently	Products managed as a portfolio
Quality variable	Total Quality Management (TQM)
Reluctance to cannibalize products	Cannibalization as part of product line renewal
Uniform business objectives by product	Business objectives tailored by product and segment
Waste products and packaging ignored	Environmental concerns important

THE PRODUCT PORTFOLIO CONCEPT

The firm's **product portfolio** is a collection of products. The firm does *not* optimize overall profits by maximizing short-run profits from each individual product. Rather, the firm should use a **portfolio approach** to product management, balancing objectives and resource allocations across all products. The firm optimizes shareholder value when its **product portfolio** is balanced; an **imbalanced** portfolio puts shareholder interests at risk. Imbalances occur when the firm funds too many new products and creates shortages of cash and other resources. Imbalances also occur when the firm has too many old products; good short-term financial results may mask a failure to invest sufficiently in the future.

The major approaches for allocating resources are financial analysis and portfolio analysis.

FINANCIAL ANALYSIS METHODS

Superior financial performance is critical for delivering increased value to shareholders. Approaches include:

- **Return on investment (ROI).** ROI calculations project future accounting data. They compare the product's forecasted rate of return with a target (**hurdle**) rate. If the forecast rate exceeds the target rate and resources are available, the firm invests.

- **Payback.** Payback is the forecast time to pay back the investment. In general, shorter paybacks are better than longer paybacks. Payback's problem is ignoring profits earned after the payback period.

Neither *ROI* nor *payback* distinguishes among time periods. Because of this defect, most firms use approaches that take into account the time value of money:

- **Net present value (NPV)** and **internal rate of return (IRR).** NPV and IRR use discount factors to account for the time value of money. Both methods use actual cash flows rather than financial and cost accounting data. They assess cash inflows (like sales revenues) when earned and cash outflows (like costs and investments) when paid out.

  - *NPV* uses a predetermined discount factor, typically the firm's cost of capital. The firm calculates NPV for various opportunities, then ranks by monetary value.

  - For *IRR*, the firm calculates the discount rate that equalizes cash inflows and cash outflows. IRR typically ranks those opportunities whose IRR exceeds the hurdle rate.

More recently, firms are using *economic profit* or *economic value added (EVA)*. EVA equals the firm's annual profit less an explicit charge for capital.

ADVANTAGES OF FINANCIAL ANALYSIS (FA): LACK OF AMBIGUITY. Pluses for FA are:

- **Clarity.** Decisions flow clearly from FA. So long as opportunities exceed a target number, the firm makes selections in attractiveness order.

- **Conceptual simplicity.** Calculations may be complex, but each approach is conceptually simple. The inputs — investments, revenues, costs — are generally readily available.

- **Comparable results.** Each approach ultimately produces a single figure — the firm can easily compare several opportunities.

DISADVANTAGES OF FINANCIAL ANALYSIS. Problems with FA are:

- **Internal political dynamics.** FA can lead to organizational game-playing. Opportunity-champions may **hockey stick** sales revenue estimates up, and costs and investments down — marginal opportunities become spectacular performers!

- **Potential misallocation of investment funds.** FA leads some firms to allocate investment funds based on historic profitability. These firms invest in mature, low-growth products, but starve high-growth products, where current profits are low and uncertainty is high.

- **Silence on strategic issues.** FA ranks opportunities by financial performance but generally does not consider strategic imperatives. FA does not consider marketing issues like brand building.

- **Uncertainty in the estimates.** FA relies on estimates of sales units, prices, costs, and investments. Estimating short-term investment requirements for even well-defined opportunities is difficult; predicting sales units and prices several years in the future is daunting.

> *Marketing Question*
>
> Suppose the products in your business unit span the range from introduction to decline. Corporate has sent a finance VP to assess your business unit and to *help you*! What would you be most concerned about?

PORTFOLIO ANALYSIS

Portfolio analysis (PA) is central to many firms' strategic planning processes. PA is best viewed as an *additional* tool for allocating resources, but not as an *alternative* to FA. PA is a systematic, organized, and easily communicable way of assembling, assessing, and integrating important information about products and markets. PA helps the firm set strategic direction, establish investment priorities, and allocate resources. The firm can use portfolio analysis to evaluate both businesses and products. Two important PA methods are the **growth-share matrix** and the **multifactor matrix**.

THE GROWTH-SHARE MATRIX. The Boston Consulting Group (BCG) developed the original PA. Dimensions are growth and share: *forecast long-run market growth* and *relative market share (RMS)*. In the BCG framework, RMS is the firm's market share divided by the market share of its nearest competitor.

Each dimension is bisected to produce a four-cell classification. Matrix entries represent products (or businesses). The growth-share matrix places heavy emphasis on the financial characteristics of products in each cell. High-share products are typically more profitable than low-share products. Growth products typically require significant investment in fixed assets, working capital, and market development. Conventional labels, classic characteristics, and strategic recommendations for products in each cell are:

CASH COWS. LOW MARKET GROWTH/HIGH MARKET SHARE – GENERATE CASH

Classic characteristics of cash cows are:

- Low costs. From experience curve effects
- Premium prices. As market leader, cash cows may command premium prices.
- Low reinvestment. Low-growth, mature products require relatively little investment.

Cash cows should be highly profitable and are often the firm's primary internal cash source.

STARS. HIGH MARKET GROWTH, HIGH MARKET SHARE – INVEST

Stars are relatively rare; few products enjoy dominant positions in high-growth markets. Stars are often profitable in accounting terms, but use significant cash because their growth requires substantial investment.

DOGS. LOW MARKET GROWTH, LOW MARKET SHARE – CRITICALLY ANALYZE FOR RETENTION OR DIVESTMENT

Dogs is a pejorative term for products with unfavorable characteristics:

- High costs relative to the leader; do not enjoy the same economy-of-scale advantages.
- Prices may be lower than the market leader.

Dogs are often unprofitable or earn only low profits. Firms with dogs should consider:

- Developing new segmentation approaches that strengthen their positions.
- Refreshing products with additional value from new features.
- Maximizing short-run cash flows by liquidating or divesting.
- Implement a *kennel* strategy by acquiring similar product to achieve viable scale.

PROBLEM CHILDREN (AKA LOTTERY TICKETS, QUESTION MARKS, WILDCATS). HIGH MARKET GROWTH, LOW MARKET SHARE – INVEST CAUTIOUSLY IN A LIMITED NUMBER

Problem children combine the uncertainties of high-growth markets with non-dominant market shares. The key choice for problem children is often *double or quit*!

- Double. Large strategic investments can move the product to market leadership.
- Quit. Exit, immediately or gradually. The product may command a good price from an aggressive follower.

Marketing Question

Suppose 20 percent of all products are in *high-growth* markets and 80 percent are in *low-growth* markets; and that 10 percent of all products are market leaders. What percentage of products are Cash Cows? Dogs? Stars? Problem Children? What does your result imply for the challenges you will face as an executive?

The best way to view the growth-share matrix is as a device for raising and discussing *what-if* (contingency) questions. Like any decision-making aid, the matrix has value only if its assumptions are valid. Issues include:

- **Long-run market growth** is the exclusive measure for market attractiveness. Problems may arise because the framework ignores other factors.
- **Relative market share** captures the firm's competitive strength. The firm can usually validate RMS in mature markets, but this is more difficult in growth markets.
- **The market share/profitability relationship** may not be universal, in part because market boundaries are not always clear-cut. Also, market definition affects measures of long-run market growth and RMS and placing products in the matrix.
- **Downward-sloping experience curves** imply an inverse relationship between RMS and costs. The matrix assumes comparable cost curves across competitors, but small focused firms often have lower costs than relatively well-managed major players.

THE MULTIFACTOR MATRIX. The growth-share matrix spawned many other portfolio approaches, some public and some proprietary. The most popular is the **multifactor matrix**, aka GE/McKinsey screen. This matrix redefines the growth-share axes. *Long-run market growth becomes market attractiveness; relative market share becomes business strengths.* The user identifies several factors to measure each dimension. (See Chapter 8 for a similar approach to assessing market segments.)

THE GROWTH-SHARE AND MULTIFACTOR MATRICES. The *growth-share matrix* has only two criteria: long-run market growth and RMS. Once managers agree on the market definition, the firm can measure these objectively. The *multifactor matrix* addresses the realism issue by using several criteria and so embraces many factors that the growth-share matrix omits. But reasonable managers may disagree about the criteria, and weightings and ratings are often highly subjective. In sum, it is generally easier to evaluate and communicate about a firm's diverse products using the *growth-share matrix* than the *multifactor matrix*, but the *multifactor matrix* is more comprehensive.

OTHER IMPORTANT PRODUCT INTERRELATIONSHIPS

Products compete for resources; they may also be interrelated in other strategic ways.

INTERRELATIONSHIPS AT THE CUSTOMER

Some products are directly complementary like razors and razor blades, and printers and toner. Sometimes product interrelationships at the customer are positive, but they can also be negative.

POSITIVE COMPLEMENTARITY. In many markets, customers who buy one type of product are more likely to buy another related product — **positive complementarity**. Sometimes positive complementarity occurs because customers trade up to higher-quality products.

NEGATIVE COMPLEMENTARITY. Customer dissatisfaction with one product can negatively affect sales of another. Negative complementarity at one customer can also negatively affect the firm's relationships with other customers.

INTERRELATIONSHIPS AT THE FIRM

Sometimes firm products have important internal interrelationships with each other.

STRATEGIC ROLES. Different products have separate yet mutually reinforcing strategic roles — like profit, growth, and acting as a firewall.

> *Marketing Question*
>
> Movie theaters offer popcorn and soft drinks as complements. How would you design a new movie house to enhance service and offer a broader variety of complementary products and services?

MULTIPLE BUSINESS UNITS. Interrelationship issues occur with products from different business units when they address (or could address) the same market. The firm has three options:

- **Develop separate missions.** Products from different business units have different missions — Chapter 7. The firm does not *squander* resources by having multiple business units address a single market opportunity.
- **Intra-firm collaboration.** The firm develops processes for separate business units to work together. But when business units do not work together, the firm may miss significant opportunities.
- **Intra-firm competition.** This Darwinian approach allows products from different business units to pursue overlapping missions. As long as one business unit seizes the opportunity, the firm accepts efficiency losses in product development and promotion.

PRODUCT LINE BREADTH: PROLIFERATION VERSUS SIMPLIFICATION

PRODUCT PROLIFERATION

Variety in customers' needs often drives **product proliferation** as firms add products to fill product-line gaps. Sometimes firms tap different customer needs by offering products in different versions or variations. Common differentiators of versions are:

- **Access and functionality.** Some firms offer differing versions of information or media products for different audiences based on: user interface — simple for casual users, complex for serious users; speed of operation — slow for casual users, fast for professional users; and other dimensions.
- **Product performance.** Some firms, like plastic producers, make high-quality products for high prices and degraded products for price-sensitive customers.
- **Time availability.** Package delivery firms like FedEx and UPS offer next-day delivery before 10 a.m., after 10 a.m., and second-day delivery.

PRODUCT PROLIFERATION AND MARKET SEGMENTATION. The difference between product proliferation and market segmentation confuses many students. **Product proliferation** refers to product variety. **Market segmentation** explores differences in customer needs and developing strategies for market segments. The firm may not require a broad product line to target multiple segments. A single product generates multiple offers by varying the brand name and other implementation elements.

SIMPLIFYING THE PRODUCT LINE

Firms typically streamline product lines due to pressure from increased competition and/or distribution-channel consolidation, where growth in store brands and rising buyer power pressure sellers for lower prices. The firm may reap significant benefits from simplifying the product line, but should make product deletion decisions carefully. Firms often use a single criterion for dropping products — *bottom-line* profits. These firms often discover that these products were carrying a large share of overhead. The remaining products must assume this overhead; their costs increase, and overall firm profits fall!

Marketing Question

Visit the toiletries aisle at your local supermarket or drugstore. How many toothpaste skus can you identify? Do you think Colgate and/or Crest should reduce the number of product items?

OTHER PRODUCT-LINE ISSUES

Now we examine several other issues for managing the product line:

BUNDLING

The firm can sell products as single *unbundled* items; it may also combine products or products and services as **bundled offers**. Sometimes firms bundle attractive products with less-attractive products but the firm risks losing sales to more focused competitors. In *mixed bundling*, the firm sells the products both unbundled and bundled.

COUNTERFEITING

Illegal product copying and brand piracy are increasingly prevalent globally. Copied products include car parts, fashion items, medicines, mobile phones, recorded music, software, and tobacco products. Customer desires for branded products and increasing sales on eBay and other websites fuel counterfeiting. The best protection is continual vigilance regarding trademark, copyright, and design patents. The firm should keep tight control over suppliers and distributors and work with local law enforcement, but problems multiply when counterfeiters operate internationally.

EVOLVING THE PRODUCT LINE

The firm must address several key issues in evolving the product line: extending product life, improving the product mix, product cannibalization, product replacement, and limitations on product availability.

EXTENDING PRODUCT LIFE. Firms often use several means to extend product life.

IMPROVING THE PRODUCT MIX. Firms can increase profits by introducing higher-margin products, possibly by replacing lower-margin products.

PRODUCT CANNIBALIZATION. To pre-empt or stave off competitive threats and/or address new market segments, firms often introduce lower-margin products that may cannibalize sales of higher-margin products. When contemplating cannibalization, the firm should consider three important issues:

- **Balancing effects.** A new product entry may cannibalize existing products and cause an immediate profit reduction. But the firm should enjoy incremental value from improved market share and/or brand presence.
- **Fear of lower profits.** When the firm introduces a new lower-profit product, customers may switch from the original high-profit product to the new entry, reducing overall firm profits. Because of this fear, internal pressures may build up against a new entry and can immobilize the firm.
- **How to decide.** Many firms make product entry decisions by comparing their most recent history with *forecast* results after introducing the new product. This practice is incorrect. The firm should always compare *forecast* profits *with* the new product to forecast profits *without* the new product.

PRODUCT REPLACEMENT. When the firm secures differential advantage with a better product, competitors often imitate and reduce price. The best approach is to replace the older product with an innovative successor. Ideally, the firm introduces a higher-value replacement shortly before the competitor's launch. Successful pre-emption weakens competitor resolve to compete against the incumbent.

LIMITATIONS ON PRODUCT AVAILABILITY. Some firms deliberately under-produce so as to create customer value via scarcity.

PRODUCT QUALITY

Product quality is very important to customers and has improved in many industries. Increasingly, any serious competitor must offer high quality products.

PRODUCT SAFETY

In many jurisdictions, regulatory bodies like the FDA and CPSC (U.S.) enforce laws protecting consumers from product hazards. Regardless, producers have a special responsibility to ensure their products do not harm customers.

SECONDARY MARKET PRODUCTS

Owners of durable products like automobiles often sell them in the **secondary market**. For customers purchasing new cars, the forecast resale price is often an important product attribute. Most financial markets are secondary markets; the firm's share price is important for raising capital and measuring shareholder value.

DISPOSAL: PRODUCTS AND PACKAGING

Packaging and product disposal are not pressing issues for all producers today, but firms should be aware of growing environmental concerns. To address disposal issues, cost concerns, and the potential impact on brand image, many firms make new products with parts from discarded products.

....
TRUE / FALSE QUESTIONS

1. The firm's product portfolio is a collection of products. ❏ **TRUE** ❏ **FALSE**

2. The growth-share matrix has only two criteria: market growth rate and firm growth rate.
   ❏ **TRUE** ❏ **FALSE**

3. It is generally easier to evaluate and communicate about a firm's diverse products using the multifactor matrix than the growth-share matrix. ❏ **TRUE** ❏ **FALSE**

4. Positive complementarity takes place when customers who buy one type of product are more likely to buy another related product. ❏ **TRUE** ❏ **FALSE**

5. Product proliferation refers to product variety while market segmentation explores differences in customer needs and developing strategies for market segments. ❏ **TRUE** ❏ **FALSE**

....
MULTIPLE CHOICE QUESTIONS

1. Which of the following financial analysis approaches focuses on the opportunity's annual profit less an explicit charge for capital?

   a. payback
   b. net present value
   c. internal rate of return
   d. economic profit

2. Advantages of using financial analysis for product management include all of the following EXCEPT:

   a. having a single figure
   b. comparable markets
   c. conceptual simplicity
   d. clarity

3. Which of the following Boston Consulting Group Matrix labels apply to products that have high market growth and high market share?

   a. cash cow
   b. star
   c. dog
   d. problem children, question mark, lottery ticket, wildcat

4. All of the following are options for effectively managing multiple business units EXCEPT:

   a. developing separate missions
   b. intra-firm competition
   c. intra-firm collaboration
   d. competitor strategic alliance

5. Which of the following is NOT one of the common differentiators for a firm offering a product in different versions or different variations?

   a. time availability
   b. product performance
   c. limitations on access and functionality
   d. market penetration pricing

Answers on page 205

CHAPTER 13

MANAGING SERVICES AND CUSTOMER SERVICE

SOME FIRMS PRODUCE AND SELL *TANGIBLE* PRODUCTS like cars, computers, kitchen equipment, and TVs. But many other firms produce and sell *intangible* services like information technology services, retail distribution, tax preparation, and transportation. Because they are intangible, services can pose a real managerial challenge. Yet well-designed and well-delivered services create customer satisfaction and loyalty, positive word of mouth, differential advantage, and high profits.

THE CHANGING VIEW

OLD WAY	NEW WAY
Customer expectations ignored	Customer expectations crucial to satisfaction
Customer service an afterthought	Customer service a key competitive weapon
Customer service separate from marketing	Customer service crucial to customer retention
Low tech	High tech
Management of peak demand rare	Management of peak demand ubiquitous
Mass services, common to all customers	Customized (or personalized) services
Most services provided internally	Many services provided via outsourcing
Narrow view of service	Broad view of service
Products important — services relatively unimportant	Services critical sources of revenues and profits
Relatively narrow range of services available	Explosive growth in service variety
Service performance unmeasured	Service performance carefully tracked
Services and customer service blurred	Services and customer service distinct parts of the market offer
Services distinct from products	Products morphing into services

PRODUCTS, SERVICES, AND CUSTOMER SERVICE

The distinction between *products* and *services* remains one of marketing's great confusions. Some people use the term *product* to describe any core offering — including both physical products and services. More precisely, a **physical product** can be touched or kicked, but a **service** is *any act or performance that one party can offer another that is essentially intangible and does not result in the ownership of anything.*

Fundamental to marketing is the underlying notion that *customers do not want your products or services; they want the benefits and values your products and services provide.* Today, firms offer many products like automobiles and railroad cars as services that customers can rent or lease.

The firm can enhance the value of its offer by adding **customer service** like delivery, information, repair, sales support, technical support, and warranties.

GROWTH IN THE SERVICE SECTOR

The service sector of advanced economies has grown dramatically in recent years, making product, service, and customer-service distinctions increasingly important. Services account for upward of 70 percent of total employment and GDP in developed countries. Many service firms now populate the *Fortune 500*, and social enterprises like government and non-profit organizations (NGOs) almost exclusively offer services. Other important factors in the private sector are:

Marketing Question: Next time you call a customer service department, ask the representative where they are located. It may be South Dakota, but most likely another country where English-speaking skills are well developed. Ask how they like their jobs, and their biggest challenges. What are the implications for firms outsourcing customer service?

- **Customer behavior changes.** Customer preference for purchasing is decreasing, leading to growth in financial services like credit, leasing, and rental.
- **Deregulation.** Deregulation in industries like electricity, financial services, natural gas, telecommunications, and transportation eases market entry and fuels growth.
- **Franchising.** Franchising is the backbone of the hospitality, restaurant, and tax preparation industries, but businesses like closet installation, commercial property restoration, onsite computer repairs, and window-cleaning are also growing via franchising.
- **Globalization.** Innovations in technology and communications make products and services accessible to global markets. Firms conduct business across the world using many service strategies to meet the diverse needs of new customers.
- **Leveraging core competence.** Some firms find that in-house activities are valuable to other firms, so they repackage and sell these activities as services.
- **Outsourcing.** Many firms are narrowing their missions to focus on core competencies and outsource activities and processes previously performed internally. Outsourcing provides suppliers with service opportunities.
- **Technology.** Technological advances allow firms to connect with customers and deliver ongoing and complementary services.

CHARACTERISTICS OF SERVICES

Physical products differ from services in several important ways:

INTANGIBILITY

Services that focus on *people* generally require the customer's physical presence or interactivity; focus on *products and information* does not. Tangible service elements often play an important role in forming expectations of (and evaluating) the service experience. Service tangibles include equipment, facilities, and personnel. Some firms provide additional tangibility via service guarantees.

SERVICE FACILITIES. Where the firm delivers the service comprises an:

- **Exterior.** Includes the location, outside view, and signage.
- **Interior.** Has two dimensions:
  - **Offstage.** Out of customer sight
  - **Onstage.** Where customers experience deeds, efforts, and performances.

SERVICE EQUIPMENT. Service equipment quality often influences the service experience. Many passengers prefer airlines with new planes (like Singapore Airlines) versus those with older fleets.

SERVICE PERSONNEL. Some work offstage; others work onstage. The customer experience depends on how well all service personnel — offstage and onstage — perform their functions.

SERVICE GUARANTEES. Guarantees about the service experience provide tangible elements of value if the firm does not keep its promises. Good service guarantees are unconditional, painless to invoke, and easy and quick to collect. The service agreement should be simple to understand and communicate, and meaningfully related to the service it guarantees. Guarantees are most appropriate when:

- Customer ego is involved.
- Customers have little experience with the service.
- Customers make frequent purchases.
- Firm and customer display a lack of trust.
- Industry image for service quality is poor.
- Sales are strongly affected by word of mouth.
- Service failure has high negative consequences.
- Service price is high.

> ### Marketing Question
>
> Think about your most recent purchase of cell phone service. Was there a service guarantee? Did the guarantee meet the noted criteria? Did the provider communicate the guarantee well? What could the provider have done better? Have you received a guarantee for any other purchase?

INSEPARABILITY

For services, provider and customer are inexorably linked — production and consumption are innately *inseparable*. Because firms cannot inventory services, demand forecasting is critical. To address supply/demand imbalances, the firm must modify supply and/or demand.

MODIFY SUPPLY. The firm can *increase* short-run supply by stretching capacity like working longer hours and outsourcing; the firm can *decrease* supply by scheduling employee training, maintenance, and renovations.

MODIFY DEMAND. The firm should analyze demand patterns, answering such questions as:

- Does service demand follow a regular, predictable cycle? If so, is the cycle length daily, weekly, monthly, or annually?
- What causes these fluctuations — climate, paydays, school vacations, or work schedules?
- Are there random demand fluctuations — births, crime, or weather?
- Can we disaggregate use patterns by market segments or profitability?

Based on the answers, the firm must decide which segments to target — then *increase/decrease* demand as necessary.

VARIABILITY

In general, *variability* in service delivery implies reduced customer satisfaction. Lack of consistency follows directly from human involvement in service delivery. Firms address variability in product manufacturing using quality tools but these are more difficult to use for services. Nonetheless, approaches like **Six Sigma**, a data-driven methodology that eliminates defects in any process, are effective for service systems.

FOCUS ON HUMAN CAPITAL. Employee selection and training are important for improving employee performance and reducing service variability.

SUBSTITUTION OF CAPITAL FOR LABOR. The firm can remove variability via automation like using dispensing machines for cash, drinks, sandwiches, and subway cards. Cost reduction objectives often drives these innovations, but they reduce variability nonetheless. The downsides: Machines can break down, and some customers prefer human contact.

PERISHABILITY

Perishability is tightly linked to inseparability and the inability to inventory services, but focuses on situations where supply is committed but demand is not. Two situations are important:

- **Demand apparently sufficient but unpaid** — Reminder systems (and black lists) attempt to address this problem.
- **Demand insufficient.** As discussed earlier, the firm has several options for increasing demand.

DIVISIBILITY

Many core and surrounding services comprise a sequence of activities conducted over time. The activity sequence functions as a service *blueprint* for identifying and dealing with service problems. The service blueprint can help redesign service delivery by adding, subtracting, or reorganizing service elements.

LACK OF ACQUISITION

People acquire and frequently own products, but not services. They experience the physical manifestation of services. Typically the service is, at best, a set of associations in memory. Positive associations drive repurchase and positive word of mouth. Negative associations lead customers to avoid the service provider and dissuade others.

ROLE OF CUSTOMERS

Firms rarely refuse to sell products to customers because of the effect on other customers. But customers experience many services in group settings, so customer-customer interaction is a critical issue for many service firms.

SERVICE QUALITY

In general, high customer satisfaction drives customer loyalty, repurchase, and positive word of mouth, and enhances shareholder value. The converse is also true. The **SERVQUAL** model relates customer satisfaction to service quality via **expectations disconfirmation**.

- **Customer satisfaction.** Perceived service is *better* than expected service.
- **Customer dissatisfaction.** Perceived service is *worse* than expected service.

Marketing Question

Think about a recent positive service experience. Did you buy the service again? Did you tell friends, family, and colleagues? Did they buy the service?

Think about a recent negative service experience. Did you buy the service again? Did you tell friends, family, and colleagues? Did they buy the service?

In SERVQUAL, customer dissatisfaction is greater if:

- The firm does not understand the customer's expectations.
- Service quality specifications do not reflect firm beliefs about service expectations.
- Service delivery performance does not meet service specifications.
- External communications about service quality do not reflect service performance.

Marketing Question

Think about your favorite coffee shop. How do you perceive service quality? Evaluate tangibles, reliability, responsiveness, assurance, and empathy.

MEASURING AND MANAGING SERVICE QUALITY

In SERVQUAL, five key variables influence perceived service quality:

- **Tangibles.** Appearance of communication materials, equipment, personnel, and physical facilities.
- **Reliability.** Ability to perform the promised service accurately and dependably.
- **Responsiveness.** Willingness to help customers and provide prompt service
- **Assurance.** Employee courtesy, knowledge, and ability to convey confidence and trust.
- **Empathy.** Provision of caring, individualized attention to customers.

The 22-item SERVQUAL scale measures these variables.

LIMITATIONS OF CUSTOMER SATISFACTION

Achieving high customer satisfaction is critical for most firms. But increasing competition implies that high satisfaction no longer guarantees high customer retention; defecting customers may be highly satisfied!

ISSUES IN IMPROVING SERVICE QUALITY

To improve service quality, the firm should consider several issues:

- **Customer co-production.** Some firms improve service quality via customer participation in service delivery like self-service restaurants and self-checkout supermarkets.
- **Improving the offer.** The firm enhances service quality by adding customer service. Additional customer service is particularly important in mature markets.
- **Maintaining the service environment.** The output from some services negatively affects the physical environment, like dirty tables in restaurants. Quickly restoring the environment improves service quality.
- **Service performance and information.** Customers want high service quality, but they also want to know when they will receive the service.
- **Service quality failures and service recovery.** To minimize customer defections, the firm should deal swiftly with service failure and aggressively manage service recovery. Done well, formerly unhappy customers become loyal, even advocates.

CUSTOMER SERVICE

Customer service is an act, performance, or information that enhances the firm's core product or service. Customer service is critical for **customer relationship management (CRM)** and can be as important as the core product. Positive word of mouth follows from great customer service; negative word of mouth can be devastating.

TYPES OF CUSTOMER SERVICE

The **flower of customer service** embraces eight dimensions for augmenting the core product/service:

- Information — data provided in response to customer questions and in anticipation of their needs
- Consultation — dialogue to probe customer requirements and develop tailored solutions
- Order-taking — accepting applications, orders, and reservations
- Billing — requests for payment
- Payment — action to pay the bill
- Exceptions — supplementary services lying outside the normal service delivery routine; special requests, special communications, problem-solving, and restitution
- Hospitality — consideration and courtesy in attending to customer needs
- Safekeeping — looking after customer possessions

We can also classify customer service by phase of the purchase process. Customers have different requirements at each phase; hence, different customer services are appropriate:

- **Pre-purchase.** Assists customers preparing for purchase by helping them identify needs and by providing promotional information about products and purchase locations.
- **During purchase.** Includes help with selection, customization agreements, financing, personal selling, product assortments, product trial, and quality assurance.
- **Post-purchase.** Most marketing activity occurs pre- and during purchase; most customer service occurs after purchase. Post-purchase service helps customers pay for, transport, receive, install, use, return and exchange, repair, service, and dispose of products.

DELIVERING EXCEPTIONAL CUSTOMER SERVICE

The firm has several levers for delivering outstanding customer service:

- **Top management support.** Top managers should over-communicate that serving customers well is crucial — they should build a culture where all employees emphasize customer service.
- **Customer service strategy.** The firm should formulate a **customer service strategy** by focusing on customer *needs for customer service.* Customers with similar product- or service-based needs may have very different customer service needs, and vice versa.
- **Human resource management.** The firm should develop good HR policies and apply them rigorously. Traditional recruiting, selecting, training and developing, appraisal, recognition, reward, and retention tools are important to ensure a good fit with the firm.
- **Service infrastructure.** The firm must design the appropriate infrastructure, like technology and human resources, to support the customer service strategy. Some customer services — like repairs, depend heavily on people; others — like web-based reservation systems, depend on technology.
- **Measuring customer service quality.** *If you can't measure it, you can't manage it.* Customer satisfaction is a good measure of service quality, but across-the-board quality improvements by many firms have made it somewhat less useful. Customer defection rate is better.

Marketing Question

Recall when you ordered something over the phone, like a product or airline reservation. Where did the provider do well — billing, consultation, exceptions, hospitality, information, order-taking, payment, or safekeeping? Where could it improve?

TRUE / FALSE QUESTIONS

1. A service is any act or performance that one party can offer another that is essentially intangible and does not result in the ownership of anything. ❑ **TRUE** ❑ **FALSE**

2. The variability concept in services marketing is tightly linked to inseparability and the inability to inventory services. ❑ **TRUE** ❑ **FALSE**

3. The SERVQUAL model relates customers satisfaction to service quality via expectations disconfirmation. ❑ **TRUE** ❑ **FALSE**

4. Most marketing activity occurs post-purchase and most customer service occurs before and during purchase. ❑ **TRUE** ❑ **FALSE**

MULTIPLE CHOICE QUESTIONS

1. Which of the following is NOT a factor related to the delivery at a service facility?

   a. exterior
   b. interior
   c. offstage
   d. indivisible

2. Service guarantees are most appropriate for each of the following EXCEPT when:

   a. The service price is low.
   b. The customer's ego is involved.
   c. Sales are strongly affected by word of mouth.
   d. There are high negative consequences of service failure.

3. Which of the following does NOT represent one of the key variables that influence perceived service quality?

   a. responsiveness
   b. reliability
   c. variability
   d. assurance

4. During which of the following phases of the purchase process should the firm assist customers by helping them identify needs and by providing promotional information about products and purchase locations?

   a. pre-purchase
   b. during purchase
   c. post-purchase
   d. cross-purchase

Answers on page 205

CHAPTER 14

DEVELOPING NEW PRODUCTS

NEW PRODUCTS ARE CRUCIAL FOR ENHANCING SHAREHOLDER VALUE. Winning firms in the 21st century will have much greater expertise than competitors in innovation, in developing and launching new products, and in providing customers with new and improved product choices. Today, many firms are dissecting and improving internal systems and processes and culture to increase innovation capabilities, and sharpening external searches for new products.

THE CHANGING VIEW

OLD WAY	NEW WAY
Bureaucratic and slow	Entrepreneurial and fast
Financial criteria only	Market and financial criteria
Functional orientation	Cross-functional teams
Ideas generated internally	Ideas encouraged from many sources
Innovation seen as risky	Managing innovation and risk critical to success
Innovation strategy unfocused	Innovation strategy clearly focused
Innovation viewed as secondary importance	Innovation seen as primary importance
Not-invented-here (NIH) syndrome	Best-in-class benchmarking
Poor risk assessment	Risk profiles assessed
Poor support tools	Advanced support tools, like quality function deployment (QFD), computer-aided design (CAD), rapid prototyping processes (RPS)
Sequential processing	Parallel processing

WHERE AND HOW INNOVATION OCCURS

In general, successful innovation provides better, cheaper, and/or faster benefits and values to customers. Many people make a distinction between *sustaining* and *disruptive* innovations:

- **Sustaining innovations** improve established products on performance dimensions valued by major customers.

Marketing Exercise

Select two modern-day successful entrepreneurs. Use the Internet and your analytic skills to assess why each has been successful.

- **Disruptive innovations** offer new and very different value propositions. Initially, these innovations may underperform existing products or processes, but a few fringe customers recognize value. Later, as cost-benefit ratios improve, they surpass the old technology and broaden their appeal.

WHAT FOSTERS PRODUCT INNOVATION

Firms vary widely in their abilities to develop innovative new products. A Columbia Business School study classified less than one-third of firms in a *Fortune 500* sample as *product innovators*, but these firms earned the best returns on capital. Three factors were most important for success:

- **Market selection.** High-growth markets stimulate innovation.
- **Organization.** Formal structures to foster R&D efforts; supportive cultures.
- **R&D.** Significant and consistent R&D spending, especially applied versus fundamental.

NEW PRODUCT DEVELOPMENT

Approaches to innovation and new product development are deeply embedded in the firm's culture. If innovation performance is unsatisfactory, the firm's culture may have to change. Firms that focus on new product success often set aggressive product-development targets.

Four approaches to new product development are:

- **Basic technology research.** Typically aimed at disruptive innovations rather than immediate new products.
- **Applied technology research.** Uses basic technology to develop new products.
- **Market-focused development.** Focuses on marketable products, often by improving ease of use or developing complementary products.
- **Market tinkering.** Makes minor modifications to current products.

These four approaches lead to five new product types — *new-to-the-world products, new product lines, additions to existing product lines, improvements/revisions of existing products*, and *repositioning existing products to new segments*.

The way the firm incurs costs strongly influences its approach to new products. For many FMCG firms, distribution and promotion (for commercialization) may consume up to one half of the product development budget; B2B firms generally spend more on actual product development. When approaching new product development, marketers should think carefully about several areas:

- **Problem focus.** New product development should address important customer needs.
- **Market knowledge.** Market knowledge is always valuable. Sometimes innovative firms ignore market information and overestimate the value of technological novelty.
- **Firm competence.** A new product must be made, distributed, sold, and serviced. The firm must possess (or acquire) the appropriate competencies.
- **Complementer products.** During product development, the firm should also consider complementer products.
- **Effectiveness measures.** The firm should measure the effectiveness of its new product development process. Specifically, the firm should isolate where it performs well in new product development and where it performs poorly.
- **Stage-gate process (next section).** Successful new product development requires tough go/no go decisions at several stages in the process.

The Stage-Gate Process for New Product Development

The stage-gate process is a systematic way of generating, then pruning, a large number of ideas into a small number of products the firm successfully launches. At each gate, two errors are possible:

TYPE I ERROR. Investing in a project that ultimately fails.

TYPE II ERROR. Rejecting a project that would have succeeded.

Firms that minimize **Type I errors** accept only the safest alternatives. Failure is low, but developing products with significant financial returns is unlikely. Firms that minimize **Type II errors** develop many products that fail, but some may succeed. The firm must balance these two error types in setting criteria for passing through each *gate*. Type I errors are ultimately highly visible and measurable. Type II errors are more difficult to identify, but are no less real.

IDEA GENERATION

It takes a large number of high-quality ideas to create a new product development portfolio that drives long-term growth. The firm should document then assess the most promising ideas. Typically the firm quickly discards many ideas, but discarded ideas help generate others with greater promise. Critical issues are:

NUMBER OF IDEAS

Successful firms eliminate many ideas during the development process. Hence, they must identify a large number of ideas to find the one idea that produces a successful product.

SCOPE OF SEARCH

Focused search within the firm's mission typically generates better ideas than unfocused search. As the firm's mission evolves, so should its scope of search.

NEW IDEA SOURCES

The firm should secure ideas from many sources, both inside and outside the organization. The firm must resist the *not-invented-here* (NIH) syndrome that denigrates ideas from outside sources. P&G embraces a *reapplied-with-pride* (RWP) approach. Specific sources include:

INTERNAL GENERATION. R&D is often a major source. Success rates depend on factors like budget and type of people hired, and their motivations.

CUSTOMERS. In some industries, many key innovations start with customers. Sometimes firm employees spend time with customers to observe their likes, dislikes, difficulties, and *pain points* with current products and processes.

COMPETITORS. Some firms just copy competitor products; others identify improvement options; and still others seek opportunities via product-line gaps.

INDEPENDENT INVENTORS. These persons can be a vital source of ideas.

REGULATIONS. Regulations often cause market inefficiencies that stimulate ideas to build businesses.

Marketing Exercise

Four Wharton graduates founded Warby Parker (WP), an Internet eyewear retailer. WP operates through a mail-order, home-trial program. Get together with a few classmates; can you generate some new product ideas on which to found a business?

SERENDIPITY. New product ideas sometimes arise unexpectedly, like Viagra.

IDEA LIBRARIES. Ideas have their own right time. The environment changes and ideas with no value at time A may have great value at time B.

NEW IDEA PROCESSES

The two main approaches for generating new product ideas are:

- **Structured thinking.** Uses logical methods to generate new product ideas — can be very effective for generating ideas to improve current products.
- **Unstructured thinking.** Comprises a family of approaches that attempt to *break the mold* and develop totally new ideas by thinking *outside the box.*

PRELIMINARY SCREENING

The goal of **preliminary screening** is to create a balanced portfolio of high-potential new product ideas. Preliminary screening typically involves securing opinions from knowledgeable marketing and/or technical personnel, customers, and even suppliers.

CONCEPT DEVELOPMENT

The **product concept** (**concept definition**) describes the product idea. Good concepts detail deliverable customer benefits. Product concepts must appeal to customers and should guide development teams.

BUSINESS-CASE ANALYSIS

Business-case analysis (BCA) sits between *concept approval* and *development.* BCA assesses the concept's financial viability and considers various risk factors. The heart of BCA is a draft marketing plan; the firm lays out its market strategy, given successful development. Forecast financial performance depends on estimates of sales revenues, costs, and investment. Typically, revenue estimates (unit volumes × prices) are the most uncertain, especially for new-to-the-world products.

Four considerations underlie forecast financial performance:

- **Sales revenues.** As discussed; these forecasts can be highly uncertain.
- **Cost of goods sold (COGS).** All ongoing costs to make and sell the product. **Gross profit** equals sales revenues less COGS. The firm may incur losses in the launch phase.
- **Investment costs.** Include all costs to develop the product, plus fixed investment for factories and equipment. The firm incurs many of these costs before it earns any revenues.
- **Discounting.** The firm must discount all future cash flows to the present.

DEVELOPMENT

A successful business-case analysis sets the stage for **development**. Development typically occurs deep in the firm. Design, engineering, and R&D focus initially on product design and functional performance, but the firm must also involve other groups. Input from manufacturing and service helps ensure the firm can make and service the product efficiently. Development also benefits from customer involvement.

Marketing Question

Many drivers use cars as on-the-road offices. Show how you would design any mid-size model for office use. Would this change if the car were also the family vehicle?

PRODUCT DESIGN

As product quality improves, design becomes increasingly important for customer satisfaction. In addition to products, design is also important for packaging: Opening ease (*frustration-free packaging*) and eye-catching display are especially important in B2C. During development, the firm must make performance trade-offs among product attributes, but it should always keep the value proposition squarely in mind.

QUALITY FUNCTION DEPLOYMENT

Quality function deployment (**QFD**) brings producers and users together. QFD maps customer needs into design, development, engineering, manufacturing, and service functions. QFD helps firms identify spoken and unspoken needs and translates these needs into actions and designs. QFD also helps various business functions to communicate and focus on achieving a common goal.

CO-CREATION

Some firms form collaborative relationships with customers and independent individuals/organizations to increase the number, and broaden the scope, of new product development. Open collaboration (OC) requires tight rules for community involvement but volunteer control may be significant. By contrast, closed collaboration (CC) relies on selected collaborators whose ideas are generally more focused.

NEW PRODUCT DEVELOPMENT PORTFOLIO

For most firms, the new product development portfolio is a critical element in the entire venture portfolio, along with insourcing, outsourcing, acquisition, strategic alliance, licensing and technology purchase, and equity investment — Chapter 7. Specifically, four goals are important:

- **Portfolio value.** The firm should consider forecast profits, risk, timing, and required resources.
- **Portfolio balance.** Ensure projects are appropriately dispersed among high/low risk, short/long term; across various product forms, markets, and technologies; and across types of development efforts — basic technology research, applied technology research, market-focused development, and market tinkering.
- **Strategic alignment.** The product innovation strategy should be directly linked to the business strategy via resource allocation into *strategic buckets*.
- **Right number of projects.** Resources are limited. Too many projects and the entire product development process slows leading to missed deadlines including product launches.

PRODUCT TESTING

The firm should test its new product for aesthetic, ergonomic, functional, and use characteristics.

The two major types of test are:

- **Alpha tests — in-company.** For most new products, firm employees provide critical feedback. Several alpha tests may run simultaneously; alpha tests often lead to further development.
- **Beta tests — with customer.** Beta test typically follow successful alpha tests. But firms sometimes conduct beta tests on product features before they finish development. Beta tests give customers an early look at developing/soon-to-be-introduced new products.

MARKET-FACTOR TESTING

The product is only one element in the firm's market offer. First-rate products fail if the firm poorly designs and/or implements the rest of the marketing mix. The firm should evaluate implementation elements, like advertising and distribution via **market-factor testing**.

SIMULATED ENVIRONMENTS

In B2C, the firm can test advertising messages via split cable TV or in movie houses. The firm can test packaging, pricing, and shelf placement in mock-up store displays placed in trailers adjacent to shopping malls.

VIRTUAL TESTING

Virtual testing is a new approach to customer testing. The firm creates an online shopping display and customers shop as in a real store, with all the distracting clutter. An important benefit of virtual testing is the ability to modify displays quickly and analyze results instantaneously. Both virtual testing and simulated testing are artificial. Test marketing provides greater realism.

TEST MARKETING

Test marketing simulates actual market conditions. Typically, the firm selects two geographic areas with similar market and customer profiles, considering issues like seasonality. The firm implements the full market launch program in one geography; the other geography acts as a control to isolate product launch results. For any test market, measurement is crucial and includes:

- **Input measures** — advertising, training, sales effort
- **Intermediate measures** — customer awareness, interest
- **Output measures** — sales, profits, customer satisfaction

Test marketing has pros and cons. *Pros* include:

- **Fine-tunes launch.** Test marketing provides invaluable data for fine-tuning actual launch.
- **Provides unexpected insight.** Test market failures may provide unexpected data.
- **Saves launch costs:** The firm can withdraw products that perform poorly in test markets and avoid spending resources on products that would have failed.

Marketing Question

Have you ever been part of a test market in your local grocery store or retail outlet? Did you try the product? Did the firm launch it successfully, or was it killed?

Cons for test marketing include:

- **Alert competitors.** The test market may show firm intentions and reduce its time-to-market advantage.
- **Competitors' actions.** Competitors can interfere with the firm's test market.
- **Excessive attention.** The firm may make a test market successful by putting in special effort. If the firm cannot duplicate this effort at launch, it may introduce a product it should have cancelled.
- **Expense and time.** Test marketing is expensive and may take a long time. Also, the firm forgoes revenues from an otherwise successful launch.

COMMERCIALIZATION

Successful completion of the stage-gate process results in a product ready for launch and **commercialization.** The firm assigns resources to construct facilities and expend marketing effort. The launch strategy must consider issues like forecast sales, time to bring facilities on line, production and inventory requirements, adherence to planned launch date, competitive lead time, expected competitive response, patent or trade secret protection, and available resources.

PRODUCT ADOPTION

The firm should anticipate five categories of customer adoption behavior:

- **Innovators.** The first to adopt the innovation but are only a small part of the population.
- **Early adopters.** Follow the innovators. Are more *respected* in their communities and are opinion leaders for others.
- **Early majority.** Motivated by current problems and make decisions *deliberately*, based in part on the experience of early adopters.
- **Late majority.** A *skeptical* group that adopts only when half the population has adopted.
- **Laggards.** These *traditionalists* are suspicious of change, are averse to novelty, and adopt when most customers have adopted and use is widespread.

Identifying potential customers by **adoption category** for a new product innovation is a critical marketing challenge. In B2C, early adopters tend to be better educated, socio-economically advantaged, and younger. A product innovation must cross the **chasm** from early adopters to early majority and the mainstream market to be successful. Many new products fail to cross the chasm; for others, it takes a long time.

The **ACCORD** acronym summarizes several factors that affect the speed of adoption and commercial success:

- **Advantage.** Offers customer value over alternatives.
- **Compatibility.** Does not require significant change in customer behavior.
- **Complexity.** Degree of customer learning requirements.
- **Observability** (Communicability). Customer benefits easy to understand and communicate.
- **Risk.** Customer experiences little risk in trying the product.
- **Divisibility.** (Reversibility). Customer can easily switch back to previous alternative.

Marketing Question

The Segway is a battery-driven personal-transportation vehicle developed by Dean Kamen. Launched in 2002, the Segway has been less successful than its inventor predicted. What barriers to adoption did the Segway face? Could Segway have done a better job in addressing these barriers?

TRUE / FALSE QUESTIONS

1. Sustaining innovations offer different value propositions. Initially, these innovations may underperform existing products or processes, but a few fringe customers recognize value. ❏ **TRUE** ❏ **FALSE**

2. Type II errors are more difficult to identify than Type I errors. ❏ **TRUE** ❏ **FALSE**

3. Firms that minimize Type II errors accept only the safest alternatives. Failure is low, but they are unlikely to develop products with significant financial return. ❏ **TRUE** ❏ **FALSE**

4. Early adopters are the first to adopt an innovation, but represent only a small part of the population.
   ❏ **TRUE** ❏ **FALSE**

5. Product innovation must cross the chasm from early adopters to early majority and the mainstream market to be successful. ❏ **TRUE** ❏ **FALSE**

MULTIPLE CHOICE QUESTIONS

1. Which of the following is NOT one of the four approaches to new product development?

   a. physiological profile research
   b. applied research technology
   c. market-focused development
   d. market tinkering

2. All of the following are considerations that underlie the forecast of a firm's financial performance EXCEPT:

   a. sales revenues
   b. investment costs
   c. cost of goods sold
   d. market tinkering

3. Which of the following is an advantage for test marketing a new product concept?

   a. Test marketing may alert competitors.
   b. Competitors may interfere with the test market.
   c. Test market failures may provide the firm with unexpected insight.
   d. The firm may invest extra effort to make the test market successful.

4. Which of the following categories of consumer behavior is a skeptical group that adopts only when half the population has adopted?

   a. early adopters
   b. early majority
   c. late majority
   d. laggards

Answers on page 205

Design the Market Offer

CHAPTER 15

INTEGRATED MARKETING COMMUNICATIONS

INTEGRATED MARKETING COMMUNICATIONS captures the idea of coordinating all communications messages with the *right* communication tools and techniques to the *right* audiences at the *right* times. This chapter reviews communications strategies and tactics for reaching target audiences and achieving the firm objectives.

THE CHANGING VIEW

OLD WAY	NEW WAY
Broad appeal	Targeted messaging
Customers are sole communications target	Multiple communications targets — including complementers, customers, employees, governments, influencers, shareholders, and suppliers
Limited media/vehicle choices	Proliferating media/vehicle choices
Mass communication	Interactive communication
Siloed communications effort	Integrated communications effort
The firm communicates with customers	The firm communicates with customers; customers also communicate with the firm
Word of mouth may provide relevant communications	Managing Internet-based word of mouth a critical managerial challenge

COMMUNICATIONS CHALLENGES

An integrated marketing communications program is critical for successfully implementing the firm's market strategy and achieving its objectives. The firm must address many challenges from both outside and inside the organization.

Marketing Question

The FDA approves drugs for specific indications — medical conditions. Physicians can *use* an approved drug for different indications, but drug firms cannot *promote* such *off-label use* without FDA approval. The FDA approved Natrecor (J&J) for *short-term* treatment of heart-failure patients with breathing problems. Nurse practitioner Regina Massaro worked closely with Dr. Altschul, the physician who pioneered Natrecor use for *longer-term* treatment of heart-failure patients — an off-label use. J&J paid Massaro to make nationwide trips to discuss heart-failure management. Massaro couldn't promote Natrecor for off-label use, but she could answer questions about her experiences — many physicians ask about *longer-term* Natrecor treatment.[3] How do you assess J&J's actions in arranging and funding Massaro's trips?

EXTERNAL CHALLENGES

As the firm tries to determine the right mix of tools and techniques for reaching various audiences, it must address several external challenges:

- **Competitive communications.** Competitors and the firm have similar communications targets. Competitors use varied communications approaches to promote their products and disadvantage the firm.
- **Evolving communications technologies.** Communications choices are expanding rapidly. Growth in digital media allows firms to modify product placement and promotions for different audiences through different communications channels.
- **Multiple information sources.** Customers receive information about the firm and its products from many sources. Communications may be negative, neutral, or helpful to the firm; they can also be very powerful.
- **Noise.** Customers and other audiences live in information-rich environments. Myriad messages (*clutter*) bombard them daily. Effective communications must cut through the clutter so firm messages resonate with intended targets.
- **Public perception.** Sometimes firms face public criticism for their communications activities and feel compelled to change.
- **Regulators.** Firms are biased information providers; hence government agencies review firm communications to ensure fairness and accuracy.
- **Social media.** The explosion of social media on the Internet has vastly increased the volume of unmanaged communications about the firm and its brands. Positive communications can help the firm, but negative communications from these sources may severely damage the firm's reputation.

INTERNAL CHALLENGES

Communication challenges occur inside the firm as well as outside. Often-heard internal opinions about firm communications are:

- **We don't need it.** Many technically oriented firms assume the *best* product, as defined by their engineers, will *win*. "Our product will sell itself." But customers must believe that the entire offer (including the product) provides the best value.
- **We've already done that.** The firm believes it has already communicated enough.
- **It's an unnecessary expense.** Many firms prefer to spend resources for tangible assets like land and plant and equipment, rather than on communications.
- **We need different messages for different audiences.** The firm has multiple communications targets like current and potential customers, complementers, employees, suppliers, and shareholders — sometimes even competitors. Achieving communications consistency can be very difficult.

COMMUNICATIONS: PROCESS AND TOOLS

THE COMMUNICATIONS PROCESS

The *sender* sends a *message* to a *receiver*; the *receiver* receives the message. In some communication processes, the *receiver* also communicates with the *sender*. Ideally, the receiver *receives* the message the sender *intended* to send. If this does not occur, there is **miscommunication** — typically not a good outcome. Three main sources of miscommunication are:

- **Encoding error.** Typically, some person or organizational entity decides on the intended message, but this message is not sent.
- **Distortion.** The firms sends the intended message, but communication is distorted; the receiver does not receive the sent message.
- **Decoding error.** Communications targets have selective attention, perception, and/or retention. Hence, the message is misperceived and/or misunderstood.

COMMUNICATIONS TOOLS

Communications tools are the ways marketers interface with target audiences. Two traditional categories the firm drives are **personal communication** and **mass personal communication**. We embrace two extra categories — **digital communication** and **word-of-mouth communication (WOM)**.

PERSONAL COMMUNICATION. Interpersonal (often *face-to-face*) communication occurs among individuals or groups. Most **personal communication** in marketing occurs when salespeople and other firm representatives, like technical- and customer-service personnel, interact with customers individually or as team members.

MASS COMMUNICATION. Much marketing communication occurs without interpersonal contact between sender and receiver, particularly in B2C marketing. Typically, the firm has greater control over the message content in mass communication than in personal communication:

- **Advertising.** The firm pays for communications directed at a mass audience.
- **Direct marketing.** Includes all paid and sponsored communications directed at individuals.
- **Packaging.** Packaging's main value is to protect the product. But packaging is a communications vehicle, delivering information and visual appeal.
- **Publicity & public relations (P&PR).** Publicity is communication for which the firm does not pay directly. PR embraces publicity but is broader; PR includes other ways of gaining favorable responses for the firm. Typical PR activities include sponsoring events, giving speeches, and donating money to charity.
- **Sales promotion (SP).** SP communications provide extra value for customers; firms often design SP to induce immediate sales. Special forms of SP are:
  - **Product placement.** The firm places products in movies and TV shows.
  - **Trade shows.** Suppliers (vendors) display and/or demonstrate products to large numbers of current and potential customers, at one time, in one convenient location.

DIGITAL COMMUNICATION. The Internet has provided firms with many additional options for communicating with customers. Some methods are electronic analogues of traditional communication tools like various types of advertising on third-party websites and direct marketing via e-mail. Other methods are specific to the medium, like firm websites, blogs and microblogs, and social networking. Traditional and digital communications can also be linked via technologies like O-codes and QR codes for print media. Interaction and feedback without human involvement, usually via artificial intelligence, is **quasi-personal communication** (QPC). Customers talk to computer servers via voice recognition software.

WORD-OF-MOUTH (WOM) COMMUNICATION. Communication among customers and potential customers can impact many purchase elements like brand choice, distribution channels, and timing. Communications about a firm or product can be positive or negative, depending on the customer experience. Generally, firms have little control over **WOM**, but increasingly they are orchestrating **buzz-marketing**, **guerilla-marketing**, and **viral-marketing** campaigns.

Marketing Question

In the past month, have you recommended a product or service to someone — or did someone give you a recommendation? Did the firm take any action to encourage WOM?

DEVELOPING THE COMMUNICATIONS STRATEGY

The firm's communications strategy embraces communications targets, communications objectives, communications messages, communications tools, and budgeting and timing.

COMMUNICATIONS TARGETS

The firm has two major types of communications targets: *directly related* to firm offers and *not-directly related* to such offers.

DIRECTLY RELATED COMMUNICATIONS TARGETS. The firm should be most concerned with reaching customers specified in the positioning statement of its market strategy — Chapter 9. These include current and potential customers, direct and indirect customers, and third-party specifiers and advisors.

Broadly speaking, communications strategies are either **push** or **pull**:

- **Push strategy.** Communication focuses on *direct* customers.
- **Pull strategy.** Communications focus on *indirect* customers further down the channel like final consumers or other end-user customers.

Large FMCG firms often use a combination of *push* and *pull* strategies.

NOT-DIRECTLY RELATED COMMUNICATIONS TARGETS. These include targets like shareholders, investors, legislators, and special-interest groups.

COMMUNICATIONS OBJECTIVES

Typically, long-run marketing communications objectives are to increase sales units and/or revenues, and repeat purchase of firm products. Prior requirements may be securing awareness, knowledge, liking, and/or trial. Major considerations are type of target and the firm's market strategy.

COMMUNICATIONS TARGET. The firm typically has different objectives for direct and indirect customers, and competitors and complementers:

- **Direct and indirect customers.** Objectives for a direct customer like a wholesaler may be both to purchase but also to make significant efforts to sell the firm's products. For an indirect customer like a consumer, the objective may be awareness, liking, trying, and/or continuing to purchase.
- **Competitors and complementers.** Communications objectives are very different from firm objectives for customers. Typically, the firm tries to influence competitor and complementer actions so customers perceive firm offers more favorably.

THE FIRM'S MARKET STRATEGY. The firm identifies customer targets in the positioning statement of the market strategy — Chapter 9 — these are also the firm's communications targets. The firm must align communications objectives with selected alternatives in the *strategic focus* to increase unit sales volume:

- Increase customer retention (reduce defection)
- Increase customer use
- Attract customers from competitors
- Secure new business

Marketing Question

Develop a communications plan for your favorite local restaurant. How does your plan improve on the restaurant's current actions?

COMMUNICATIONS MESSAGES

Constructing the appropriate message for a customer target is central to developing the communications strategy. The core underlying principle is that message design should reflect the value proposition (positioning element) in the firm's market strategy.

COMMUNICATIONS TOOLS

Communications objectives drive firm choice of communication tools. Selecting the *right* tool(s) is critical in developing effective communications to reach target audiences. Among firm options are personal selling, telemarketing/telesales, individual service personnel, sales and service teams, advertising, direct marketing, publicity & public relations, website, blogs and microblogs, social media, and mobile marketing.

BUDGETING AND TIMING

Budgeting and timing the firm's communications efforts are critical for determining the most effective communications strategy. Both budgeting and timing relate directly to communications objectives and selected communication tools.

A critical budgeting issue concerns the firm's choice of push versus pull communication strategies; they have very different cost parameters:

- **Pull strategies.** Firms generally spend heavily on advertising to generate *pull*. These *fixed-costs* expenditures require large cash outflows for uncertain revenues. Hence, pull strategies are generally more popular with well-financed large firms than with small firms.
- **Push strategies.** Firms generally incur high *variable costs* from margins, discounts, and sales commissions earned by intermediaries like wholesalers and retailers. Payments directly relate to firm sales, limiting upfront cash outflows. Smaller firms generally favor push strategies.

INTEGRATING COMMUNICATIONS EFFORTS

The firm's core challenge is to develop an effective **integrated marketing communications** program to maximize impact of its strategy and achieve objectives. The four types of integration are:

A. Communications for all targets in a single market segment.

B. Communications with other marketing implementation variables — product, service, distribution, and price.

C. Communications for all targets in several market segments.

D. Communications for all targets — market segments, markets, businesses, corporate.

A — Integrate communications for all targets, in a single market segment strategy. This communications integration is fundamental. The firm should blend various communications campaigns (using different tools) to be mutually reinforcing and, if possible, synergistic.

B, C, and D — Reflect higher levels of integration. In each case, the firm must ensure its messages are consistent and even strive for *synergy*.

Increasingly sophisticated segmentation and *mass customization* practices, along with proliferation of communication tools, are creating more opportunities for marketers to deliver targeted and relevant messages in a granular way.

Marketing Question

Identify a firm(s) that relies heavily on a *pull* strategy. Is the firm successful? If so, why? If not, why not?

....
TRUE / FALSE QUESTIONS

1. Publicity is usually defined as communication for which the firm does not pay directly.
   ❏ TRUE ❏ FALSE

2. Interaction and feedback without human involvement, usually via artificial intelligence, is mass communication. ❏ TRUE ❏ FALSE

3. Typically, firms have little control over word-of-mouth communication, but are increasingly orchestrating buzz-marketing and guerilla-marketing campaigns to encourage positive word-of-mouth.
   ❏ TRUE ❏ FALSE

4. The firm has two major types of communications targets: early adopters and late adopters.
   ❏ TRUE ❏ FALSE

5. Increasingly sophisticated segmentation and mass customization practices, along with the proliferation of communication tools, are creating more opportunities for marketers to deliver targeted and relevant messages in a granular way to customers. ❏ TRUE ❏ FALSE

....
MULTIPLE CHOICE QUESTIONS

1. Which of the following is NOT an example of communication challenges that occur within or outside the firm?

   a. "We don't need it."
   b. "We've already done that."
   c. "We need different messages for different audiences."
   d. "Advertising is not effective for small businesses."

2. Which of the following is NOT one of the three causes of miscommunication?

   a. encoding
   b. distortion
   c. feedback
   d. decoding

3. Which of the following types of mass communication is usually defined as communication for which the firm does not pay directly?

   a. publicity
   b. direct marketing
   c. advertising
   d. public relations

4. Which of the following is NOT one of the four types of integration a firm should strive to attain to maximize impact of its strategy and achieve objectives?

   a. Integrate communications with other marketing implementation variables like product, price, distribution, and service.
   b. Integrate communication for all targets in a single market.
   c. Integrate communication for all targets in several markets.
   d. Integrate communications, in parallel with competitor actions, mirror market share growth.

Answers on page 205

Design the Market Offer

CHAPTER 16

MASS AND DIGITAL COMMUNICATION

ADVERTISING IS THE MOST VISIBLE FORM OF MASS COMMUNICATIONS and consumes the largest percentage of many FMCG firms marketing budgets. No matter what communications approaches the firm chooses, it must set objectives, select specific tools, execute the program, and measure results.

THE CHANGING VIEW

OLD WAY	NEW WAY
Creativity desirable in messaging	Creativity essential in everything
Direct response methods are rare	Direct response methods are ubiquitous
Exposure-driven	Impact-driven
Intermediaries are usually involved	Movement to direct marketing
Intuition	Measurement/tracking
Local/national advertising strategies	Regional/global advertising strategies
Media scheduling is pedestrian	Media scheduling creativity is essential
Passive audience	Active/interactive audience
Short-term promotions common	Long-term brand equity a key concern

Mass Communications

ADVERTISING FOUNDATIONS

At its essence, advertising is a service. The advertiser pays the media firm to *bundle* its advertising with content like articles in a newspaper/magazine story or a TV show, but receives nothing *directly* in return. The advertiser receives its value *indirectly*. Customers receive value from highly subsidized (or free) content; advertisers receive value from customer attention to their messages. These customers have immense value to advertisers.

In many industries, particularly FMCG, advertising is central to implementing market and communications strategies. Firms make investments today for financial returns tomorrow. In implementing market strategy, the firm should consider advertising as an *investment*. Today's advertising should achieve short-term results, but may also have long-run impact, like building the brand, and lead to future customer purchases.

The Advertising Program

TARGET AUDIENCE: WHOM ARE WE TRYING TO INFLUENCE?

A key element in formulating the market strategy is deciding which segments to target. For each target segment, the positioning statement identifies customer targets with whom the firm wishes to communicate. For a *push* strategy, the firm focuses on direct customers; for a *pull* strategy, the firm focuses on indirect customers.

How advertising *works*. Advertising effectiveness is perhaps the most-studied marketing topic. **Hierarchy-of-effects** models are central to understanding how advertising works. Typically, the firm's ultimate goal is to reinforce the brand and encourage *purchase* and *repeat purchase*.

High involvement. The customer believes the purchase, like a new automobile, involves financial and/or psychosocial risk. The customer engages in a staged learning process:

- **Awareness.** Learning that the product is available for purchase.
- **Knowledge.** Understanding product attributes, features, benefits, and values.
- **Liking/preference.** Developing favorable/positive feelings about the product.
- **Trial.** Testing the product before purchase and use.
- **Purchase.** Exchange money or other resources for the product.
- **Repeat purchase.** Purchasing the product again. Advertising can reinforce positive feelings that lead to repeat purchase.

Marketing Exercise

Apply a hierarchy-of-effects model to your purchase of a HDTV set.

Low involvement. Customers see little risk and require little pre-purchase knowledge. Advertising's role is to create high *awareness* and motivate customers to *trial*.

ADVERTISING OBJECTIVES: WHAT ARE WE TRYING TO ACHIEVE?

Once the firm has validated advertising as the appropriate communications vehicle, it should formulate **advertising objectives**. There are two considerations:

- **Output objectives** — what the firm ultimately wants to achieve, like sales, repeat purchase, market share, and brand loyalty.
- **Intermediate objectives** — relate to hierarchy-of-effects models and include awareness, knowledge, liking/preference, trial, and emotional commitment (to a brand).

MESSAGING: WHAT CONTENT SHOULD THE TARGET AUDIENCE RECEIVE?

The firm's advertising message derives directly from the market strategy. The positioning statement has four elements:

Convince	[customer target]
In the context of other alternatives	[competitor targets]
That they will receive these benefits	[value proposition]
Because we have these capabilities/features	[reasons to believe]

The firm's advertising message should follow directly from its positioning statement, with special emphasis on the value proposition. The message should focus upon core benefits and values and reflect unique claims where the firm has a differential advantage. Clear positioning statements provide excellent guidance for creative personnel in advertising agencies to develop effective messages.

Firms active in multiple countries must decide whether, and to what extent, they should *standardize* messages globally or *localize* them for national/regional markets. National markets differ in cultural norms, living patterns, and income distribution, so these variables provide useful *hooks* for developing messages. But standardization can provide cost and efficiency savings. Recently, standardization has become easier as advertising agencies have *gone global*.

EXECUTION: HOW SHALL WE COMMUNICATE THE MESSAGE?

Execution focuses on the method (style) firms use to turn core messages into effective advertising. The essence of creativity seems to be a willingness to alternate between divergent and convergent thinking, between brainstorming and analytic reasoning, between pushing the limits and being reasonable and practical.

Advertising executions come in two major forms — *rational* and *emotional*:

RATIONAL APPEALS

Rational appeals focus on people's sense of logic. Five main styles are:

- **Comparative (attack).** Successful comparative advertising focuses on demonstrating superiority over competition.
- **Demonstration.** Shows the product in use and focuses on performance. Many B2B communications use demonstration ads; they are also common in sales force materials.
- **One-sided and two-sided. One-sided advertising** focuses only on positive product attributes; **two-sided advertising** presents both positive and negative messages.
- **Primacy or recency.** Research shows that items at the beginning of a message — *primacy* — and at the end — *recency* — are more effective than items in the middle.
- **Refutational.** A special case of two-sided advertising explicitly mentions competitor claims, but then directly refutes them.

> *Marketing Exercise*
>
> Use available resources like print media and YouTube to identify advertisements using each of the rational and emotional appeals discussed. Bring to class.

Marketing Question

View Go Daddy's *Censorship Hearing* advertisement (www.godaddy.com). Do you think it is funny? Why or why not? Bring your favorite humorous advertisement to class.

EMOTIONAL APPEALS

These advertising approaches appeal to emotions. Four main styles are:

- **Celebrity endorsement.** Advertisers often use well-known people to endorse products, especially on TV.
- **Fear.** Fear appeals create anxiety; behaving as the advertising suggests removes the anxiety. Examples are *physical danger, social disapproval, monetary loss*, and *female insecurities.*
- **Humor.** Humor is widespread in advertising but should be used carefully. Humor helps create awareness, sets a positive tone, and enhances memory; but improperly crafted humor may distract from the core message.
- **Storytelling. Storytelling** can be a very effective way of appealing to people's emotions. MasterCard's *Priceless* campaign and Nike's *Just Do It* are good storytelling examples.

MEDIA SELECTION AND TIMING: WHERE AND WHEN SHALL WE PLACE OUR ADVERTISING?

To select appropriate media, the firm must answer five related questions:

- **Media objectives.** What should our media strategy accomplish?
- **Type of media.** Which media classes shall we use — print, broadcast, outdoor?
- **Specific media.** Which media vehicles shall we use — *Vanity Fair, Survivor*, bus stops?
- **Timing.** When will our advertising appear?
- **Media schedule.** Specifically, where and when shall we place our ads?

MEDIA OBJECTIVES

WHAT SHOULD OUR MEDIA STRATEGY ACCOMPLISH? Key concerns are reach, frequency, and impact:

- **Reach.** Number of targeted individuals exposed to the advertising at least once.
- **Frequency.** Average number of times a target individual is exposed to the advertising.
- **Reach and frequency.** Reach and frequency calculate gross rating points (GRPs).

Gross rating points (GRPs) = Reach × Frequency

Generally, advertisers trade off reach and frequency. When the firm uses different media types, duplication is an issue. Suppose the firm decides to advertise on both radio and TV; two relevant measures are:

- **Duplicated reach:** Receive a message from *both* radio and TV.
- **Unduplicated reach:** Receive a single message, *either* radio or TV, but not both.

- **Impact.** Impact is directly related to creativity in generating advertisements — indeed, many *creatives* view the media department's job as boring and routine. But mass media has fragmented, and consumers' media habits are more varied; hence the media task is increasingly challenging.

TYPE OF MEDIA

WHICH MEDIA CLASSES SHALL WE USE? A **media class** is a group of closely related media. Media classes differ from one another on dimensions like time availability and intrusiveness. A common category system (with examples) is:

- **Broadcast** — television and radio; exist for short time periods — significant intrusion.
- **Online** — e-mail and web alerts; delivered in real time. Read at leisure — more intrusive than print.
- **Outdoor** — billboards and in-store; long presence — relatively non-intrusive.
- **Print** — newspapers and magazines; read at leisure — relatively non-intrusive.

Each media type has advantages and disadvantages for advertisers.

SPECIFIC MEDIA

WHICH MEDIA VEHICLES SHALL WE USE? A **media vehicle** is a specific entity in a media class. The *newspaper* media class includes *The New York Times*, *The Boston Globe*, and *The San Francisco Examiner*. The *magazine* media class includes *Good Housekeeping*, *Time*, and *Vanity Fair*. The *television* media class includes *60 Minutes*, *American Idol*, and *Days of Our Lives*, and in-store (e.g., Walmart, Tesco). Critical issues in choosing media vehicles are:

- **Audience size.** How many readers/viewers/listeners are there? Audited readership, listenership, or viewership statistics are available for most media vehicles.
- **Audience type.** Does the audience fit with the communications target? Specifically, does it have the right demographics — age, gender, lifestyle, marital status, and product-use characteristics?
- **Cost.** Two costs are important in assessing media vehicles:
  - **Absolute cost.** Total out-of-pocket cost — the price for one advertisement in *The New York Times* or a 30-second commercial on *60 Minutes*.
  - **Cost per audience member.** A breakdown cost for comparing media vehicles, based on audience size. A popular measure for print media is:

    Cost per thousand (**CPM**) = Total cost of advertising space **x** 1000/Circulation
- **Nature of the vehicle.** How does the message interact with the media vehicle? Readers generally pay more attention to advertisements in magazines than in newspapers.

TIMING

WHEN WILL OUR ADVERTISING APPEAR? The four main timing patterns are:

- **Concentration.** Commit all expenditures at one time.
- **Continuous.** A regular periodic advertising pattern.
- **Flighting.** Repeated high advertising levels followed by low (or no) advertising.
- **Pulsing.** Combines continuous and flighting. Pulsing can occur within a media vehicle, within a media class, or across multiple media vehicles and classes.

MEDIA SCHEDULE

SPECIFICALLY, WHERE AND WHEN SHALL WE PLACE OUR ADS? The firm tries to optimize media objectives like reach, frequency, and GRPs subject to a budget constraint.

Marketing Question

A Sunny Day is a full-length feature film sponsored by Starbucks and PepsiCo to introduce bottled frappuccino drinks to China. *A Sunny Day* plays in Shanghai's modern subway system on 4,000 flat screens, in subway cars and at 95 stations, for a few minutes daily for 40 weekdays. What do you think of this communications initiative? Can you suggest other innovative communications approaches?

ADVERTISING BUDGET: HOW MUCH SHALL WE SPEND ON ADVERTISING?

The **advertising response function (ARF)** relates advertising spending to advertising objectives like sales. The ARF is crucial for setting the **advertising budget** but its shape is typically not known. The firm faces two questions in deciding its advertising budget:

- What shape is the ARF?
- Where is the firm currently operating?

If the firm can answer these two questions, budgeting is simply a matter of marginal analysis: Set the budget where marginal revenue equals marginal cost. Marginal analysis underpins computer-based, decision-calculus models like ADBUDG.

> **Marketing Question**
>
> The price of advertising on the U.S. Superbowl is around $3 million for 30 seconds. Is it worth it?

OBJECTIVE AND TASK

This *bottom-up* approach focuses on advertising objectives. The firm uses historical and/or experimental data to estimate the budget for each task, then sums the costs to calculate a total.

OTHER BUDGETING METHODOLOGIES

Firms sometimes use *top-down* methods to calibrate budgets they develop by *objective* and *task*:

- **Percentage of sales.** The advertising budget is a **percentage of sales (A/S)**; *sales* is current sales, anticipated next-year sales, or some combination.

  Practical problems using percentage of sales include:

  - **Advertising new products.** Because sales are low, the firm is biased against advertising spending even though it may be vital.
  - **Basing the budget on anticipated sales.** The firm would reduce advertising when it expects sales to dip, yet maintaining or increasing advertising may be the best strategic action.
  - **Basing the budget on last year's sales.** Suppose sales would grow if the firm increased advertising; the firm would not increase its budget.
  - **Seduction.** The firm makes competitive comparisons based on A/S ratios; but these ratios do not specify actual advertising spending.

- **Competitive parity.** The firm bases advertising on competitor actions. The firm may match the competitor dollar-for-dollar or use competitor spending as a benchmark. Some firms base their budgets on their competitor spending per market share point.

- **What the firm can afford.** There is no rational basis for this approach. Unfortunately, it is not that uncommon.

PROGRAM EVALUATION: HOW SHALL WE TEST OUR ADVERTISING AND MEASURE ITS EFFECTIVENESS?

The firm may test individual advertisements, different levels and types of spending, and/or evaluate the entire advertising program:

TESTING INDIVIDUAL ADVERTISEMENTS. The firm tests ads with target customers (subjects), individually or in groups; in a laboratory or experimental field setting. Some examples of testing techniques are:

- **Laboratory/print.** Show several advertisements or mock publications with advertising inserted; subjects view these at home or at a central location.

- **Laboratory/broadcast.** Insert advertisements in a TV program or movie; subjects view these in a theater or shopping mall.
- **Field setting.** Similar to the laboratory, but with real publications and TV programs.

Laboratory testing lets researchers manipulate several advertising elements, exercise tighter control over the subject interaction with the advertisement, and limit costs. The major downside is lack of realism. Field settings reverse these pros and cons. **Advertising effectiveness measures** for both field and laboratory tests include:

- **Recognition.** Widely used for print advertising. The researcher asks subjects which advertisements they recognize.
- **Unaided recall.** Widely used for broadcast advertising. The researcher asks subjects what advertising they remember, *without* prompting.
- **Aided recall.** Widely used for broadcast advertising. The researcher asks subjects what advertising they remember, *with* prompting.
- **Purchase.** Used in field settings. Customer panel members present ID cards at grocery stores when they make purchases.

TESTING DIFFERENT LEVELS AND TYPES OF SPENDING

The firm tests alternative spending patterns using experimental design procedures.

EVALUATING THE ENTIRE ADVERTISING PROGRAM

The firm may wish to evaluate an entire advertising program. **Tracking studies** measure customer responses over time, using either a customer panel or randomly selected respondents.

THE ADVERTISING AGENCY SYSTEM

Most major U.S. advertisers outsource advertising program development to advertising agencies, but some firms like The Prudential and Ryanair running simple advertisements in print media conduct advertising activities in-house. By outsourcing, firms have better access to creative talent and greater flexibility. The firm usually works with three agency groups:

- **Account/relationship managers** — the key agency interface and help craft the strategy;
- **Creative department** — develops advertising messages and executions;
- **Media department** — prepares the media schedule and provides supporting data.

Traditionally, firms paid advertising agencies a fixed percentage of advertising spend or commitment. More recently, firms and agencies negotiate fees. The firm may also pay for results to more closely align firm and agency interests.

CORE ELEMENTS OF THE CREATIVE BRIEF

The core agency job is to translate firm market strategy into an advertising message, and execute on that message. Firm and agency personnel should jointly develop a **creative brief** — a *contract* between the firm and agency. Core elements include:

- **Marketing objective.** What the firm wants to achieve — output and intermediate objectives.
- **Assignment.** The type of campaign including media type, timing, and approval process.
- **Customer insight.** Informs the creative process — critical insight into target market; identifies rational and emotional factors that drive product purchase/use.

- **Competitive insight.** Informs the creative process — includes barriers to achieving firm objectives.
- **Target audience.** Whom the firm wishes to influence — customer types and segments — includes demographics, psychographics, and current products.
- **Key benefit.** The most important benefit/value the firm wishes to emphasize.
- **Reasons to believe.** Why the target customer should believe the firm's claims.
- **Brand identity.** How the firm wants the target audience to feel about its product. Should be important to the audience, deliverable by the firm, and unique to the brand.
- **Mandates.** Elements outside the advertiser's control — must or must not be included — like corporate and/or legal requirements advertising must meet.
- **Measurement.** How the firm will know if the campaign has been successful.

Marketing Question

Suppose your school, college, or university plans advertising to increase student applications. Develop a creative brief for developing a campaign idea.

Some important institutional changes are occurring in the advertising agency industry. These changes have major implications for advertisers:

- **Formation of large groups.** Many well-known individual agencies are now part of four major groups: Interpublic and Omnicon (U.S.), WPP (Britain), and Publicis (France).
- **Globalization.** Advertising agencies have developed global scopes to serve clients globally.
- **Broadening of services.** Advertising agencies are taking a more holistic view of communication by expanding outside of advertising.

Other Mass Communications Options

DIRECT MARKETING

Direct marketing is a fast-growing communications tool embracing many ways of requesting a customer response. Today, direct marketing includes traditional print and broadcast advertising, packaging, package inserts, warranty cards, take-ones, and newer digital options like fax, e-mail, and the Internet. Low bulk postal rates, online shopping, and widespread credit card use help grow direct marketing. Other factors include:

- **Delivery systems.** Package delivery firms like FedEx and UPS increasingly offer greater service variety.
- **Demographics and lifestyles.** The growth of dual-income families facing increasing time pressures, especially in developed countries.
- **Internet.** The Internet allows far greater personalization/customization and immediacy than other direct marketing methods.
- **Product quality.** The generalized increase in product quality has reduced customer risk when buying products remotely.
- **Professionalism.** Direct marketing firms are more professional and sophisticated, especially in segmenting, targeting, and communicating.
- **Technology.** Using advances in computer- and telecommunications technologies, firms can develop, manage, and mine customer databases.

Although direct marketing may be more expensive than advertising on a CPM basis, it offers several advantages:

- **Ability to identify prospects.** By relating customer profiles to purchase patterns, direct marketers can identify high-quality prospects.
- **Ability to tailor the offer.** Direct marketers know the products customers purchase; hence, they can tailor messages and offers to individuals.

- **Action-oriented customer response.** Advertising programs typically work via an effects hierarchy. By contrast, direct marketing is more action-oriented and typically requests purchase.
- **Better customer knowledge.** Many direct marketing firms have extensive information on customers.
- **Better measurement.** The firm can test program elements like message, price, incentives, and/or type of direct marketing to assess their impact on sales and adjust accordingly.
- **Flexibility.** The firm can develop some direct marketing campaigns, like e-mail, much more quickly than mass advertising.
- **Predictability.** Because direct marketing typically requests purchase, sales forecasts for direct marketing programs can be fairly accurate. Budgeting for direct marketing is simpler than for advertising.

PUBLICITY AND PUBLIC RELATIONS

Publicity and public relations (P&PR) are closely related; publicity is really a subset of public relations. **Publicity** focuses on securing neutral or favorable short-term press coverage. **Public relations (PR)** is broader in scope and more multifaceted. PR embraces corporate reputation, crisis management, government relations (lobbying), internal relations, press relations, product publicity, and shareholder relations. P&PR generally relies on intermediaries to transmit messages (hopefully positive) to target audiences. The advantage for P&PR is that the audience may view the intermediary as impartial, and the firm does not pay for media space and time.

SALES PROMOTION

Sales promotion (SP) is a complex blend of communications techniques providing extra customer value, typically for trial to stimulate immediate sales. Sometimes SP has longer-run objectives like increasing awareness. The three main SP types are:

- **Consumer promotion** — manufacturer to consumer
- **Trade promotion** — manufacturer to retailer
- **Retail promotion** — retailer to consumer

Consumer and retail promotions include cash refunds, contests, coupons, deals, games, rebates, point-of-purchase displays, premiums, prizes, samples, and sports sponsorships. *Trade promotions* include advertising and merchandising allowances; contests, deals and prizes; special price deals; *spiffs*; and trade shows. Firms are continually creating new SP techniques. Generally, SP is not a good standalone approach; the firm should tightly integrate SP with other communications. The firm should always keep in mind SP's long-term impact, particularly if SP involves short-term price reductions.

> *Marketing Exercise*
>
> Three African countries — Mozambique, Swaziland, and South Africa — formed the *East3Route* initiative to attract European tourists. *East3Route* has issued an RFP (request for proposal) to develop a P&PR campaign to support the initiative. Prepare a proposal.

Digital Communications

The first section of this chapter focuses on traditional mass communications approaches. Section 2 addresses digital communications options. The Internet does three things traditional communication methods do not. The Internet:

- Communicates globally 24/7/365;
- Makes it easy for customers to communicate with the firm;
- Makes it easy for customers to communicate with each other.

On the Internet, the firm can follow customers as they visit websites, blogs and microblogs, view advertisements, and make purchases. We discuss five digital communications topics: online advertising and public relations, websites, blogs and microblogs, social networking, and mobile marketing.

ONLINE ADVERTISING AND PUBLIC RELATIONS

As a communications tool, the Internet offers many ways for marketers to communicate with customers, each with its own characteristics:

SEARCH

Generic search has two important facets for marketers — **paid search** and **search engine optimization:**

PAID SEARCH. Advertisers pay to appear next to, and be associated with, search results based on keywords.

SEARCH ENGINE OPTIMIZATION. Success in appearing at higher page positions (free) requires understanding the mechanics of search engines and *optimizing* the firm's website by selecting significant key words.

DISPLAY

Display advertising comprises banner ads on websites. The basic banner ad has been standard for many years but new sizes include tall, skyscraper-like and medium-rectangle ads.

CLASSIFIEDS

Online classifieds are typically text listings for specific types of products and services like automobiles, jobs, real estate, yellow pages, and time-sensitive auctions.

VIDEO

Internet video is increasing dramatically. Firms place videos on their own and other firm websites, and on public sites like YouTube.

E-MAIL

Out-bound e-mail communication is a popular way for firms to maintain contact with current customers. To avoid the spam problem, many firms encourage prospective customers to provide e-mail addresses, then allow *opting out*. E-mail is a two-way street. *In-bound* e-mail allows the firm to deal with customers on a personal basis, but it must develop processes to address in-bound communications fully and promptly.

WEBSITES

At a minimum, the firm's website is a form of mass communications (brochureware); it can also enable sales promotion by offering free samples and discounts. The website's true potential is its

Marketing Question

Many firms have developed creative approaches to using the Internet as a communications device. What is your favorite example of an Internet campaign? Was it successful? Why or why not?

ability to engage customers and build brand equity. Customers form links to the brand and can join with like-minded customers to form online communities.

Simple websites are inexpensive to establish and take down, but complex websites may be more cost-effective. Some firms encourage customers to use the Internet for routine tasks like product information search, placing orders, and checking delivery status. Many firms use the Internet to generate sales directly.

BLOGS AND MICROBLOGS – TWITTER

Blogs are platforms to offer opinionated comments. Blogs are often highly specialized (celebrities, food, travel, wine); some bloggers have enormous followings and are important opinion leaders. Hence, bloggers offer marketers the ability to target specialized audiences. But blogging can backfire if bloggers view the blog as commercial interests invading a non-commercial domain.

Twitter is a microblogging service; users send and read other users' messages — *tweets* — text posts of up to 140 characters displayed on the author's profile page. Users send tweets to friends' lists and subscribe to other authors' tweets.

SOCIAL MEDIA

Social media (**SM**) are online tools and platforms that allow Internet users to share insights and experiences for business or pleasure, share content (words, pictures, audio, video), entertain each other, offer reviews and opinions, and collaborate.

THE BRIGHT SIDE OF SOCIAL MEDIA

SM include blogs and microblogs, Internet forums, networks, photo and video sharing, podcasts and webinars, and wikis for meeting like-minded people. Many firms engage in community building by bringing together users. These communities offer excellent opportunities to stimulate positive word of mouth, gain awareness, enhance brand image, build brand equity, and drive sales.

Many firms use customer reviews for product redesign; other firms engage customers in new product development.

THE DARK SIDE OF SOCIAL MEDIA

Much social media activity by firms aims to create favorable mentions about the firm and its brands, but customer-to-customer communications (C2C) can also be negative. Defecting customers may encourage network members to defect and/or broadcast dissatisfactions widely. Increasingly, firms are training employees to monitor the Internet for negative communications and implement ways to mitigate brand damage.

Marketing Question

Firms are increasingly using blogs for commercial purposes. Search the Internet. Which company blog do you think is most effective? Why? What are the benefits and limitations of blogs?

Marketing Question

As book publishers have embraced electronic publishing (iPad, Kindle, Nook), some are assessing the opportunity to secure additional revenues by placing advertising in both electronic and printed books. As a publishing marketing executive, how would you approach an assignment to investigate this opportunity?

Marketing Question

What is your favorite example of a mobile marketing campaign? Why is this campaign your favorite?

MOBILE MARKETING

Hand-held personal digital assistants (PDAs), smart phones, and tablet computers free web surfers from personal computers. Digital communications can now occur *on the go* 24/7/365. Mobile marketing will increase in importance. Mobile devices offer new options for marketers:

- **Short message service (SMS)** — short text messages (up to 160 characters) that remain stored until the user opens the mobile device.
- **Multimedia message service (MMS)** — similar to SMS but may include graphics, video clips, and sound files.

Marketers may send permission-based or unsolicited messages. For permission-based (*opt in*) options, users subscribe to a service like *foursquare* or *shopkick*. Opt-in communications are preferable in many situations.

TRUE / FALSE QUESTIONS

1. The two major forms of advertising executions are scientific and rational approaches.
❏ TRUE ❏ FALSE

2. Fear-based advertising is an example of a main style of rational advertising. ❏ TRUE ❏ FALSE

3. Advertising frequency is the average number of times a targeted individual is exposed to an advertisement. ❏ TRUE ❏ FALSE

4. A media vehicle is a specific entity in a media class. ❏ TRUE ❏ FALSE

5. The advertising response function relates advertising spending to advertising objectives like sales.
❏ TRUE ❏ FALSE

MULTIPLE CHOICE QUESTIONS

1. Which of the following is NOT a main style of rational advertising?

   a. demonstration advertising
   b. celebrity endorsement-based advertising
   c. comparative advertising
   d. primacy or recency advertising

2. All of the following represent main styles of emotional advertising EXCEPT:

   a. humor-based advertising
   b. fear-based advertising
   c. refutational advertising
   d. storytelling-based advertising

3. Which of the following represents the correct formula to calculate gross rating points (GRPs)?

   a. reach + frequency
   b. reach/frequency
   c. (reach + frequency)/2
   d. reach x frequency

4. Which of the following advertising timing patterns has repeated high advertising levels followed by low (or no) advertising?

   a. concentration
   b. continuous
   c. flighting
   d. pulsing

5. Which of the following is NOT one of the three main types of sales promotions?

   a. consumer promotion
   b. trade promotion
   c. retail promotion
   d. concentrated promotion

Answers on page 205

C H A P T E R 1 7

D I R E C T I N G
A N D M A N A G I N G
T H E F I E L D
S A L E S E F F O R T

IN MANY FIRMS, THE SALES FORCE IS THE ONLY GROUP SPECIFICALLY CHARGED with making sales and securing revenues. In B2B marketing, the field sales force has always been critical; salespeople typically introduce firm products/services to customers. By contrast, in B2C marketing, advertising is often the main communication channel to consumers — the sales force has played a supporting role, but this is changing as the retail industry concentrates. Chapter 17 addresses four main topics: the marketing/sales interface, leading the selling effort, the tasks of sales force management, and managing key/strategic accounts.

THE CHANGING VIEW

OLD WAY	NEW WAY
Evaluation based on sales volume	Evaluation increasingly based on profit contribution
Firms seek profits by cost reduction	Firms seek profits through revenue growth
Focus on making sales	Focus on building long-term, profitable customer relationships
Many low-powered sales personnel	Fewer high-powered sales personnel
Sales and marketing clearly separate	Sales and marketing increasingly intertwined
Sales efforts managed domestically	Sales efforts for global customers managed globally
Sales force organization and processes are fixed for long periods of time	Sales force organization and processes are modified to reflect environmental and strategic changes
Sales force/service linkages poor or loose	Sales force closely linked to customer service
Salespeople act in an ad hoc fashion	Salespeople developing planning skills
Salespeople individualism emphasized	Salespeople increasingly team players
Salespeople undervalued in the firm	Salespeople increasingly valued — the only firm function responsible for generating revenues
Salesperson as seller	Salesperson as educator and problem-solver

CONTINUES ON NEXT PAGE

OLD WAY	NEW WAY
Salesperson skill requirements relatively low	Salesperson skill requirements increasingly high
Salesperson the sole interface with customers	Salesperson manages the organizational interface with many personnel
Transactions-based sales	Relationship-based partnerships

MARKETING'S ROLE IN THE FIELD SALES EFFORT

Marketing and sales must be on the same team, each performing its own critical functions. Marketing tends to have a long-run view; sales must deliver short-term performance. To be truly effective in the marketplace, marketing and sales must work hand-in-hand to seamlessly implement the market strategy. Well-managed firms have processes that tightly coordinate marketing and sales efforts.

LEADING THE SALES EFFORT

Sales receives short shrift in many firms. Many CEOs have financial, science, marketing, legal, or manufacturing backgrounds — but no sales experience. These CEOs don't realize the firm will fail if the sales force generates insufficient revenues. This stark reality places a premium on leadership at each level in the sales organization. All sales managers, junior and senior, should *lead from the front*, spending time in the field with their salespeople. The most effective sales managers lead by example, encouraging two-way communication with customers, and collaborating with other organizational functions.

The most effective sales leaders *advance the science of sales and the art of the customer relationship* by making fact-based decisions, like allocating sales resources — salespeople, strategic (key) account managers, telesales — across customer segments and sales channels.

Sales leaders create a *risk-taking* culture where failed experiments for delivering customer value are *accepted* and *expected*. They celebrate and reward learning from honest mistakes, but penalize repeated mistakes. Sales leaders discover and develop best practice by following the *fail or scale* principle.

Perhaps the most critical leadership function is encouraging sales people to *live the mission* — to provide a rationale for the sales job over and above financial rewards. Salespeople who internalize a greater purpose build credibility and trust with customers and develop a powerful differentiator for defeating competitors.

> *Marketing Exercise*
>
> Interview a senior sales executive and ask two core questions:
> - What works well in your relationship with marketing? Why do these things work?
> - What works poorly in your relationship with marketing? Why do these things not work?

The Tasks of Sales Force Management

To mount an effective selling effort, sales managers must focus on six tasks. Three sales force management tasks address *developing* sales strategy; three tasks deal with *implementing* sales strategy:

Developing the sales strategy	Implementing the sales strategy
Task 1: Set and achieve sales objectives.	Task 4: Design the sales organization.
Task 2: Determine and allocate selling effort.	Task 5: Create critical organizational processes.
Task 3: Develop sales approaches.	Task 6: Staff the sales organization.

TASK 1: SET AND ACHIEVE SALES OBJECTIVES

Sales objectives are the firm's desired results; achieving objectives is the sales force central task. The firm makes profits, survives and grows, and enhances shareholder value only by selling products/services to customers. Achieving sales objectives takes precedence over all other activities like collecting payments, delivering goods, entertaining, and gathering information. Sales objectives turned into specific performance requirements are called **sales quotas**.

DEFINING SALES OBJECTIVES

The firm can choose among several sales force performance measures. Most firms set sales objectives in terms of volume like gross sales revenues (dollars) or gross sales units. Some firms also set profitability objectives like profit contribution — gross profits less direct sales force costs. Well-set objectives specify *how much* and *by when* the sales force must meet targets.

RELATING SALES OBJECTIVES TO MARKETING OBJECTIVES

A useful way of driving marketing and sales integration is to rigorously translate marketing objectives into sales objectives. Translating market segment objectives into sales objectives by product can be a complex undertaking.

BREAKING DOWN SALES OBJECTIVES

Typically, the sales force breaks down overall sales objectives into **control units** like sales regions, sales districts, and individual sales territories. Senior sales managers gain significant insight by comparing actual sales performance versus sales objectives for individual control units; they see if a particular region, district, or territory is performing well or poorly. Firms also establish sales objectives in time units like quarterly, monthly, and weekly. **Calendarizing** allows the firm to monitor performance continuously and sets the stage for making course corrections when performance deviations are negative.

ALTERNATIVE SALES PERFORMANCE MEASURES

Sales and profit-type objectives are the most popular performance measures, but there are many others. The firm should choose carefully based on the nature of the business and its strategic situation.

- **Customer retention.** The proportion of customers from the start of the year who are still customers at the end of the year — the opposite of customer defection (churn).
- **Market share.** This measure focuses on firm performance versus competitors.
- **Price realization.** The extent to which the firm achieves planned price levels.
- **Close rate.** The proportion of sales attempts resulting in actual sales.
- **Customer satisfaction.** Specific metrics focusing on the customer experience.

ACHIEVING SALES OBJECTIVES

Most salespeople are ethical and positively motivated to successfully sell products/services to target customers. Although relatively uncommon, sometimes firms pressure salespeople to make sales by any method — including giving customers improper payments, kickbacks, and/or all-expense-paid trips. When this type of behavior comes to light, it damages the firm's reputation and reduces shareholder value.

TASK 2: DETERMINE AND ALLOCATE SELLING EFFORT

The best way to determine and allocate selling effort is by examining four interrelated decisions:

- **Sales force size.** How much selling effort should the firm expend in total? In particular, how many salespeople should sell its products?
- **Sales force activities.** What activities should salespeople do? What proportion of total time should salespeople spend actually *selling*?
- **Selling effort allocation.** How should salespeople allocate selling time among firm products and segments?
- **Telesales.** What proportion of overall selling effort should the firm allocate to telesales? What should telesales people do?

SALES FORCE SIZE

For effective selling effort, the firm must have the *right* number of well-trained, motivated salespeople. Managing *headcount* is typically a crucial HR function, and sales managers often wage difficult internal battles to optimize sales force size. When selling effort is low, the firm makes few sales. As selling effort increases, sales increase. Ultimately, sales *top out* or reach a maximum level, even if the firm adds extra salespeople. The firm should continue hiring until the marginal revenue from adding a salesperson equals that salesperson's marginal cost. Approaches to the sizing decision are experimental or analytic.

EXPERIMENTAL METHOD. Sales managers change sales force size and see what happens. Two broad hypotheses are:

1. The sales force is too small.
2. The sales force is too large.

Sales managers should decide what criteria would support/reject each hypothesis. Then they select one or more sales districts/regions for a trial and comparable districts/regions as controls.

ANALYTIC METHOD. The analytic approach has three steps:

1. **Estimate the total number of selling hours required to achieve sales objectives:** Two broad approaches for calculating *required number of selling hours* are:
   - **Single-factor models.** The firm classifies current and potential customers into A, B, C, and D categories (I) by a value measure like sales potential (II). Then the firm: a. identifies the number of customers in each category (III); b. estimates the required selling hours annually for customers per category (IV); c. multiplies III × IV to secure the required selling hours annually per category. Summing the results across categories provides the total number of selling hours. Single-factor models are simple to use but may not fully capture the complexity of selling to various customers. Portfolio models may do a better job.
   - **Portfolio models.** The firm forms a matrix by classifying customers on multiple dimensions like *customer potential* and the firm share of customer business — *customer share.* The firm identifies the number of customers in each matrix cell and required selling time per customer. The analysis proceeds as with the single-factor model.
2. **Calculate the number of available selling hours per salesperson.** Salespeople conduct many activities. Sales managers must calculate the time available for selling.
3. **Calculate the required sales force size — divide 1 by 2.** Dividing *required number of selling hours* by *number of available selling hours per salesperson* provides a *ballpark* estimate for sales force size. The firm should expect some variation from actual size, but significant variation demands action.

Marketing Question

If you, a friend, or a colleague have worked in sales, what percentage of time was *face time* with customers? What other activities were part of the job? Were the time allocations good? Why or why not? What were the challenges of increasing face time?

SALES FORCE ACTIVITIES

The main sales force job is to make sales. But claims on salespeople's time include checking credit and inventories, collections, customer service, delivering products, education and training, gathering market intelligence, internal communications, meetings, qualifying sales leads, receiving payments, record-keeping, report writing, sales planning, and travel. Many firms increase salesperson **face time** by using less-critical personnel for time-consuming activities or introducing technological solutions. Typically, time allocations differ from one sales territory to another.

SELLING EFFORT ALLOCATION

The firm's selling effort (selling time allocation) should mirror the *structure* of its sales objectives. For sales objectives by product, the firm should allocate selling effort by product. For sales objectives by product and market segment, the firm should allocate selling effort by product and market segment. Sales objectives by old versus new products require a similar selling effort allocation. Two important issues are:

- **Percentage allocations.** Although the *structure* of selling effort allocations and sales objectives should be identical, generally, the *proportions* are different — some types of sales are easier to make than others.
- **Actual time allocations.** Similar to sales objectives, the firm should break down selling effort allocations by individual control units — sales regions, sales districts, and sales territories.

Sales managers must make these selling effort allocations and ensure salespeople stick to the guidelines. If managers do not lead, salespeople will set their own priorities.

TELESALES

In recent years, many firms have reduced sales costs by adding telesales departments. Telesales functions differ markedly from firm to firm:

- **Lead generation.** Some firms use telesales to make cold calls and appointments for on-the-road salespeople.
- **Potential customers.** Telesales may be more effective than impersonal communication methods for contacting potential customers.
- **Current customers.** Some firms assign small current customers to telesales.
- **Partner with field sales.** Some firms pair field sales and telesales. Less-expensive telesales conducts many customer-facing activities as well as field sales.

TASK 3: DEVELOP SALES APPROACHES

Because customer needs differ by segment, the firm should offer a different value proposition for each market segment. Hence, salespeople selling multiple products to multiple segments must have multiple **sales approaches**. Aided by sales managers and product managers, salespeople should develop messages for specific customers and competitive threats. In particular, they should:

- Secure insight into specific needs and competitive threats at individual customers.
- Understand the various perspectives of the customer decision-makers and influencers.
- Develop sales approaches that address customer needs, answer objections, and counter competitors' sales approaches.

The traditional sales approach has two major components:

1. Tailoring the sales message for different customer targets, and
2. Designing a process to explain values and benefits in the firm's offer.

TAILORING THE SALES MESSAGE FOR DIFFERENT CUSTOMER TARGETS

Customer needs and competitive offers drive the value proposition and the sales approach. Salespeople must decide whom to target and how to tailor sales messages for each person. The salesperson must orchestrate the value proposition into a sales approach for each customer role (and individual). In designing the sales approach, salespeople should sharpen competitive focus.

DESIGNING A PROCESS TO EXPLAIN THE FIRM'S BENEFITS

Selling is a process to facilitate customer buying. A completely standardized process is undesirable, but sales managers should guide salespeople via coaching, counseling, and well-designed training programs. Teaching employees to *sell* is daunting; good sales managers break the selling task into discrete easy-to-learn steps like:

- **Call objectives.** Know the desired results from each sales call and at each stage in the buying process. A pre-call planning process can help.
- **Sales interview tone.** Decide how strident or aggressive to be in different situations.
- **Need elicitation.** Develop procedures to elicit customer needs.
- **Presenting product benefits.** Present product benefits in the context of customer needs.
- **Handling objections.** Anticipate customer objections and know how to address them. Objections differ from product to product and from customer to customer.
- **Communications timing and closing the deal.** Communicate in a strategic sequence; learn how to close a sale and ask for the order.

TASK 4: DESIGN THE SALES ORGANIZATION

The sales organization should reflect the firm's strategic realities. For example, if the firm's product line is complex and heterogeneous, perhaps it should have multiple sales forces. Three critical issues are:

- Should firm employees conduct the selling effort? Or should the firm outsource selling?
- How should an employee-based sales force be organized? Or reorganized?
- How should the firm design sales territories?

SHOULD FIRM EMPLOYEES CONDUCT THE SELLING EFFORT? OR SHOULD THE FIRM OUTSOURCE SELLING?

Three issues are important:

- **Control.** Employee-based sales forces are more likely to follow managerial directions. Outsourced agents, brokers, and reps earn commissions; hence, the firm may exercise little control, particularly if the outsourcee sells other firm (even competitor) products.

Marketing Question

Baby food firm Gerber fired 250 salespeople and sold to grocery store chains via food brokers. In the education market, by contrast, Apple shifted from third-party sellers to an employee-based sales force. Why did these firms move in opposite directions? When is outsourcing the better decision?

- **Cost.** Employee-based sales forces typically incur substantial fixed costs like salaries, and travel and entertainment. By contrast, third-party sellers on commission are a variable cost: No sales, no costs!
- **Flexibility.** To modify an employee-based sales force takes time and almost always involves HR. Third-party sellers typically work with strict performance criteria and short-term contracts.

HOW SHOULD AN EMPLOYEE-BASED SALES FORCE BE ORGANIZED?

Three interrelated design variables for choice of organizational design are *degree of centralization/decentralization, number of management levels,* and *managerial span of control.* As many firms have downsized, sales forces have decentralized, with fewer management levels and larger managerial spans of control, especially for first-line sales managers; such *hollowing out* makes directing and coaching salespeople more difficult.

Specialization is one of the most important design variables. Essentially, sales organizations can be unspecialized or specialized:

- **Unspecialized.** Two organization forms are generally considered unspecialized:
  1. No geographic bounds on a salesperson's search for sales opportunities.
  2. Territories organized by geography where salespeople sell all products, to all customers, for all applications in specified geographic areas.
- **Specialized.** Specialization can be by product, maintenance/new business, distribution channel, market segment, and/or customer importance (strategic accounts).

... OR REORGANIZED?

As the firm's environment evolves, so must its market and sales strategies evolve. The sales organization must also evolve. Examples of reorganizations include:

- From a geographic-based sales force to a sales force with no geographic boundaries.
- From a product-based sales force to strategic account managers (SAMs).
- From a geographic-based sales force to a product-based sales force.
- From a geographic-based sales force to a distribution-level-based sales force.
- From an undifferentiated account-based sales force to a strategic account-based sales force.

HOW SHOULD THE FIRM DESIGN SALES TERRITORIES?

Within the sales organization structure, the firm must design (redesign) **sales territories.** The two key variables are **sales potential** — available sales; and **salesperson workload** — time to complete required activities. The four sales territory design steps are:

- **Initial design by sales potential.** The firm identifies geographically contiguous territories with roughly equal *sales potential.* Some trial territories are geographically larger than others.
- **Calculate workload.** Use sales-effort allocation decisions to determine *workload.*
- **Adjust for workload.** Make territory design adjustments to optimize sales potential and salesperson workload.
- **Continuous monitoring.** Sales managers must monitor salespeople and their territories and continually adjust.

TASK 5: CREATE CRITICAL ORGANIZATIONAL PROCESSES

All sales organizations employ a variety of organizational processes like sales planning, pipeline analysis and sales forecasting, evaluation methods, and reward systems to help implement planned selling effort.

SALES PLANNING

The firm should actively engage salespeople in a detailed sales planning process. Time is the salesperson's critical scarce resource; the sales action plan drives the selling effort by specifying where the salesperson will place effort in the upcoming year, plus identifying shorter-term action steps.

PIPELINE ANALYSIS AND SALES FORECASTING

The sales pipeline comprises stages in the selling process that customers traverse in moving from prospects (potential customers) to buyers. **Pipeline analysis** tracks firm success in moving customers through these stages and is particularly important for sales forecasting.

EVALUATION METHODS

For salespeople, the most critical measure is sales performance versus sales objectives. But sales managers should also assess the quantity and quality of selling effort. Sales managers should use several measures to evaluate selling effort as a single measure can be misleading. For example, high sales per existing account may seem like great performance, but perhaps the salesperson is opening few new accounts.

REWARD SYSTEMS

Reward systems are powerful motivators for salespeople. To establish a truly motivating system, salespeople should answer "yes" to the following questions:

- Can I *achieve* my sales objectives?
- Do I *value* the rewards I will receive for meeting my sales objectives?
- Do I believe I will truly *receive* the rewards I earn?
- Is the reward system fair?

Sales reward systems can have several components:

- **Financial compensation.** The firm combines three financial rewards in various ways:
  - **Base salary.** Paid to the salesperson regardless of sales performance (in the short run).
  - **Bonus.** Reward paid for achieving quota — typically a target sales or profit level.
  - **Sales commission.** Variable compensation based on sales or profits.
- **Recognition.** This important reward is relatively inexpensive but can be a powerful motivator.
- **Promotions and work assignments.** Promotions and more interesting and responsible job possibilities are highly motivating for some salespeople.

Generally, financial compensation is a salesperson's most important motivator. The firm should ensure its incentive compensation drives required behavior. A well-designed compensation system can be highly motivating, but a poorly designed system can be highly demotivating.

> *Marketing Question*
>
> Think about jobs you have had. How were you compensated? What types of incentives did the employer provide? What did you find demotivating?

TASK 6: STAFF THE SALES ORGANIZATION

Sales managers must ensure the sales force is fully staffed and all territories filled at all times. Far too often, sales managers do not plan for natural attrition, dismissal, promotions, and/or transfers, and are forced to scramble when a salesperson leaves. Sales managers should *inventory* salespeople and have their own *pipeline* of candidates ready to move to a territory when one opens up.

Marketing Question

What are the challenges of consistently motivating a sales team? How would you address these challenges?

If the firm has a policy of recruiting salespeople internally, it can create a career path in related departments like sales support or customer service. If the firm recruits externally, sales managers should continually interview candidates, develop short lists, and be ready to hire when needed. Staffing trade-offs include:

- **Availability.** If experienced competent salespeople are not available, as in new and growing industries, the firm must be ready to provide significant training.
- **Hiring philosophy.** The firm may require salespeople *uncontaminated* by *bad habits* from previous selling experiences.
- **Time.** If a new hire must perform effectively and immediately, there may be no time for a broad search and significant training.
- **Tolerance for failure.** Hiring only the best salespeople may be critical. In other cases, a sink-or-swim approach can be more effective.

The staffing process to hire and prepare effective salespeople involves several steps:

- **Recruiting.** Sizing and defining the pool from which the firm will select salespeople.
- **Selecting.** Using selection criteria to choose salespeople from the recruitment pool.
- **Training.** Ensuring salespeople have the knowledge, skills, and abilities (KSAs) to be effective.
- **Coaching.** Continuous efforts by first-line sales managers to improve selling effectiveness.
- **Retaining.** Maintaining high-performing salespeople.
- **Replacing.** Weeding out and replacing poorly performing salespeople.

RECRUITING

The recruitment pool reflects the firm's hiring philosophy. Two broad approaches are:

- **Experience.** Hire experienced sales professionals.
- **Inexperience.** Hire high-potential individuals with zero (or limited) sales experience. The firm may focus on recent college graduates or employees in telesales or non-sales functions.

SELECTING

Selection criteria can be loose or tight. The firm must minimize two key selection errors:

- **Type I error** — Hiring a salesperson who eventually fails.
- **Type II error** — Not hiring a salesperson who would have succeeded had they been hired.

Sales managers should track hiring errors so the firm can sharpen its recruiting and selecting policies.

TRAINING

Successful training turns newly hired salespeople into effective performers by making their KSAs congruent with the selling job. Training requirements depend on the firm's recruiting and selecting policies. The firm should offer sales force development programs periodically.

COACHING

Training typically occurs intermittently; coaching is ongoing. First-line sales managers should work with their salespeople to ensure they are being as effective as possible and not making classic salesperson mistakes.

RETAINING

High-performing salespeople are valuable assets, and the relationships they forge with customers are often vital for long-term firm success. When a high-quality salesperson moves to new responsibilities or to a different company, firm/customer relationships become vulnerable.

REPLACING

The firm should quickly replace underperforming salespeople. Sometimes the firm makes a hiring error; sometimes a previously high-performing salesperson cannot adjust to a new strategy.

SALES MANAGEMENT

Securing effective salespeople is one thing; finding effective sales managers is quite another. Regrettably, many firms thoughtlessly promote their best salespeople to be sales managers. The firm may lose a great salesperson and gain a poor sales manager! Sales managers must carry out the six tasks of sales management. Senior sales managers should also have the skills to interface with marketing and other firm functions.

> **Marketing Question**
>
> How would you go about identifying potential candidates for first-line sales manager positions?

KEY/STRATEGIC ACCOUNT MANAGEMENT

Realizing the 80:20 rule, many firms are implementing strategic account (SA) programs. These firms identify the most important current and potential customers, then invest in them. In most SA programs, **strategic account managers** (**SAMs**) are responsible for building and sustaining relationships with individual strategic accounts.

> **Marketing Question**
>
> How does the SAM job differ from the salesperson's job?

Successful strategic account programs adopt the *congruence model*, requiring critical decisions in four areas:

- **Strategy.** Includes overall resource allocation, number of SAs and revenue and profit targets, nominating and selecting criteria for SAs, and types of firm/SA relationships.
- **Organization structure.** Concerned with organizational placement of the SA program, reporting structure, and interfaces with other functions, notably the sales force.
- **Human resources.** Securing the appropriate personnel to be SAMs; includes other classic HR functions like training, retaining, and compensation.
- **Systems and processes.** Methodologies for helping SAMs do their jobs like SA planning systems, customer profitability, benchmarking, and best practice sharing.

SA programs have evolved in two important ways:

- **Managing global accounts.** To better serve global customers, suppliers are adopting SA practices at a global level. **Global account managers** (**GAMs**) develop plans for multinational accounts and manage global account teams that implement their strategies.
- **Customer tiers.** Rather than classify major customers as either strategic accounts or regular accounts, leading firms partition SAs into several tiers based on current and potential revenues — like Tier I (platinum), Tier II (gold), and Tier III (bronze) — and allocate resources accordingly.

Nine critical success factors for managing strategic accounts are:

- Establish the scope — size and boundaries — of the SA program
- Secure senior management commitment
- Select the *right* strategic accounts
- Design the line organization for managing SAs
- Secure effective SAMs
- Develop effective SA plans
- Establish the supporting organizational infrastructure
- Deliver and document the creation of incremental value
- Put it all together — align the success factors in SA management

TRUE / FALSE QUESTIONS

1. Calendarizing allows the firm to monitor performance on a continuous basis and sets the stage for making course corrections if performance deviates negatively from objectives. ❏ **TRUE** ❏ **FALSE**

2. The firm's selling effort or selling time allocation should mirror the structure of its sales objectives.
   ❏ **TRUE** ❏ **FALSE**

3. For salespeople, the most critical measure is sales performance versus sales objectives.
   ❏ **TRUE** ❏ **FALSE**

4. An example of a Type I selection error is not hiring a salesperson who would have succeeded had they been hired. ❏ **TRUE** ❏ **FALSE**

5. Successful strategic account programs adopt the congruence model, requiring critical decisions in the areas of budgeting, manufacturing, innovation, and social responsibility. ❏ **TRUE** ❏ **FALSE**

MULTIPLE CHOICE QUESTIONS

1. Sales objectives turned into specific performance requirements are called

   _____.

   a. sales quotas
   b. control units
   c. portfolio models
   d. spiffs

2. Which of the following is NOT one of the three interrelated decisions to examine when determining and allocating the selling effort?

   a. sales force size
   b. sales force activities
   c. sales force compensation
   d. selling effort allocation

3. In determining whether or not to outsource the selling effort, a firm must address each of the following critical issues EXCEPT:

   a. control
   b. cost
   c. flexibility in modification
   d. globalization

4. Which of the following is NOT one of the three basic financial rewards in determining financial compensation for a salesperson?

   a. base salary
   b. sales commission
   c. bonus
   d. spiff

5. Which of the following is NOT one of the three basic financial rewards in determining financial compensation for a salesperson?

   a. base salary
   b. sales commission
   c. bonus
   d. spiff

Answers on page 205

CHAPTER 18

DISTRIBUTION DECISIONS

FIRM PRODUCTS REACH CUSTOMERS VIA DISTRIBUTION CHANNELS. Distribution can be direct from supplier to customer, but may also be highly complex involving many intermediaries. Power inequalities may prevent firms from making distribution innovations. Yet no distribution system lasts forever, and new approaches that add value and reduce costs can unseat market leaders.

THE CHANGING VIEW

OLD WAY	NEW WAY
Conflict models dominate	Cooperative models ascendant
Customers patient	Customers impatient
Direct marketing rare	Direct marketing common
Distribution arrangements fixed	Distribution arrangements changeable
Distribution — local/regional	Distribution — regional/national/global
Fast delivery rare	Delivery speed highly valued
Information technology poorly used	Information technology essential
Manufacturer as channel captain	Retail power increasing
Overnight distribution unavailable	Overnight distribution increasing
Push inventory systems (loading intermediaries common)	Pull inventory (efficient consumer response systems)
Slow progression: exclusive → selective → intensive	Fast progression: exclusive → selective → intensive
Telecommunications infrequent	Telecommunications ubiquitous

DISTRIBUTION SYSTEMS AND THEIR EVOLUTION

A **distribution channel or network** comprises various intermediaries that facilitate supplier goods and services reaching consumers and/or other end-user customers. The functions intermediaries perform and their interrelationships are always in flux. Leading indicators of impending change include: unhappy consumers, end-user customers, and/or suppliers; complacent intermediaries; deteriorating system economics; market coverage gaps; new technology; outdated system interfaces; poor logistics; and unexplored channels. The effectiveness of any distribution system changes over time, but suppliers often have difficulty making adjustments.

Developing a Distribution Strategy

To develop distribution strategy, the firm must make several critical decisions:

- **Distribution functions.** What exactly must be done in the distribution channel?
- **Distribution channel: direct or indirect?** Should the firm deal directly with consumers and/or end-user customers? Or should the firm use intermediaries, and if so, which ones?
- **Distribution channel breadth.** How many intermediaries should there be at each distribution level?
- **Criteria for selecting and evaluating intermediaries.** How should the firm decide whether a particular intermediary is appropriate for handling its products?

DISTRIBUTION FUNCTIONS

By completing many functions, distribution closes gaps in physical location and time between factory-finished products and consumers/end-user customers. Sometimes the supplier undertakes a particular function; other times intermediaries or end users do so. In a complex distribution channel, some functions, like physical movement, must be done several times.

DISTRIBUTION CHANNELS: DIRECT OR INDIRECT?

Essentially, the firm has two options:

- **Direct channels.** Suppliers manage most contact with consumers and end users.
- **Indirect channels.** Intermediaries like the distributors, wholesalers, and retailers play a major role in transferring products to consumers and end users. Some indirect channels have a single intermediary; others have multiple intermediaries.

REACHING CONSUMERS THROUGH DIRECT CHANNELS

Direct distribution, combined with database marketing, is a serious alternative to indirect distribution. In B2C, **direct distribution** has several forms:

FACE-TO-FACE DIRECT SALES. Direct customer contact can give suppliers intimate insight into customer needs. Some firm salespeople sell and deliver products direct to customers.

DIRECT SALES VIA DIRECT MARKETING, MASS MEDIA, AND TELEMARKETING/TELESALES. The firm makes contact with individual customers; they receive purchased products directly by package delivery from remote locations.

INTERNET. The Internet is the fastest-growing *inbound* communications method for many product forms. Customers initiate the buying process at the supplier's website.

SPECIALIZED RETAIL DISTRIBUTION. The suppler firm controls product display and customer experiences in retail outlets. Retail outlets are either wholly owned by the supplier or franchised to a third party.

Marketing Question

Fingood (disguised name) distributed products to consumers via distributors and retailers. To spur consumer demand, Fingood cut prices to distributors by 20 percent, but Fingood's leading distributor held prices firm so as to increase its margins. The price reduction failed. What were Fingood's mistakes? How should Fingood proceed?

REACHING CONSUMERS THROUGH INDIRECT CHANNELS

Many B2C firm products reach consumers via *indirect distribution*: Distributors, wholesalers, and/or retailers provide *physical location* and *time* value. By constructing product assortments from many suppliers, indirect channels reduce customer search costs and provide an entire shopping experience. Intermediaries may provide market access that would otherwise be very expensive (or impossible) for the firm to secure. Efficiencies from using channel partners also reduces costs for suppliers:

- Agents, manufacturers' representatives, and brokers — selling economies.
- Banks and financial institutions — financing economies.
- Distributors, wholesalers and retailers — inventory, selling, and transportation economies.
- Independent warehouses — inventory economies.
- Package delivery and transportation companies — transportation economies.

REACHING ORGANIZATIONAL CUSTOMERS

B2B firms use both direct and indirect distribution to reach organizational customers:

- **Direct distribution.** Firms sell directly to end-user customers via on-the-road sales forces, telemarketing/telesales, direct marketing, and/or the Internet.
- **Indirect distribution.** Some suppliers reach customers, especially small businesses, through retail stores — like Office Depot and Staples for office supplies.

Distribution speed is increasingly important as firms use **just-in-time** (**JIT**) inventory systems to increase operating efficiencies.

DISTRIBUTION CHANNEL BREADTH

Marketing Question

Best Buy discovered that many customers were examining products in its stores, then searching the Internet for better prices and placing orders online. How would you advise Best Buy?

Distribution channel breadth refers to the number of channel members the firm uses at a particular distribution level — like wholesalers or retailers. The firm should also consider different *types* of distributor. Adding a new distributor type can be important when customers have preferred outlets. When the firm distributes through multiple channels, channel crossing becomes an issue — customers secure product information and/or try the product in one (or more) channels (showrooming), but purchase from a third channel.

Firms have three broad channel breadth options:

INTENSIVE DISTRIBUTION. When customers minimize search, products should be easily available. The firm maximizes the number and type of outlets.

EXCLUSIVE DISTRIBUTION. When customers are willing to search and travel, the firm should be very careful in selecting outlets. When retailers provide brand equity and positive shopping experiences, B2C firms may choose a few prestigious outlets.

SELECTIVE DISTRIBUTION. Selective distribution is a compromise between intensive and exclusive distribution. Too many outlets can lead to excessive competition; too few outlets and firm products are difficult to find.

Distribution breadth is equally important in B2B and B2C marketing, and raises three related exclusivity issues:

DISTRIBUTORS — GEOGRAPHIC EXCLUSIVITY. Should the supplier give distributors geographic exclusivity? Exclusivity eliminates *free* riding and intra-brand competition by providing geographic monopolies. Exclusivity also motivates distributors to invest in promotion and improves service, but may also breed complacency.

DISTRIBUTORS — PRODUCT EXCLUSIVITY. Productivity exclusivity may reduce conflict, satisfy channel partners, and better meet end-customer needs. Sometimes firms offer different product designs and/or brands to different distribution channels.

SUPPLIER EXCLUSIVITY. Some suppliers require that intermediaries focus entirely on their products; others insist on exclusivity within a product class.

CRITERIA FOR SELECTING AND EVALUATING INTERMEDIARIES

Clear and unambiguous criteria for selecting channel partners favor both suppliers and distributors. The firm should clearly specify the functions and performance standards distributors must meet. Both the firm and distributors should recognize their separate obligations. To improve success probabilities, the supplier should ask several questions of potential distributors:

- Does the distributor have adequate market coverage?
- How competent is distributor management?
- How does the distributor rate on aggressiveness, enthusiasm, and taking initiative?
- Is the distributor the appropriate size to do business with us?
- What is the distributor's credit and financial condition?
- What is the distributor's general reputation among suppliers and customers?
- What is the distributor's selling capability? What is its historic sales performance?
- Will the distributor forgo competitive products? Does it welcome the supplier's products?

PUTTING IT ALL TOGETHER: THE DISTRIBUTION STRATEGY

An eight-step way to develop distribution strategy requires:

Step 1. Identify end-customer segments.

Step 2. Identify and prioritize segment requirements regarding channel functions.

Step 3. Benchmark supplier and competitor channel capabilities — compare with customer requirements.

Step 4. Creatively identify channel options for each segment — consider switching costs and potential conflicts.

Step 5. Evaluate benefits and costs of various channel options.

Step 6. Elaborate channel overlaps — make serious choices.

Step 7. Appoint distributors — trade off securing market coverage and avoiding channel conflicts.

Step 8. Clearly assign distributor territories.

MANAGING DISTRIBUTION CHANNELS

Ensuring top performance from distributors day by day can be a significant challenge. We discuss intermediary compliance, power inequalities, conflict, and the emerging-partnership model.

Marketing Question

Have you or a friend or colleague ever been involved in distribution? Which issues in Table 18.5 in the main text posed problems? How did you solve them?

INTERMEDIARY COMPLIANCE

The firm must ensure that channel intermediaries stick to their agreements and implement its market strategies. When firms compensate intermediaries with standard commissions for all products and customers, they may encounter compliance problems. The firm can better direct distributors by varying commissions by product and customer type. The firm should continuously evaluate intermediary performance. But the firm must remember that intermediary relationships are a two-way street. Distributor also evaluates supplier performance.

POWER IN DISTRIBUTION SYSTEMS

Power and conflict are endemic in distribution systems. **Power** is one channel member's ability to get another member to act as it wants. Typically, some channel members have more power than others; they also have different objectives. When a supplier is more powerful, it can impose demands. Over time, power tends to shift from one channel member to another — among manufacturers/brand owners, distributors/wholesalers, retailers, and end-user customers.

MANUFACTURERS/BRAND OWNERS. In the early 20th century, manufacturers grew and increased power over distributors and wholesalers. Manufacturers researched customer needs, designed good products, and reduced costs and prices via mass production. Many retain significant power.

DISTRIBUTORS/WHOLESALERS. Today, these once-powerful intermediaries have less power than in the late 19th century, but still play a major role in many industries. Newer intermediaries like **value-added resellers** (**VARs**) build additional software modules on other firm platforms, and modify computer hardware for niche markets. **Systems integrators** add value by installing and servicing software and hardware (IT integration services) from many vendors and making them work together.

RETAILERS. Strong retail chains have evolved via industry concentration. Major retailers are often price leaders. They use buying power and efficient logistics to drive down costs. Online retailers like Amazon are placing increasing pressure on *bricks-and-mortar* retailers. Major retailers also force suppliers to make direct payments to secure shelf space — aka **slotting fees**.

END-USER CUSTOMERS. In B2C markets, individual consumers seldom have significant power, but consumer groups can profoundly influence producers. In B2B, mergers and acquisitions, have left the few remaining corporate customers in several industries with significant power.

Marketing Question

Many local retailers make short-term offers at highly discounted prices via Internet firms like Groupon that maintain e-mail subscriber lists. As consultant to a small retailer, would you advise signing up? Why or why not?

CONFLICT IN DISTRIBUTION SYSTEMS

Because distribution channel members have multiple organizational relationships, the potential for conflict is high. *Operational conflict* occurs daily due to reasons like late shipments, invoice errors, and unfulfilled promises. *Strategic conflict* is more serious and may lead to significant change in channel relationships.

STRATEGIC CONFLICTS INITIATED BY DOWNSTREAM CUSTOMERS.

- **End-user customers grow and desire direct-to-supplier relationships.** Many suppliers start out using distributors to reach end-users (especially small businesses). As these customers grow, they believe that distributors provide insufficient value for their margins. End users believe they can secure lower prices from direct supplier relationships.

- **Distributors become large and change the power balance.** The emergence of multiple-location mega-auto dealers selling huge volumes from several producers has shifted the power balance from manufacturers to retailers.

- **Distributors supply private-label products.** Sometimes innovative distributors disrupt channel relationships by offering their own branded products, secured from other suppliers or by self-manufacture.
- **New buying influences enter the distribution channel.** In some industries, independent buying groups amass buying power for their members.

STRATEGIC CONFLICTS INITIATED UPSTREAM BY SUPPLIERS.

- **To reach end-user customers more efficiently, the supplier goes direct.** Sometimes suppliers believe they can be more effective than distributors. Suppliers bypass distributors by selling direct to end-user customers. Distributors typically resent these initiatives.
- **The supplier addresses a new market that competes with its distributor.** The supplier/distributor relationship may be fine, but the supplier introduces products that compete with its distributor, and strains the relationship.
- **For better market penetration, the supplier adds new distributor types.** Suppliers sometimes initiate *horizontal conflict* by adding additional distributors and/or new distribution channels. Current distributors are often unhappy with these initiatives.

PLANNING FOR POWER CHANGES

All things equal, the firm is better off having a stronger (versus weaker) power position relative to other channel members. If the firm initiates strategic conflict, it must assess the likely impact on other channel members and anticipate how they may respond.

THE PARTNERSHIP MODEL

When firms exercise power and generate strategic conflict, the underlying assumption is a *zero-sum game*. If the firm *wins*, another channel member *loses*, and vice versa. The **partnership model** assumes the possibility of a *positive-sum game*. By developing trust and working together, several channel members win; there are no losers. Supplier-customer partnerships are at the heart of strategic account management — Chapter 18.

> *Marketing Question*
>
> Walmart is well known for driving tough bargains with suppliers to secure low prices. Yet Walmart has a partnership agreement with P&G. Why? Why does P&G partner with Walmart?

LEGAL ISSUES IN DISTRIBUTION

Other than pricing, distribution issues are more subject to legal concerns than any other marketing-mix variable. The legality of various distribution practices varies by industry and legal jurisdiction. In the U.S., distribution is the focus of many **antitrust** lawsuits. Sometimes offended competitors file lawsuits; other times, the federal government initiates legal action — typically, the FTC and/or DOJ-ATD. Critical U.S. issues are:

- **Exclusive territories.** Generally, the courts look unfavorably on arrangements that give distributors exclusive territories when this reduces competition.
- **Price discrimination.** The Robinson-Patman Act prohibits suppliers from setting different prices for different buyers, where this would reduce competition.
- **Resale price maintenance (RPM).** Suppliers set *retail* prices. RPM used to be illegal, but a 2007 Supreme Court decision allowed its reestablishment in many situations.
- **Selecting and terminating distributors.** Generally, suppliers are free to select and terminate distributors.
- **State and local laws.** Many local laws focus on distribution.
- **Tying agreements.** Strong suppliers force resellers to sell their entire product line. **Full-line forcing** is illegal if it reduces competition.

TRUE / FALSE QUESTIONS

1. Distribution channel depth is the number of channel members the firm uses at a particular level.
   ❏ **TRUE** ❏ **FALSE**

2. Power is one channel member's ability to get another member to act as it wants. ❏ **TRUE** ❏ **FALSE**

3. Value-added resellers are a new type of intermediary, building additional software modules on other firms' platforms, and modifying computer hardware for niche markets. ❏ **TRUE** ❏ **FALSE**

4. Strategic conflict occurs daily due to reasons like late shipments, invoice errors, and unfulfilled promises. ❏ **TRUE** ❏ **FALSE**

5. When firms exercise power and generate strategic conflict, they assume a positive-sum game, if the firm wins, another channel member loses, and vice versa. ❏ **TRUE** ❏ **FALSE**

MULTIPLE CHOICE QUESTIONS

1. Which of the following is NOT a critical decision that a firm must make to develop its distribution strategy?

   a. Determine distribution functions.
   b. Determine whether the distribution channel will be direct or indirect.
   c. Determine the distribution channel depth.
   d. Determine the criteria for selecting and evaluating intermediaries.

2. All of the following represent broad distribution channel breadth options EXCEPT:

   a. pulsing distribution
   b. intensive distribution
   c. exclusive distribution
   d. selective distribution

3. Which of the following does NOT represent an important question that the supplier should ask of potential distributors to improve the chances of success?

   a. What is the distributor's credit and financial condition?
   b. Does the distributor have adequate market coverage?
   c. How does the distributor rate on aggressiveness, enthusiasm, and taking initiative?
   d. All of the questions are important in improving the chances of success.

4. Which of the following is NOT a strategic conflict initiated by upstream suppliers?

   a. Supplier goes direct to reach end-user customers.
   b. Supplier addresses a new market that competes with its distributor.
   c. Supplier adds new distribution types for better market penetration.
   d. All of the selections represent strategic conflicts initiated by upstream suppliers.

5. _____ prohibits suppliers from setting different prices for different buyers, where this would reduce competition.

   a. The Sherman Antitrust Act
   b. The Robinson-Patman Act
   c. The Civil Rights Act
   d. The Occupational Health and Safety Administration

Answers on page 205

CHAPTER 19

CRITICAL UNDERPINNINGS OF PRICING DECISIONS

PRICING IS CRITICAL FOR EARNING PROFITS AND CREATING SHAREHOLDER VALUE. Pricing is also pivotal for entering new markets, introducing new products, and changing firm objectives and/or strategy. Price decisions have a greater profit impact than other profit levers. Reasons include:

- Price affects profit margin since margin equals price *less* cost.
- Price affects volume via the demand curve.
- Because price affects volume, it also affects costs via economies of scale.
- Price often affects customer quality and value perceptions.

THE CHANGING VIEW

OLD WAY	NEW WAY
Customer ill-informed	Customer well-informed
Focus on costs	Focus on perceived customer value
Full-cost systems pervasive	Activity-based costing becoming prevalent
Inflation permitted easy price increases	Low inflation/foreign competition hold prices down
Perceived customer value ignored	Perceived customer value measured and tracked
Prestige sometimes ahead of value perceptions	Value consciousness pervasive among customers

Pricing strategy is the firm's overall approach to setting price. Four critical considerations should enter into pricing decisions:

- Perceived customer value
- Costs
- Competition
- Strategic objectives

Too much emphasis on one single element leads to suboptimal pricing decisions, like the destructive, downward pricing spiral that can follow from an excessive focus on competitors.

PERCEIVED CUSTOMER VALUE

When increased competition brings more options, customers invariably seek lower prices. As customers turn elsewhere, the firm may believe it has a pricing problem. More likely, it has a **perceived value** problem. We focus on three value-related issues: creating, measuring, and capturing value.

CREATING VALUE

The firm creates value in its offer primarily through non-price elements in its marketing mix:

- **Product.** Typically delivers the major portion of the value proposition.
- **Service.** Adds additional value to the core product.
- **Promotion.** Conveys information about value, but sometimes provides value in its own right — like reassuring customers they made a good purchase.
- **Distribution.** Provides value through time and place convenience.

Price can also create value by inferring product quality and contributing to brand image.

MEASURING VALUE

Measuring the value customers perceive in firm and competitor offers is critical. Some approaches are:

DIRECT VALUE ASSESSMENT. The firm simply asks customers what they would pay for various products. Downward response bias is a concern, but carefully phrased questions can provide helpful data.

DOLLARMETRIC METHOD. For each pair of options, customers say which they prefer and how much extra they would pay. Summing positive and negative differences reveals the relative value of the options.

PERCEIVED VALUE ANALYSIS. Five steps measure an offer's perceived value. The firm develops perceived value scores for each supplier. Price does *not* enter into the analysis, but is important for interpretation.

1. Identify customer-required benefits/values.
2. Weight relative importance of benefits/values to customers.
3. Rate each offer from the various suppliers.
4. Develop benefit/value scores: multiply step 2 × step 3 for each benefit/value.
5. Sum the scores from step 4 across benefits/values to develop perceived value scores.

Marketing Question

The prices for printed and pdf versions of *Managing Marketing in the 21st Century* (600 pages) and *Capon's Marketing Framework* (300 pages) are identical. Do you agree with this pricing decision? Why or why not?

ECONOMIC ANALYSIS – ECONOMIC VALUE FOR THE CUSTOMER (EVC). Many B2B firms use EVC — the maximum price customers will pay — to calculate the economic value of new products. EVC analysis depends critically on competitive products in the customer's choice set. EVC helps clarify firm options: Should the firm add more value for a higher price or provide less value for a lower price?

PRICE EXPERIMENT. The firm offers the test product at different prices in different market areas, like geographic locations. Sales levels at different prices reflect customer value.

CAPTURING VALUE

The firm incurs many costs to create an offer; it creates value if these costs are less than the value customers perceive. High prices imply that the firm retains most value; low prices imply that the firm transfers most value to customers. A critical firm decision is the degree to which the firm retains or transfers value.

CUSTOMER PRICE SENSITIVITY

Sometimes customers are **price sensitive**; other times they are **price insensitive**. Classical microeconomics focuses on price sensitivity at the market level.

MARKET-LEVEL PRICE SENSITIVITY.

- **Price elastic.** When price goes down a little, volume increases significantly; when price goes up a little, volume decreases significantly.
- **Price inelastic.** Volume does not change much, even with significant price changes.

Price elasticity of demand (PED) = Percentage change in demand/percentage change in price.

Pundits often advise marketers to set prices at what *the market will bear*. This advice is *useless*. All markets *bear* many prices. The firm should decide what volume it wants to sell, then set the appropriate price.

INDIVIDUAL CUSTOMER PRICE SENSITIVITY. Markets are rarely homogeneous. Customers with full information on alternatives, benefits/values, and prices tend to be more price sensitive than those with less information. Other factors affecting willingness to pay include brand loyalty, frequency of use, past experience, product availability, and seasonality. Sometimes the firm affects customer price sensitivity. Price-sensitive customers feel pain when prices are high.

When making pricing decisions, the firm must consider several factors:

- **Competitive comparison.** Can customers easily and fairly compare alternative offers? Without purchasing?
- **Education.** Do firms educate customers to focus on price by fierce price competition?
- **End benefit.** What end benefit/value does the offer deliver? How price sensitive are end-user customers?
- **Expenditures.** How significant are absolute purchase expenditures?
- **Fairness.** How does the current price compare to customer experience with similar products? What do they expect to pay? Is the price justified?
- **Inventory.** Do buyers hold inventory?
- **Non-monetary costs.** What effort, time, and/or risk must customers expend to make a purchase?
- **Perceived substitutes.** What competitive offers and prices do customers consider? Can the firm influence customers' price expectations with positioning decisions?
- **Price/quality.** Are price and quality related for competitor products?

> *Marketing Question*
>
> Create two columns. In column 1, list the products or services for which you are most price sensitive. In column 2, list the products or services for which you are least price sensitive. What factors differentiate the two lists? Specifically, what factors or conditions make you more price sensitive?

Marketing Question

As the newly appointed marketing director for a chain of movie houses, you find that prices are identical for all seats for all movies. How might you improve profits by adopting a different pricing approach?

- **Shared cost.** Do customers pay the full costs? If not, what portion do they pay?
- **Switching costs.** What costs/investments would customers incur if they switched suppliers? Are they locked into current suppliers?
- **Terms.** Are financing options available and clearly communicated?
- **Unique value.** How do customers weigh elements of the firm's offer that influence their decisions?

COSTS

Costs are important for setting prices. After all, costs represent one-half of the profit equation: *Profit = sales revenues minus costs*. In practice, many firms use costs for setting prices, but they often do so inappropriately.

THE INAPPROPRIATE ROLE FOR COSTS: COST-PLUS PRICING

Cost-plus pricing is a pricing methodology used by most firms. Cost-plus pricing proceeds by identifying product costs, then adding a pre-determined profit margin.

Advantages of cost-plus pricing are:

- **Profitability.** All sales seem profitable as price must, by definition, be above cost.
- **Simplicity.** If the firm knows its costs, pricing is simple. Anyone can do the math.
- **Defensibility.** Legally acceptable and often required for government and other cost-plus contracts.

Regardless, cost-plus pricing has four main disadvantages:

PROFIT LIMITATIONS. Customer value has no role in price-setting:

- **Prices are too low.** Customers value the offer at more than the cost-plus price.
- **Prices are too high.** Customers value the offer at less than the cost-plus price.

Cost-plus pricing leads to over-pricing in price-sensitive markets and under-pricing in price-insensitive markets. Cost-plus pricing also leaves the firm vulnerable to competitors.

INAPPROPRIATE TREATMENT OF FIXED COSTS. Firms frequently classify costs as fixed and variable.

- **Variable costs.** Vary directly with the volume of sales and production. Variable costs increase as volume increases and decrease as volume decreases.
- **Fixed costs.** Do not vary with the volume of sales or production, over a reasonable range. Fixed costs include overhead and allocated items like depreciation, rent, salaries, and SG&A (selling, general, and administrative).

In practice, many firms arbitrarily assume some sales level to calculate fixed costs per unit. Because price and volume are related, these firms essentially use *price* to calculate *price*. This makes no sense.

ARBITRARY OVERHEAD ALLOCATIONS. Suppose a firm has two business units, A and B; A is comfortably profitable but B is not. Corporate may reduce B's overhead allocation and increase A's. B's fixed costs are reduced, but A's are increased. Such financial machinations are typical of firms striving to even out profits across products. But they can be highly demotivating to A's managers!

MISMATCH WITH MARKET REALITIES. When demand falls, logic suggests the firm should lower prices. Pure cost-plus pricing does not allow such action. As sales fall, and the firm spreads its fixed costs over lower volumes, fixed costs per unit increase — and so must price! When

Marketing Question

What would be the implications for Apple and Verizon if they based prices for the iPod and cell phone service, respectively, on cost?

demand surges, logic suggests the firm should raise prices. But the firm spreads fixed costs over larger volumes, and fixed costs per unit decrease — and so must price! Variable mark-ups based on demand can partially solve this problem.

APPROPRIATE ROLES FOR COSTS

Cost-plus pricing is the lazy way to set prices. Regardless, costs are important in three critical situations:

BIRTH CONTROL. Costs are particularly important for new product introduction. Typically, a new product must meet or exceed financial criteria like the firm's **hurdle rate** to receive go-ahead approval. The firm bases cash flow estimates on target prices, volumes, and costs. The relevant costs are *fully loaded costs*, meaning they include all incremental costs related to the new product, *including* incremental overhead.

DEATH CONTROL. Costs are also important when the firm is considering dropping a product. The relevant cost is the *marginal cost* — the cost to make and sell one additional unit. Marginal cost includes all variable costs and some incremental fixed costs, but excludes all allocated over-head.

The marginal cost is the **floor price**; only in rare circumstances should the firm set prices below the floor price.

PROFIT PLANNING. Birth control and death control are special cases; the major role for costs is profit planning. The firm explores various possible prices and estimates unit volumes and unit costs. The firm uses these data to calculate sales revenues and profits.

COMPETITION

The firm should always consider competitor prices. Basing the firm's price on the competitor prices is legal and ensures price parity, but focusing too heavily on competitors' pricing strategies has distinct disadvantages:

- *Price parity* with competitors devalues features, benefits, and values and tends to *commoditize* products. Customers then focus buying decisions on price.
- An excessive *price focus* may lead to losses for everyone, both the firm and competitors.

Generally, the firm should not focus on beating the competitor's *price*. Rather, the firm should beat the competitor's *offer* — product, service, and other marketing-mix elements. Price plays a critical balancing role. Two issues are crucial:

1. How will competitors respond to firm price changes?
2. How should the firm respond to competitor price reductions?

HOW WILL COMPETITORS RESPOND TO FIRM PRICE CHANGES?

When making price changes, the firm should always consider likely competitor responses. Basically competitors have three pricing options — *raise*, *hold*, or *lower*. Whether or not firm price moves are successful depends on competitor choices. Some questions about competitors the firm should be able to answer:

- Has the competitor been raising or lowering prices?
- How comparable are the various competitive offers in terms of perceived customer value?
- How many firms are competing? What are their market shares?
- What are the competitor's costs and profits?
- How is the competitor's product positioned relative to the firm's?

HOW SHOULD THE FIRM RESPOND TO COMPETITOR PRICE REDUCTIONS?

The firm's response depends on its market position. Generally, strong firms should match price cuts only after exhausting other options. But weak firms with minimal sustainable differential advantage may have to respond right away. Only the low-cost producer wins when price-cutting is rampant; how that firm uses its cost advantage determines other competitors' fates.

Firms with dominant market share often face severe price competition from small competitors and/or new entrants. These competitors may believe the leader:

- Has not carefully managed costs, and assumes its own costs are lower.
- Does not know individual product costs because of difficulties allocating overhead.
- Will not retaliate directly because it would sacrifice profits on its much larger volume.

Unless demand is *price elastic*, the firm should minimize direct price-cutting responses. The nature of the competitive price reductions governs the firm's price and non-price options:

PRICE OPTIONS. Price retaliation can range among indirect and direct actions:

- **Indirect price retaliation.** The firm signals disapproval by cutting prices in the competitor's strong markets.
- **Selective price competition.** If the competitor attacks part of the firm's product line with low prices, the firm has two sorts of options:
  - **Selective price cuts.** The firm may cut prices directly against the attack and/or offer lower prices in selected channels like the Internet.
  - **Introduce a *fighting* brand.** The firm cuts prices against the attack but with a specially designed *fighting* brand.
- **Cut prices across the board.** Ultimately the firm may have to cut prices broadly. But this approach will not succeed unless the firm also cuts costs, especially variable costs.

NON-PRICE OPTIONS. The firm uses its creative abilities to compete in areas other than price. Alternatives for defending its position across the board include:

- **Change the basis of competition.** Rather than compete product versus product, the firm changes the type of competition. Specifically, it may bundle products to remove a competitor's price advantage.
- **Clarify and reinforce the price/value relationship.** The firm creates price/value expectations — higher/lower prices imply higher/lower value. This approach is especially important if product failure is a major concern.
- **Invest in fixed-cost marketing expenditures.** The firm reinforces its position and builds switching costs by making marketing expenditures like advertising, better quality and delivery, customer service, and loyalty programs. The firm spreads these fixed costs over large volume.
- **Make pricing opaque.** Price transparency increases customers' bargaining power, so the firm may make pricing opaque.
- **Signal the firm's position.** Communicate the firm's capabilities and/or intentions.

If none of these actions work and the firm is in severe trouble, it may seek government help. If it cannot withstand competitive attack, the firm may withdraw, partly or totally:

- **Partial withdrawal.** The crucial decision is which market segment(s) to cede to competitors and which to retain. The firm must develop a razor-sharp focus on retained segments and take appropriate actions — redesign products, add services, and/or offer long-term contracts.

Marketing Question

Select a product and then search the Internet for different prices. Do the prices vary? Why? If you were to purchase, which supplier would you use? Why?

- **Total withdrawal.** When facing a competitor with significant cost advantage pursuing a low-price strategy, discretion may be the better part of valor. The firm withdraws and plays a different game.

STRATEGIC OBJECTIVES

Choosing strategic objectives is a major component of developing market strategy. The three major options are increase in volume and/or market share, maximize profits, and maximize cash flow. Generally, each strategic objective relates to a particular pricing strategy:

MAXIMIZE GROWTH IN VOLUME AND/OR MARKET SHARE. The firm must offer high customer value — a value-to-price (V/P) ratio superior to competitors. Appropriate conditions are:

- Deep pockets to absorb initially low profit margins
- Desire to deter competitors
- Good ability to cut costs in the future
- Price-elastic market
- Sufficient capacity to fulfill increases in demand

MAXIMIZE PROFITABILITY. When the firm's paramount objective is maximizing profits, it provides less value to customers and retains more for itself as profit.

MAXIMIZE CASH FLOW. If the firm plans market withdrawal, maximizing cash flow is often a good short-term strategic objective. *Harvesting* is the approach to short-term cash-flow maximization.

....
TRUE / FALSE QUESTIONS

1. High prices imply that the firm transfers most value to customers; low prices imply that the firm retains most of the value. ❏ **TRUE** ❏ **FALSE**

2. Price-elastic items include products where volume does not change much, even with significant price changes. ❏ **TRUE** ❏ **FALSE**

3. Cost-plus pricing is a pricing methodology used by most firms and proceeds by identifying product costs, then adding a predetermined profit margin. ❏ **TRUE** ❏ **FALSE**

4. Marginal cost includes all variable costs and some incremental fixed cost, but excludes all allocated overhead costs. ❏ **TRUE** ❏ **FALSE**

5. When demand is price inelastic, the firm should maximize direct price-cutting responses to gain additional market share. ❏ **TRUE** ❏ **FALSE**

....
MULTIPLE CHOICE QUESTIONS

1. Which of the following is NOT a method used to measure the value that customers perceive on firm and competitor offers?

   a. direct value assessment
   b. dollarmetric method
   c. price experiment
   d. factor analysis

2. In the _____ approach to measuring value, the firm offers the test product at different prices in different market areas, like different geographic locations. It bases its measure of customer value on the sales levels at different prices.

   a. direct value assessment
   b. dollarmetric method
   c. price experiment
   d. factor analysis

3. Which of the following is the correct formula to calculate the price elasticity of demand?

   a. percentage change in price/ percentage change in demand
   b. percentage change in demand/ percentage change in price
   c. percentage change in price minus percentage change in demand
   d. percentage change in demand minus percentage change in price

4. All of the following are non-price options a firm can use to defend its position against the competition EXCEPT:

   a. Clarify and reinforce the price/value relationship.
   b. Make pricing opaque.
   c. Signal the firm's position.
   d. Invest in variable-cost marketing expenditures.

5. All of the following represent conditions for a high value-to-price strategy EXCEPT:

   a. good ability to cut costs in the future
   b. sufficient capacity to fulfill increases in demand
   c. a desire to deter competitors
   d. a price-inelastic market

Answers on page 205

....

PART D – GETTING PAID FOR CUSTOMER VALUE

CHAPTER 20

SETTING PRICES

CHAPTER 20 IS THE SECOND OF TWO PRICING CHAPTERS. This chapter builds on the foundations from Chapter 19 and focuses on actually *setting prices*.

THE CHANGING VIEW

OLD WAY	NEW WAY
Antitrust considerations minimal	Growing enforcement in U.S. and European Union
Destructive pricing tactics common	Growing sophistication in using the pricing toolkit
Inefficient product markets	Efficient product markets — role of the Internet
List-price mentality	Varied pricing tactics
Price and offer homogeneity	Price and offer heterogeneity
Pricing complexity limited by human factors	Pricing complexity driven by software
Pricing decisions disorganized	Intellectual capital development in pricing
Standard pricing	Customized pricing

SETTING PRICE FOR A NEW PRODUCT

Because *cost-plus pricing* and *competitive equivalence pricing* fail to take into account many key variables, we recommend a three-step approach to pricing:

- **Step 1.** Determine the maximum price — the economic value to the customer (EVC).
- **Step 2.** Determine the minimum price — the fully loaded cost, including overhead allocations.
- **Step 3.** Set the price based on strategic objectives and likely competitive response.

Possible strategic objectives are *toehold* (just require a market presence), *short-term profit*, and *market share*. When setting price, the firm should consider potential customer lifetime value (CLV). Is this a one-time purchase, or will customers purchase additional items?

CHANGING THE PRICE OF AN EXISTING PRODUCT

The firm has many reasons to change price. Sometimes external competitive pressures are critical, but other pressures may be internal. Financial managers may want increased profit margins by raising prices. Critical questions are:

- Can the firm *increase price* without losing significant volume? How much volume will it lose? Will the incremental profit margin offset the lost volume?

- If the firm *decreases price,* will it gain significant volume? How much volume will it gain? Will the extra volume offset the reduced profit margin?

A recommended five-step process for considering price changes is:

Step 1: Reconfigure the traditional income statement. Partition costs into two categories: variable costs and fixed costs.

Step 2: Calculate current contribution margin per unit. Contribution margin (CM) must cover fixed costs; any remainder is profit. CM equals (is identical to) sales revenues less variable costs. Contribution margin per unit (CMU) is CM on a per-unit basis.

Step 3: Proposed price change: Calculate new contribution margin per unit — at each proposed price.

Step 4: Determine new sales targets. Determine the necessary sales volume at each proposed price to make the same profit.

Step 5: Assess the risk/reward trade-off. The firm must assess the likelihood it can meet (or exceed) the new volume target. The answer depends, in part, on competitive response.

Marketing Question

The sales force is pressuring you to cut prices, so they can increase sales. Finance pushes for price increases to raise margins. How would you respond?

AVOIDING PRICE CHANGES

Many firms address pricing issues by assessing the value they offer customers, and then deciding on the price. This approach often leads to considerable customer pressure to reduce price — *fixed offer, variable price.* An alternative approach for mitigating this pressure is to design several offers, each at a fixed price — *variable offer, fixed price.* The firm presents a **price menu**, including two or more product alternatives, and different delivery and/or service options like employee training, guaranteed supply, and special packaging.

The price-menu approach has two significant benefits. First, firms often add services to a base product and then charge higher prices. The price menu tests the value of extra services; if customers do not value the extra service, they will continue to buy the base product. Second, by pricing the product and service together in a single offer, the firm averages; some customers overpay (don't want services) and some underpay (use services). With a price menu, each customer selects the offer that best meets its needs.

TACTICAL PRICING

Tactical pricing is the ongoing stream of pricing decisions the firm makes on a daily basis. Generally, robust strategic pricing drives good tactical pricing, but tactical pricing has a major impact on firm performance. A common misconception is that a product has a single price; in fact, single prices are rare. The **pricing toolkit** is the variety of tools the firm can use to make price adjustments, often for individual customers. Undisciplined use of the toolkit can lead to **price waterfall** problems.

THE PRICING TOOLKIT

The firm should recognize that toolkit elements are differentially important across customers. The items in a pricing toolkit include:

Acceptable currency	Credit terms	Guarantees and warranties	Price stability
Allowances	Discounts	Inventory carrying costs	Slotting fees
Barter	Company shares	Leasing	Returns
Buy-backs	Freight	List price	Unbundling and bundling
Credit availability		Markdown money	

For an equivalent price reduction, one customer may prefer a larger discount; another may want an advertising allowance.

THE POCKET PRICE AND PRICE WATERFALL

Some firms use toolkit items appropriately, but many others have poor systems for tracking use. These latter firms do not know their **pocket prices** — the money they actually receive (in their pockets). When firms conduct pocket-price analysis, they are often surprised to find a broad price range, but little rationale. Small-volume customers may receive large discounts; high-volume customers do not. To optimize pricing, the firm must understand the pocket price for each customer and the way these prices developed — the **price waterfall**.

DESIGNING PRICING APPROACHES

Several pricing methods are available:

- **Price discrimination and variable pricing.** The firm optimizes profits by setting different prices for different customers/segments — some pay more, others pay less. The firm can amplify this effect by designing multiple offers with different values.

- **Dynamic pricing.** A special case of price discrimination when demand varies over time.

- **Variable-rate versus flat-rate pricing.** Firms selling services price by use — *variable rate*, or by time period — *flat rate*. Variable prices may earn greater revenues, but flat-rate prices are generally easier (and less costly) to administer.

- **Customer-driven pricing.** Mostly, sellers set a price and buyers can accept it or not. In customer-driven pricing, the customer names the price; the firm can accept or not.

- **Auction pricing.** A form of customer-driven pricing where customers compete with other potential buyers to purchase a product. Alternative types of auction are:

  - **English auction.** Used especially for second-hand items. Prices start low, and potential buyers bid up the price. Auctioneers seek the buyer willing to pay the highest price.

  - **Vickrey auction.** A *sealed-bid* English auction where the winning bidder pays the price of the second-highest bid.

  - **Dutch auction.** Prices start high; the seller reduces price until a buyer bids.

  - **Reverse auction.** This type of auction is for suppliers. The customer states its requirements; suppliers bid to provide the product. Prices go down and the lowest bidder wins the business.

> *Marketing Exercise*
>
> Next time you fly, ask fellow travelers what fare they paid. What is the basis for the price differences? Be prepared for them — or you — to be disgruntled!

SETTING THE ACTUAL PRICE

Several issues are important when setting the actual price:

- **Fees and surcharges.** Many firms use *fees and surcharges* to increase pocket prices, especially in difficult economic times.
- **Promotional pricing versus steady pricing.** In many situations, sales are sensitive to short-term price promotions. Firms often execute price promotions by comparing the sale price with the regular price. Despite sales increases, promotions can have negative effects:
  - **Brand image.** The promotion negatively affects the brand, especially upscale brands.
  - **Diversion.** Retailers and/or distributors may *divert* the product to non-competing outlets.
  - **Hidden cost.** Frequent price promotions can be difficult and costly to administer.
  - **Poor forecasting.** Demand exceeds forecast and customers are upset.
  - **Time-shifting.** Customers buy for inventory to avoid paying the full price later.
- **Psychological pricing.** For many customers, the psychological distance from $9.95 to $10.00 is greater than from $10.00 to $10.05; hence, many firms set prices to end with 95 cents.
- **Pricing bases.** Most industries have accepted bases for setting prices, typically by individual product, but changing the price basis may be a way to secure advantage.

SPECIAL TOPICS IN SETTING PRICES

We examine special pricing topics:

- **Complementary product pricing.** *Complementary products* are used together — hot dogs and buns, automobiles and spare parts, printers and cartridges, and movies and popcorn. The firm must make a two-part pricing decision.
- **Gray market pricing.** *Gray markets* undercut the firm's strategy. Gray markets develop when the firm sells a similar product in different markets at different prices. Customers purchase the product in a low-price market and then ship for resale to a high-price market.
- **Pay-what-you-want pricing.** Organizations using this approach rely on customers' sense of fairness.
- **Topsy-turvy pricing.** Suppliers and customers exchange value. The firm provides product/service value; the customer provides monetary value via the price. But sometimes the customer provides additional value, and the supplier, not the customer, pays the price. Hence, a medical practitioner may pay a sports team for the privilege of treating its players.
- **Transfer pricing.** Firms set *transfer prices* among business units and geographic subsidiaries. Transfer prices affect subsidiary profits and, internationally, firm tariff and tax liabilities.

PRICING MANAGEMENT

How should the firm create a **pricing management** structure? How should the firm set prices? Who should be responsible? Generally, centralized pricing provides greater control; decentralized pricing offers greater market sensitivity. But decentralized pricing may have long-run negative effects:

- **Information sharing.** Customers talk to each other about prices; those paying higher prices exert pressure for price reduction.

- **Limited perspective.** A local decision-maker like a salesperson is unlikely to consider the potential long-run impact of a local price reduction on the firm's entire customer base.
- **Negotiation.** Customers learn to place end-of-period orders when suppliers are anxious about revenues and may reduce prices. They also learn to play off multiple vendors against one another.

Three important areas of pricing capability are:

- **Human capital.** Broad pricing knowledge at decision-makers' command.
- **Social capital.** The ability to negotiate agreements on prices among firm decision-makers. Marketing may want *low steady* prices to demonstrate *good value*; salespeople may want high prices with discount flexibility.
- **Systems capital.** Supports pricing decisions using hardware and software.

LEGAL AND ETHICAL ISSUES IN PRICING

Marketers should have a working knowledge of three broad topics: anti-competitive pricing, dumping, and fairness in consumer pricing:

ANTICOMPETITIVE PRICING

Several pricing approaches are anticompetitive.

- **Discriminatory pricing.** Under the U.S. Robinson-Patman Act, firms cannot sell identical products to different customers at different prices when the effect is to lessen competition or create a monopoly.
- **Predatory pricing.** Dominant firms sometimes engage in **predatory pricing** by temporarily price very low to thwart a competitive threat.
- **Price conspiracies.** A firm and its competitors overtly collude to fix prices, make implicit agreements to price in parallel, and/or exchange price information. Higher prices and customer harm typically occur.

DUMPING

Some firms **dump** products in foreign markets at "less than fair market value," below home market prices, and often below average costs. This practice may be illegal in the receiving country.

FAIRNESS IN CONSUMER PRICING

Two important fairness issues for consumers are:

- **Bait and switch.** Retailers advertise a low price product but have only limited availability. The *bait* sells quickly, then retailers offer most customers a higher price product, the *switch*.
- **Deceptive pricing.** False prices or prices that might confuse or mislead customers are deceptive.

TRUE / FALSE QUESTIONS

1. Tactical pricing is the ongoing stream of pricing decisions that firms make on a daily basis.
   ❏ TRUE ❏ FALSE

2. A common misconception is that a product has multiple prices; in fact, single prices are most common. ❏ TRUE ❏ FALSE

3. In an English auction, the customer states its requirements and suppliers bid to provide the product. Prices go down and the lowest bidder wins the business. ❏ TRUE ❏ FALSE

4. Three important areas of pricing capability are human capital, social capital, and systems capital.
   ❏ TRUE ❏ FALSE

5. Under the U.S. Robinson-Patman Act, firms cannot sell identical products to different customers at different prices when the effect is to lessen competition or create a monopoly. ❏ TRUE ❏ FALSE

MULTIPLE CHOICE QUESTIONS

1. A _____ is the variety of tools the firms can use to make price adjustments, often for individual customers.

   a. pricing toolkit
   b. product portfolio
   c. perceptual map
   d. factor portfolio

2. Pricing services by use is referred to as
   _____.

   a. fixed-rate pricing
   b. penetration pricing
   c. marginal pricing
   d. variable-rate pricing

3. A sealed-bid auction where the winning bidder pays the price of the second-highest bid is called a(n) _____.

   a. English auction
   b. Dutch auction
   c. reverse auction
   d. Vickrey auction

4. Which of the following develop when the manufacturer sells similar products to multiple geographic markets at significantly different prices?

   a. gray markets
   b. black markets
   c. blue markets
   d. green markets

5. _____ occur(s) when a firm and its competitors overtly collude to fix prices or make implicit agreements to price in parallel or exchange price information.

   a. Predatory pricing
   b. Price discrimination
   c. Price conspiracies
   d. Bait and switch pricing

Answers on page 205

CHAPTER 21

ENSURING THE FIRM IMPLEMENTS THE MARKET OFFER AS PLANNED

TO DO A GOOD JOB OF EXECUTING MARKET STRATEGY, the firm must seamlessly align various implementation programs. Vision, mission, strategy, and values are critical, but the firm must also pay close attention to organization structure, systems and processes, and human resource practices. These tasks are much easier when the firm has customer-focused values leading to a true external orientation.

THE CHANGING VIEW

OLD WAY	NEW WAY
Customer satisfaction and loyalty are low priority	Customer satisfaction and loyalty are high priority
Hierarchy-based organization	Knowledge-based organization
Human resource factors neglected	Human resource factors highlighted
Internally oriented structures, and systems and processes	Externally oriented structures, and systems and processes
Marketing as a separate function	Marketing as everybody's business
Marketing seen as a department	Marketing seen as a philosophy
Market-share oriented	Shareholder and customer-value oriented
No customer information systems	Highly developed customer information systems
Operational focus	Strategic focus
Rigid, inflexible structures	Flexible, adaptive structures
Rules-driven	Values-driven
Sales and marketing discrete	Sales and marketing merging
Selection, training, and rewards driven by bureaucracy	Selection, training, and rewards driven by strategy

FUNCTIONAL EXCELLENCE IN SUCCESSFUL EXTERNALLY ORIENTED FIRMS

Firms deliver customer value and secure differential advantage in many ways, deploying various resources and expertise to build core competence. Expertise areas include customer service, finance, human resources, operations and the supply chain, research and development, and sales.

CUSTOMER SERVICE

Increased competition has made customer service very important for delivering customer value, securing differential advantage and attracting, retaining, and growing customers. Yet, in many firms, customer service does not report to marketing. This may not matter when an external orientation is the firm's dominant philosophy. But poor customer service generates significant customer dissatisfaction, especially if expectations are high, and can destroy an otherwise effective market strategy.

FINANCE

Financial decisions and controls play a critical role in managing the operations of any successful firm. Financial engineering is central to marketing major capital goods and services, from aircraft and earth-moving equipment to business systems. Externally oriented firms galvanize their finance and accounting functions; they contribute to the firm's marketing efforts in many ways.

HUMAN RESOURCES

Human resources (HR) is a vital function for any business, but some firms create differential advantage by developing unique approaches to developing and motivating their workforces to achieve high levels of excellence. Many consultants claim HR advantages are the most sustainable, since they are difficult to copy.

OPERATIONS AND THE SUPPLY CHAIN

Internal operations and the supply chain are important areas for the firm to improve its external focus, especially in services, where it touches the customer most often. All contemporary approaches to teaching operations systems design work back from the marketplace. The operations system is a great place for the firm to secure differential advantage.

RESEARCH AND DEVELOPMENT

R&D breakthroughs have given birth to many great firms. 3M, Apple, DuPont, GlaxoSmithKline (GSK), HP, Intel, Medtronics, Monsanto, and Xerox are just a few that achieved and maintained pre-eminence based on technological strengths. When the firm manages its R&D/Marketing interface well, the impact can be dramatic.

SALES

The sales function rarely reports to marketing yet, as with customer service, selling is critical for implementing the market strategy. Innovation in sales can be the key to success. Many B2B firms like DHL and IBM are driving successful growth by innovating with strategic (key) account and global account programs.

Marketing Question

Select three firms from Table 21.1 in the main text. What investments in resources are they making to maintain their differential advantages?

Marketing Question

Can you think of a firm whose finance operations made doing business with it easier? What specifically did you like? How could the firm improve?

Marketing Question

In your experience, which firms do the best job of managing human resources? How did this translate into marketplace success? Define key objectives and success for HR.

INTEGRATED SYSTEMS

Specific functional areas bring success to externally oriented firms. These firms succeed, not just because of a single strong suit, but because they integrate efforts from many functions.

A FRAMEWORK FOR DEVELOPING AN EXTERNAL ORIENTATION

To achieve success in increasingly competitive markets, the firm must focus resources to deliver customer value and secure differential advantage. In the final analysis, nothing else matters. The firm must keep resources aligned with the ever-changing environment. Continual realignment is difficult, but some firms do better than others. The most successful firms develop an **external orientation** culture. The inverted pyramid used by externally oriented firms places customers at the top of the pyramid and reinforces the critical role they play in firm success.

VALUES

Many firms reinforce customer importance by means of a values statement emphasizing a customer-focused culture. **Values** are a common set of beliefs that guide the behavior of all organization members. Some values are hard, like profitability and market share; other values are soft, like integrity, respect for others, trust, and customer pre-eminence.

> ### *Marketing Question*
>
> Select two of your favorite firms; identify their values. Are these firms living up to their values? If not, where are they failing? What is the marketing significance of communicating these values?

VISION, MISSION, STRATEGY

All framework elements must reflect and reinforce firm commitment to an external orientation. Many organizational transformations start at the bottom of the pyramid, developing (or re-working) external elements.

- **Vision.** A description of the firm's ideal future state — an impressionistic picture of what the future should be. Good vision statements set a broad direction — they should inspire employees for the long run. A good vision statement is not too broad, nor is it too specific nor easily achievable.
- **Mission.** Guides the firm's search for market opportunities more directly. A well-developed mission keeps the firm focused in a limited arena where success is likely.
- **Strategy.** The firm's game plan for the market, pointing the way to firm actions. The market strategy specifies what the firm is trying to achieve, which segments it will target for effort, and how it will position itself in those market segments.

The more difficult work of culture change lies in aligning the firm's **internal architecture** — organization structure, systems and processes, and HRM practices — with vision, mission, and strategy. Customer-oriented values are a good start, but architectural elements must also reflect and shape the culture. Unless the culture is externally focused, desire for the *status quo* will undermine firm efforts. Aligning the firm's architectural elements to reflect its desired external orientation must be systemic.

ORGANIZING THE FIRM'S MARKETING EFFORTS

The firm has many ways to organize its marketing effort. Some traditional structures still have great value, but contemporary approaches are breaking new ground.

***TRADITIONAL:* FUNCTIONAL MARKETING ORGANIZATION.** The firm places activities like advertising and promotion, distribution, marketing administration, marketing research, and new product development in a marketing department. Marketing is usually separate from the sales force and functions like accounting, human resources, production, and R&D.

***TRADITIONAL:* PRODUCT/BRAND MANAGEMENT ORGANIZATION.** Product/brand managers develop market plans for products and brands; they are responsible for volume, market share, and/or profits, but do not control all inputs. Product/brand managers' general management orientation provides a clear career path, but this organization structure has two significant problems: potentially destructive internal brand manager competition and brand manager turnover.

***TRADITIONAL:* CATEGORY MANAGEMENT ORGANIZATION.** This approach attempts to address problems with the product/brand management organization, in part by leveraging success from strong brands to weaker brands. The category management organization directs multiple brands in a complementary manner.

***TRADITIONAL:* MARKET SEGMENT ORGANIZATION.** The market segment organization is more externally focused than the preceding options; managers are responsible for individual market segments. The market segment organization may overlie other marketing and sales functions. (Typically, the rest of the firm is functionally organized.)

***TRADITIONAL:* COMBINED PRODUCT/BRAND MANAGEMENT AND MARKET SEGMENT ORGANIZATION.** Product/brand and market segment organizations each omit a crucial dimension. In product/brand organizations, no one is specifically responsible for market segments: In the market segment organization, no one is specifically responsible for individual products/brands. The combined organization addresses these problems.

***NEWER:* INCLUSION ORGANIZATION.** The firm groups many activities under marketing. The *inclusion organization* may work well in service businesses, where marketing and operations are difficult to distinguish, but is not appropriate for all firms.

***NEWER:* BUSINESS PROCESS ORGANIZATION.** One outgrowth of the re-engineering movement was some firms' attempts to organize around *business processes*. The firm retains a classic functional structure, but much organizational output results from cross-functional teams.

***NEWER:* CUSTOMER-MANAGEMENT ORGANIZATION.** This organization focuses specifically on customers. CRM systems that allow firms to identify customers by name, buying patterns, and history support this organization form. A specific advantage of the customer management organization is increased customer contact; hence, customer managers gain significant customer insight.

> *Marketing Question*
>
> As a current or potential customer, how do you think Microsoft classifies you? Call the customer service department or go to Microsoft's website to find out.

SYSTEMS AND PROCESSES

All organizations use systems and processes to produce organizational outputs. One end of the continuum embraces *hard systems* — typically require capital equipment. At the other end are human-resource-intensive *soft systems*.

HARD SYSTEMS. Hard systems improve operational efficiency and reduce costs. But they can also contribute to creating an external orientation, improve marketing effectiveness, optimize sales force efforts, and help secure differential advantage. Benefits include:

- **Customer information.** Customer information is more readily available and widely distributed; hence, employees better understand customer needs.

- **Customer intimacy.** Customer relationship management (CRM) systems provide significant information about customers, including purchase histories, buying patterns, and other firm interactions. Large firms can now emulate smaller high-touch organizations.

- **Customer effort.** Many firms use externally facing systems for customers to access product information and order online; customers save time, effort, and risk in purchasing. These systems help the firm get closer to customers and reinforce the brand.

SOFT SYSTEMS. People-based soft systems can also help the firm become more externally oriented. Consider the planning process. Good planning is externally driven and should involve all functional areas and several management levels. Planning brings people across the firm face-to-face with external realities. Outputs from market planning set firm direction.

MAKING THE FIRM'S SYSTEMS THE BEST THEY CAN BE. More important than any individual system are methodologies for evolving and integrating systems to drive an external orientation.

- **Best practice transfer.** A best practice system helps identify and transmit superior expertise, knowledge, and processes across the firm.

- **Benchmarking.** Best practices frequently occur in other firms. Benchmarking competitors, customers, suppliers, and firms in other industries can improve firm processes.

- **Re-engineering.** The re-engineering approach examines fundamental assumptions about firm systems and processes and seeks alternative approaches for redesign and improvement.

> ### *Marketing Question*
>
> Identify a specific customer service process — like buying a product in a store. Visit several establishments to examine their processes. What improvement suggestions do you have?

HUMAN RESOURCE MANAGEMENT

Human resource management (HRM) tools like recruiting, selecting, training, measuring and rewarding, career development, and talent management provide many opportunities to emphasize the importance of an organization-wide external focus.

MARKETING EXECUTIVES. The ideal marketer is multifaceted, possessing a blend of analytic, creative, and leadership skills. Other positive traits include committed, energetic, hardworking, inspiring, passionate, and talented.

NON-MARKETING PROFESSIONALS. To become a truly externally oriented organization, all employees (not only marketers) must become externally focused. Customer-responsive employees are critical for managing the customer experience, especially in services.

SUSTAINING AN EXTERNAL ORIENTATION

Sustaining an external orientation is easier if the firm understands its challenges:

- **Accounting systems.** The firm must produce data in the form that supports an external perspective. Many firms report profit by product; they should also measure profit by customer and/or customer group.

- **Bureaucracy.** As firms grow, departmentalization and task specialization are efficient ways to complete repetitive tasks. But rules and behaviors, reinforced by day-to-day work pressures, become embedded in the organization.

- **Centralization versus decentralization.** Centralizing and standardizing can have great value, but excessive centralization leads to standardized actions, rather than customer *responsiveness.*

- **Excessive focus on organizational efficiency.** Many firms work extremely hard to reduce costs by improving organizational efficiency. Regardless, an organizational culture dominated by a drive for efficiency can become internally focused.

Marketing Question

How do you assess your college, school, or university on its degree of external orientation? Are some parts more externally focused than others? If yes, what accounts for these differences?

- **Functional divisions.** Firms develop specialized functions to increase expertise in key areas. But specialization can lead to silo thinking and divisiveness among specialties. Functional heads must recognize the importance of cross-functional cooperation to firm success.

- **Functional view of marketing.** The firm must distinguish between marketing as a *philosophy* and marketing as a *department*. The firm that delegates all marketing problems to a marketing department will neither create nor deliver fully integrated offers.

- **Internal politics.** The CEO and/or business head must actively support institutionalizing an external orientation and frequently communicate this support. If not, some functions will be suspicious of customer-focused initiatives.

- **Inward-oriented marketing departments.** Marketing departments are sometimes their own worst enemies. They implement a not-invented-here (NIH) syndrome that quashes *foreign* ideas and initiatives to *protect their turf.*

- **Misaligned incentives.** People in organizations do what is *inspected* of them, **not** what is *expected* of them! They behave in ways that earn rewards. Conflicting and function-specific performance objectives and rewards make it difficult to integrate across functions.

- **Social fabric of institutions.** Firm employees know each other and interact daily. Customers, competitors, and suppliers are occasional *intruders* who interrupt daily life!

··
TRUE / FALSE QUESTIONS

1. The category management organization attempts to address problems with the product/brand management organization and to leverage success from strong brands to weaker brands.
❏ **TRUE** ❏ **FALSE**

2. The business process organization retains a classic functional structure, with much organizational output resulting from cross-functional teams. ❏ **TRUE** ❏ **FALSE**

3. Soft systems improve operational efficiency and reduce costs. ❏ **TRUE** ❏ **FALSE**

4. The re-engineering approach examines fundamental assumptions about firm systems and processes and seeks alternative approaches for redesign and improvement. ❏ **TRUE** ❏ **FALSE**

5. To become a truly externally oriented organization, all employees across the firm, not only marketers, must become externally focused. ❏ **TRUE** ❏ **FALSE**

··
MULTIPLE CHOICE QUESTIONS

1. Which of the following represents a description of the firm's ideal future or an impressionistic picture of what the future should be?

    a. vision
    b. mission
    c. strategy
    d. objective

2. Which of the following types of organizational structures places activities like marketing research, distribution, advertising and promotion, marketing administration, and new product development in what is traditionally called a marketing department?

    a. product/brand management
    b. functional marketing
    c. category management
    d. market segment

3. The _____ organization retains a classic functional structure, but much organizational output results from cross-functional teams.

    a. product/brand management
    b. functional marketing
    c. business process
    d. market segment

4. A specific advantage of the _____ structure is that customer contact increases, and customer portfolio managers gain significant customer insight.

    a. product/brand management
    b. functional marketing
    c. category management
    d. customer-management

5. All of the following represent challenges for a firm working toward sustaining an external orientation EXCEPT:

    a. bureaucracy
    b. accounting systems
    c. functional divisions
    d. All selections represent challenges.

Answers on page 205

CHAPTER 22

MONITORING AND CONTROLLING FIRM PERFORMANCE AND FUNCTIONING

MARKETING AND BUSINESS MANAGERS TAKE MANY ACTIONS — enter new markets and segments, introduce new products, increase and reduce advertising, add and cut salespeople, shift distribution channels, and raise and lower prices. But the firm must also know if its actions lead to intended results. A good monitor-and-control system tells if the firm's actions, individually and collectively, improved performance; leading indicators help the firm assess if it is on track, or should change direction.

THE CHANGING VIEW

OLD WAY	NEW WAY
Accounting profit	Shareholder value creation
Backward looking	Forward looking
Bottom-line oriented	Variety of measures
Fact finding	Learning and improvement
Financial focus	Business focus
Focus on firm success	Focus on firm and customer success
Internally oriented	Externally oriented
Measurement and control based on accounting performance measures	Measurement and control based on marketing performance measures
Output measures only	Emphasis also on input and intermediate measures
Post-action control	Steering control
Punitive philosophy	Analytic philosophy
Unbalanced scorecard	Balanced scorecard

KEY PRINCIPLES OF MONITOR-AND-CONTROL PROCESSES

Monitoring focuses on measuring how well the firm is doing in various business aspects. *Control* is concerned with making changes or adjustments so the firm does better. Monitor-and-control processes are the most powerful means of changing individual behavior and enhancing long-term results. Chapter 22 focuses on two complementary areas: firm performance and firm functioning.

- **Firm performance.** *Is the firm achieving planned results?* Planned results are the **standards** against which the firm measures actual results. All things equal, if actual results meet or exceed standards, performance is satisfactory and the firm continues to operate as planned. If actual results are standards, the firm should modify its actions.

- **Firm functioning.** To achieve desired results, the firm allocates resources and takes actions. *Is the firm functioning well?* For greater insight, we decompose this question into three:
  - **Implementation.** Did the firm implement its planned actions?
  - **Strategy.** Is the firm's market strategy well conceived and on target?
  - **Managerial processes.** Are the firm's managerial processes the best they can be?

Effective monitor-and-control processes rest on five key principles:
- Focus on market levers and develop alternative plans.
- Implement steering control rather than post-action control.
- Use the right performance measures at the right organizational levels.
- Model the relationship between input, intermediate, and output measures.
- Tie compensation to performance.

Marketing Question

Consider your personal objectives and strategy: Have you thought through these rigorously? Are you achieving your planned objectives? Are you functioning well in trying to achieve your objectives?

FOCUS ON MARKET LEVERS AND DEVELOP ALTERNATIVE PLANS

Market levers flow from the firm's market strategy and implementation plans; they include actions like introducing new products, increasing/decreasing advertising, adding/replacing salespeople, and enhanced training. The firm allocates resources and takes actions to achieve planned performance. Monitor-and-control efforts should focus on market levers. If actual results fall below standards, the firm should be ready with alternative plans.

IMPLEMENT STEERING CONTROL RATHER THAN POST-ACTION CONTROL

Steering control and *post-action control* are different **monitor-and-control approaches.** Firms using post-action control wait a preset time period and then compare actual results against standards. If results are unsatisfactory, they take corrective action. Firms exercising post-action control typically develop annual marketing plans and set standards by quarter. By contrast, steering control is dynamic, continuous, and anticipatory.

USE THE RIGHT PERFORMANCE MEASURES AT THE RIGHT ORGANIZATIONAL LEVELS

If possible, the firm's monitor-and-control process should use objective measures like sales, market share, and profits. When less concrete measures like customer satisfaction are appropriate, the firm should use validated scales. The firm should measure performance at multiple organizational levels, like corporate, geographic region, business unit, market segment, marketing function, customer, sales region, sales district, and/or sales territory.

MODEL THE RELATIONSHIP BETWEEN INPUT, INTERMEDIATE, AND OUTPUT MEASURES

Monitor-and-control systems must disentangle cause and effect. To ensure that the firm makes valid inferences, it must distinguish among:

- **Input measures** — actions the firm takes
- **Intermediate measures** — customer actions or changes in their state of mind.
- **Output measures** — performance variables like sales and profits.

Generally, collecting data on input and output measures is relatively easy; securing data on intermediate measures is often more resource-intensive. The firm must have confidence in the presumed relationships between inputs and intermediates and between intermediates and outputs.

TIE COMPENSATION TO PERFORMANCE

Developing the performance-to-compensation linkage is not easy. If compensation design is poor, employees may optimize individual performance and compensation. But they may harm the firm by failing to cooperate across functional boundaries and business units.

CRITICAL ELEMENTS OF THE MONITOR-AND-CONTROL PROCESS

Nine repeatable yet distinct stages for any monitor-and-control process are:

1. **Identify the process to control.** Clarify the control system's focus.
2. **Decide and define measures.** Options include input, intermediate, and/or output variables. The firm must also decide *when* to measure them, and devise a process for developing standards.
3. **Develop a measurement system.** Figure out a system to collect, integrate, and analyze relevant data and distribute results.
4. **Set standards.** Decides what standards to apply for each measure. Generally, standards flow from action programs related to market strategy.
5. **Measure results.** Using the measurement system from step 3, collect, integrate, analyze, and distribute results.
6. **Compare results against standards.** Compares results — step 5, against standards — step 4, to identify performance gaps/variances.
7. **Understand and communicate performance gaps.** Communicate data and interprepation of performance gaps to executives responsible for taking action.
8. **Generate and evaluate alternatives.** Executives identify and evaluate alternative corrective actions to close negative gaps.
9. **Select alternative and take action.** Executives select a course of action, then develop and implement an action plan.

Monitoring and Controlling Firm Performance

What performance should the firm monitor and control? The framework to answer this question is: **output → intermediate → input**.

OUTPUT MEASURES

Output measures are the *final* results the firm wants to achieve. These results can be *hard* — objectively assessed measures, or *soft measures* — like rating scales requiring more interpretation. *Internal* hard measures include sales volume, product profitability, and customer profitability; *external* hard measures include market share and market-occupancy ratio. Soft measures include customer satisfaction and brand health checks.

INTERNAL HARD MEASURES — SALES VOLUME

Sales volume includes sales units, sales revenues, and their growth rates. Overall measures are important, but breaking these down to identify components and applying the iceberg principle provides greater insight. The iceberg principle (6/7 below the surface) suggests that overperformance in one area masks underperformance somewhere else. Only by isolating underperforming areas and taking appropriate action can the firm improve overall performance. Issues with sales measures are:

- **Different sales-volume measures.** At a minimum, the firm should measure both sales units and sales revenues. Both measures are necessary to distinguish between revenue growth based on sales units and revenue growth based on price increases.

- **Sales quality.** Some firms focus on specific types of sales.

- **Accuracy and consistency of sales volume measures.** The firm must ensure that sales units and sales revenue measures are accurate, and are derived consistently from period to period.

INTERNAL HARD MEASURES — PRODUCT PROFITABILITY

Achieving good sales volume performance is important, but management is generally more interested in profits. Failure to meet profit targets may result from lack of promised resources or *unfair* corporate overhead allocations, rather than marketing problems.

To solve overhead allocation problems, the firm should focus on profit measures that exclude allocations — like **profit contribution** and **direct product profit**.

- **Profit contribution** equals sales revenue less variable costs.

- **Direct product profit** assesses profit performance after taking into account fixed costs. The firm separates fixed costs into two parts: costs *directly related* to the product (would disappear if the product were dropped) — *direct fixed costs*, and *allocated* costs — *indirect fixed costs*. Direct product profit equals profit contribution less direct fixed costs.

- **Profit return measures.** Some firms prefer **profit return** measures to absolute measures like profit contribution or direct product profit. Two popular measures are *return on sales (ROS)* and *return on investment (ROI)*. An exclusive focus on either, especially ROS, can lead to poor decisions.

> ### Marketing Question
> What is the overhead allocation problem? Why do firms face this issue?

INTERNAL HARD MEASURES — CUSTOMER PROFITABILITY

Most firms have systems to measure product profitability. By contrast, relatively few firms measure customer profitability. Yet customers provide firm revenues and are its core assets. Hence, the firm should understand the profitability dynamics of individual customers, market segments, and distribution channels.

EXTERNAL HARD MEASURES — MARKET SHARE

Marketing Question

What are the challenges of setting standards and measuring performance against them?

Market share compares firm performance directly with competitors and is the most common *market-based* measure. The firm should measure market share in both units and in revenues. These measures are identical when the firm's price equals the market average. When price exceeds the average, revenue share exceeds unit share (and vice versa).

SOFT MEASURES

The firm should regularly take its customers' pulse. Customer satisfaction and attitudes are widely employed *soft* output measures. Soft measures help track how customers are responding to the firm and competitors. Because many soft measures are tied to hard measures, they can be valuable intermediate measures.

INTERMEDIATE MEASURES

Intermediate measures sit between inputs and outputs. Success on intermediate measures does not guarantee output performance. But the firm only achieves good output performance by securing good intermediate performance. Intermediate measures have two characteristics:

- **Input effect.** The firm's marketing effort must affect the intermediate measure.
- **Output effect.** The intermediate measure must influence another intermediate measure and/or an important output measure(s).

INTERMEDIATE SALES FORCE MEASURES

The firm should base these measures on a sales pipeline model. Intermediate sales force measures differ from firm to firm. For one firm, factory trials may be a good measure; for another, dollars of co-op advertising agreed.

INTERMEDIATE ADVERTISING MEASURES

The firm should base its measures on an advertising effectiveness model geared to the market situation. For a newly launched product, *awareness* may be appropriate; for an established product, *quality perception.*

Monitoring and Controlling Firm Functioning

INPUT MEASURES

In a well-developed monitor-and-control system, input measures are closely and explicitly linked to intermediate measures. In turn, intermediate measures are closely and explicitly related to output measures. Input measure performance depends on three aspects of firm functioning:

- **Implementation control.** Did the firm implement planned actions?
- **Strategy control.** Is the firm's market strategy well conceived and on target?
- **Managerial process control.** Are the firm's processes the best they can be?

IMPLEMENTATION CONTROL

The firm's market strategy spawns many implementation programs; these programs generate action plans in marketing-mix areas like product, service, promotion, distribution, and price. The market strategy may also generate action plans in functional areas like engineering, operations, R&D, and technical service.

STRATEGY CONTROL

Strategy control answers the question: *Is the firm's market strategy well conceived and on target?* The firm typically sets strategy for the medium or long run; it should not overact to poor output performance by making hasty changes. For strategy control, post-action control is generally superior to steering control.

MANAGERIAL PROCESS CONTROL

Three broad approaches to *managerial process control* and process improvement are best practice transfer, benchmarking, and re-engineering — Chapter 21. The *marketing audit* is a comprehensive process for evaluating firm marketing practices embracing market strategy, systems, activities, and organization. To ensure confidences are kept and findings are unbiased, outsiders typically conduct the audit. A useful auditing framework has six parts:

- **Marketing environment.** What changes are occurring at customers, competitors, and suppliers? What PESTLE trends — Chapter 3 —affect the industry?
- **Market objectives and strategy.** Are the firm's market objectives and strategy realistic given the environment and the firm's strengths? Do managers understand the objectives and strategy?
- **Marketing implementation.** How do firm offers compare to competitor offers in terms of product, service, promotion, distribution, and price? Does the firm's marketing mix implement the market strategy? Are they mutually consistent?
- **Marketing organization.** Are job roles and responsibilities clear and consistent? Do measurement and reward systems motivate performance?
- **Marketing systems.** How effective are firm marketing systems, including competitor intelligence, customer advisory boards, customer database design and update, marketing research, measuring customer satisfaction, new product development, sales forecasting and pipeline management, and sales lead generation?
- **Marketing productivity.** How profitable are the firm's product lines? How profitable are the firm's customers and segments? Should some products be repriced or discontinued?

Marketing Question

Previously, we asked you to identify potential output measures for BMS introduction of Abilify, a new drug for people with schizophrenia or bipolar disorder. Recall that BMS promotional strategy is twofold: sales representatives detailing Abilify to physicians and consumer advertising. What intermediate measures would you suggest for Abilify?

Marketing audits can be a very effective diagnostic tool. The firm should look out for:

- **Considering marketing as the marketing department's job.** Customers are the firm's critical assets. Marketing is everybody's business, not just the marketing department's responsibility.
- **Cutting prices rather than increasing value.** The sales force complains and the firm cuts prices. The firm earns insufficient profit to enhance customer value.
- **Failure to invest for the future, especially in human resources.** The firm views marketing and HR as expenses, not investments. The firm under-funds marketing and training and development.
- **Failure to segment markets effectively.** Firms form simple geographic or demographic segments; they do not probe deeply enough to gain good insight.
- **Insufficient knowledge of customer attitudes and behavior.** Firms collect customer data too infrequently. Even with frequent collection, senior managers are often ill-informed, and the data do not drive marketing decision-making.
- **New product development gets delegated to the developers.** Technical employees develop new products with little marketing input and insufficient customer insight.

THE BALANCED SCORECARD

The **balanced scorecard** seeks a middle ground between using too few and too many measures. Well-balanced scorecards reflect a steering control philosophy by *balancing* input, intermediate, and output measures. The most commonly used measures for balanced scorecards are:

- **Market share** — hard output measure
- **Customer satisfaction relative to competition** — soft output measure
- **Customer retention versus industry averages** — hard output measure
- **Investment as a percentage of sales** — hard input measure
- **Employee attitudes and retention** — soft and hard input measures

Many balanced scorecards focus on four measurement categories — financial, customer, internal business processes, and learning and growth. The firm should closely align scorecards for different functional areas and managerial levels — like brand and category managers and different sales management levels. Carefully designed and aligned sets of measures improve firm chances of performing well.

*Marketing
Question*

In your educational institution, each instructor has his or her own way of measuring student performance. Can you suggest a balanced-scorecard framework that all instructors could use to measure student performance?

TRUE / FALSE QUESTIONS

1. Firms using steering control wait for a preset amount of time, then compare actual results against standards. ❏ **TRUE** ❏ **FALSE**

2. Internal hard measures include market share and market-occupancy ratio. ❏ **TRUE** ❏ **FALSE**

3. Direct product profit assesses the product's profit performance after taking into account fixed costs incurred by the product. ❏ **TRUE** ❏ **FALSE**

4. Customer satisfaction is the most common market-based measure, comparing the firm's performance directly with competitors. ❏ **TRUE** ❏ **FALSE**

5. Strategy control asks the question: "Is the firm's market strategy well conceived and on target?" ❏ **TRUE** ❏ **FALSE**

MULTIPLE CHOICE QUESTIONS

1. Which of the following is NOT one of the key principles on which a firm should build its monitor-and-control processes?

    a. Focus on market levers and develop alternative plans.
    b. Implement post-action control rather than steering controls.
    c. Use the right performance measures at the right organizational levels.
    d. Model the relationship between input, intermediate, and output measures.

2. Which of the following is NOT an example of an internal hard measure?

    a. sales volume
    b. product profitability
    c. customer profitability
    d. market share

3. Which of the following is NOT one of the basic aspects of the firm's functioning to enhance performance on input measures?

    a. implementation control
    b. strategy control
    c. managerial process control
    d. vision control

4. All of the following are important parts of an auditing framework EXCEPT:

    a. marketing environment
    b. marketing systems
    c. marketing productivity
    d. marketing demographics

5. All of the following are commonly used measures for balanced scorecards EXCEPT:

    a. market share
    b. debt to equity ratio
    c. customer retention versus industry averages
    d. employee attitudes and retention

Answers on page 205

SECTION V
SPECIAL
MARKETING
TOPICS

Managing Marketing in the 21ˢᵗ Century

SECTION I: MARKETING AND THE FIRM

CHAPTER 1
Introduction to Managing Marketing

CHAPTER 2
The Value of Customers

SECTION II: FUNDAMENTAL INSIGHTS FOR STRATEGIC MARKETING

CHAPTER 3
Market Insight

CHAPTER 4
Customer Insight

CHAPTER 5
Insight about Competitors, Company, and Complementers

CHAPTER 6
Marketing Research

TRANSITION TO STRATEGIC MARKETING

SECTION III: STRATEGIC MARKETING

IMPERATIVE 1
Determine and Recommend Which Markets to Address

CHAPTER 7
Identifying and Choosing Opportunities

IMPERATIVE 2
Identify and Target Market Segments

CHAPTER 8
Market Segmentation and Targeting

IMPERATIVE 3
Set Strategic Direction and Positioning

CHAPTER 9
Market Strategy – Integrating Firm Efforts for Marketing Success

CHAPTER 10
Managing through the Life Cycle

CHAPTER 11
Managing Brands

SECTION IV: IMPLEMENTING THE MARKET STRATEGY

IMPERATIVE 4
Design the Market Offer

PART A: PROVIDING CUSTOMER VALUE

PART B: COMMUNICATING CUSTOMER VALUE

PART C: DELIVERING CUSTOMER VALUE

PART D: GETTING PAID FOR CUSTOMER VALUE

CHAPTER 12
Managing the Product Line

CHAPTER 15
Integrated Marketing Communications

CHAPTER 18
Distribution Decisions

CHAPTER 19
Critical Underpinnings of Pricing Decisions

CHAPTER 13
Managing Services and Customer Service

CHAPTER 16
Mass and Digital Communication

CHAPTER 20
Setting Prices

CHAPTER 14
Developing New Products

CHAPTER 17
Directing and Managing the Field Sales Effort

IMPERATIVE 5
Secure Support from Other Functions

CHAPTER 21
Ensuring the Firm Implements the Market Offer as Planned

IMPERATIVE 6
Monitor and Control

CHAPTER 22
Monitoring and Controlling Firm Functioning and Performance

SECTION V: SPECIAL MARKETING TOPICS

CHAPTER 23
International, Regional, and Global Marketing

CHAPTER 23

INTERNATIONAL, REGIONAL, AND GLOBAL MARKETING

SEVERAL QUESTIONS ARE APPROPRIATE when addressing international, regional, and global marketing:

- Should the firm engage in marketing outside its domestic borders?
- How should the firm choose which foreign markets to enter?
- What foreign-market-entry options are available?
- What marketing strategy should the firm choose for foreign markets?
- What global market strategy issues must the firm address, and how should it do so?
- How should the firm organize for global markets?
- How should the firm address global customers?

THE CHANGING VIEW

OLD WAY	NEW WAY
Brand decisions made locally and regionally; supported by myriad advertising and PR agencies	Strategic brand decisions made centrally; single agency acts as global partner
Intercountry agreements on economic issues fragmented and limited in scope	Intercountry agreements on economic issues becoming the norm
International and global marketing mainly for large firms	International and global marketing an increasing option for small- and medium-size firms
International trade conducted in multiple languages	English emerging as the lingua franca of international and global business
Many international marketing decisions made at country and regional levels	Firms struggle over which decisions to centralize at head office and which to place in countries and regions

CONTINUES ON NEXT PAGE

OLD WAY	NEW WAY
Most firms group countries by geographic proximity for international and global marketing	Leading firms group countries in ways other than geographic proximity
Product and geography dominate organizational design for international marketing	Global customer organizations are increasingly important for B2B firms
Technology not a major factor in international and global marketing	Global package delivery and the Internet critical growth drivers for international and global marketing

SHOULD YOU ENTER FOREIGN MARKETS?

Before going abroad, the firm should be very clear about its purpose. Unless it has good reasons, the firm probably shouldn't bother.

Generally, firms go abroad for a variety of different reasons:

- **Diversify risk.** Domestic firms spread risk by seeking revenues in countries with different local and regional business cycles.
- **Follow customers.** When an important customer enters a foreign market, the firm may have little choice but to follow.
- **Gain knowledge.** Foreign market entry may be the best way to enhance firm intellectual capital.
- **Growth opportunities.** Revenue and profit opportunities seem greater abroad than at home.
- **Keep competitors honest.** Sometimes a foreign competitor subsidizes entry in the firm's domestic market. To *keep the competitor honest*, the firm may enter the aggressor's home market.
- **Reduce costs.** Sometimes firms base success on low-cost operations that allow low prices.
- **Small home market.** For firms based in small countries, going abroad may be the only reasonable way to grow.

The firm should only go abroad if it believes that profits from foreign market entry outweigh the risks.

HOW TO CHOOSE WHICH FOREIGN MARKETS TO ENTER

Key considerations for entering a foreign market(s) are expected financial return, risk, and timing of profits; these factors depend on foreign market attractiveness for firm products and the firm's ability to compete.

FOREIGN MARKET ATTRACTIVENESS

PESTLE factors — Chapter 3 — affect market attractiveness in different ways.

ECONOMIC AND POLITICAL/LEGAL: DOMESTIC

Economic. The crucial economic issue is current and potential market size for firm products. Greater spending power in wealthier countries implies larger markets for many products and services. The most important wealth measures are **gross domestic product (GDP)** — annual market value of all final goods and services made within a country's borders — and *GDP per capita*.

> ## *Marketing Question*
>
> In Kenya, sugar was sold in 50 and 100 kg. bags for both industrial and consumer markets. Trade liberalization and common market protocols led to severe price competition from imported sugar. How should Kensug Inc. (disguised name), a major Kenyan sugar producer, address this challenge?

Marketing Question

Segway is considering entry into Asia. Which countries should Segway enter? Why? What additional data would you require to appropriately advise Segway?

Political/legal. The political/legal environment often has an important impact on market attractiveness. Many countries develop governmental and institutional processes to benefit local firms. Some give exporters financing and tax advantages; others impose tariffs and quotas on imported goods. Regulation is often a critical entry variable.

ECONOMIC AND POLITICAL/LEGAL: INTERNATIONAL

The firm must also consider the impact of global and regional organizations.

Global organizations. Several global government-type organizations enhance foreign-market attractiveness by securing intercountry agreements to increase trade and investment:

- **International Monetary Fund (IMF).** The 186-country member IMF works to foster global monetary cooperation, secure financial stability, facilitate international trade, promote high employment and sustainable economic growth, and reduce poverty.
- **World Bank (WB).** 188 member countries own the WB, providing financial and technical assistance to developing countries.
- **World Trade Organization (WTO).** The 153-country member WTO addresses a broader scope of international agreements to liberalize trade via trade rules and dispute resolutions.

Regional organizations. Several regional organizations focus on increasing member-country trade by reducing trade barriers:

- **European Union (EU).** The EU's 27 member countries comprise an economic and political union of 500 million people generating 30 percent of global world product. People, goods, services, and capital move freely and all EU countries apply a common external tariff.
- **NAFTA.** NAFTA focuses almost exclusively on trade and investment among Canada, Mexico, and the U.S.
- **Mercosur.** Mercosur is a free-trade zone comprising Brazil, Argentina, Paraguay, and Uruguay — and several associate members.
- **ASEAN.** ASEAN is a 10-member group promoting economic growth and cultural development. Six members formed the AFTA free-trade area; unlike the EU, AFTA does not have a common external tariff.

When contemplating foreign market entry, the firm should understand the type and scope of the country's international relationships — with individual countries, regional groupings, and global institutions.

GEOGRAPHIC AND SOCIOCULTURAL DISTANCE

Geographic. *Geographic distance* concerns the ease/difficulty of transporting people and goods, and communications, between the home and target country. In addition to physical distance, important factors include presence/absence of physical land borders, separation by land/water, time zones, transportation and communication alternatives, topography, and climate. Reduced geographic distance implies increased market-entry attractiveness.

Sociocultural. Countries often differ from each other on multiple dimensions — language, religion, values and attitudes, education, social organization, technical and material, politics, law, and aesthetics.

Sociocultural distance varies widely from one country pair to another. Low sociocultural distance between the home and target countries implies reduced firm risk; high sociocultural distance can lead to failure despite other promising factors.

Marketing Question

Your firm manufactures inexpensive consumer goods. Management has asked you to identify the most attractive countries to enter taking regional organizations into account. How would you proceed?

BALANCING COUNTRY ATTRACTIVENESS FACTORS

When assessing foreign market attractiveness, the firm must consider various economic, political/legal, sociocultural, and geographic issues. In general, positive economic and political/legal factors and low sociocultural and geographic distance imply attractive opportunities, but typically the firm must balance positives and negatives.

THE FIRM'S ABILITY TO COMPETE

The firm must also consider its ability to compete — what are the firm's chances of attracting, retaining, and growing customers in the face of current and potential competitors, in the proposed market? The firm should pay close attention to strong domestic competitors and other foreign entrants. Generally, local firms are effective in catering to local tastes, use local resources efficiently, and know how to address local obstacles.

OPTIONS FOR ENTERING FOREIGN MARKETS

For *all* foreign-entry decisions, the core marketing issue is the firm's planned investment and involvement in the target country. We distinguish between *passive* entry and *active* entry. The firm must also consider how many foreign markets to enter, how quickly, and in what order.

PASSIVE ENTRY

The firm allows another organization to do all or most of the work and has little control over marketing and sales efforts. Correspondingly, risk and financial return are lower than for active entry. Options include:

EXPORTING

The firm exports products but outsources most activities by:

- Simply responding to orders arriving from abroad.
- Appointing an export agent to sell products in foreign markets.
- Deciding which foreign markets to address, then appointing local sales agents and/or distributors.

LICENSING

The firm has an asset — like product or process technology (patent or trade secret), brand name, or trademark — with value in foreign markets. The firm (licensor) agrees that another firm (licensee) can use the asset; in return, the licensee typically pays *minimum* royalties (right to use the asset) and *earned* royalties (based on sales or profits) to the licensor.

ACTIVE ENTRY

The firm plays a major role in marketing and sales, but greater profit potential comes with higher risk.

IMPORTING

Traditional. Products enter the foreign market as imports from the firm's home country and/or third countries. The firm actively markets and sells products via traveling home-based sales representatives and/or local salespeople based in foreign branches/subsidiaries.

Marketing Question

Tasks Everyday <*www.taskseveryday.com*>, based in Mumbai, India, offers virtual assistants for small, midsize, and large businesses and busy professionals. Tasks Everyday has a ready supply of university-educated graduate assistants and is seeking rapid expansion. What actions would you advise Tasks Everyday to take?

Facilitated by the Internet. The Internet and growth in air-courier transportation have helped many firms identify and serve customers in foreign markets.

LOCAL PRODUCTION

The firm has several options for offering products locally:

Acquisition. The firm acquires a firm/business unit in the foreign market. Marketing, sales, and other functions are already in place, together with local business and personal relationships. The firm surmounts many political/legal and sociocultural barriers.

Greenfield. The firm constructs local facilities from scratch. Factors driving this option include high tariff barriers, high transportation costs, local content rules, and wanting to be close to customers.

Joint Venture. A joint venture with a local partner helps the firm reduce political/legal and sociocultural risks, but degree of ownership can be a critical issue. Some governments require foreign entrants to have domestic partners, and may limit percentage ownership. Local production requires host-country investment but strengthens local institutional and customer ties. The firm becomes part of the host country's administrative and cultural fabric as supplier, customer, employer, and taxpayer. Local production also avoids quotas and tariffs.

FRANCHISING

Franchising is a popular foreign-entry mode when the firm's value proposition requires local production and/or delivery. The franchisor secures franchisees, conducts marketing and brand building, enforces standards, and may supply raw materials. The franchisee invests in local operations, local marketing and sales, and pays fees to the franchisor. Because many franchisees are local entrepreneurs, market entry can be fast.

STRATEGIES FOR INTERNATIONAL, REGIONAL, AND GLOBAL MARKETING

Firms that expand outside their home countries must decide on the scope of their foreign activities, then make serious strategic international and global marketing decisions.

SCOPE

We identify three broad approaches to international marketing.

Limited international marketing. These firms limit operations outside their domestic markets. These firms generally face five core challenges: which countries to enter, in what order, how to enter, what market strategy to employ, and how to implement the market strategy.

Regional marketing. These experienced international marketers focus their efforts on a relatively large group of countries typically, but not exclusively, within a single continent — like Europe, Latin America, or Asia Pacific.

Global marketing. Global marketers also have extensive international experience, but seek opportunities globally. The typical global marketer has multicountry presence in several continents.

Marketing Question

You have been appointed Tata Motors' Marketing Vice President for North America. Your immediate task is to launch the *Nano*, a four-door, four-passenger vehicle that sells in India for about $2,200. What will be the core elements in your three-year launch plan? Make sure you ask and answer critical strategic questions.

OBJECTIVES

The firm should consider objectives at two levels: international business overall, and its partition by region and country. In general, relevant measures are similar to those for domestic markets — revenues, profits, and market share. The firm should also set goals for the speed with which it ramps up international activity.

SEGMENTING MULTIPLE COUNTRY MARKETS

International and global marketers should answer two critical questions:

- How should we form segments for developing international market strategy? The firm can either group countries or form across-country segments.
- How should we decide which segments to address?

SEGMENTATION BY GROUPING COUNTRIES

Approaches to country grouping include:

- **Common markets and trade zones.** Related to geographic proximity but omits non-member geographically proximate countries.
- **Cultural closeness.** The firm may group countries based on various attitudinal dimensions.
- **Geographic proximity.** Options include grouping by continent, or by subcontinent.
- **Historical relationships.** Examples are the British Commonwealth, the Commonwealth of Independent States (CIS), Spain and Spanish Latin America, and Portugal and Brazil.
- **Income.** A five-category system embraces: OECD members (34 countries), other high income (39), upper middle income (46), lower middle income (55), and low income (43).
- **Language.** Has elements of geographic proximity and historical relationships but focuses specifically on language.
- **Specific purpose.** Examples are OPEC (oil production) and NATO (defense).

ACROSS-COUNTRY SEGMENTATION

The firm may form market segments regardless of geographic location:

- **Demographic characteristics.** Traditional demographic variables alone or in combination can form segments. B2C variables include age, education, gender, income, and religion. Company size, growth, industry, and profitability are useful B2B variables.
- **Values.** Roper Starch Worldwide (RSW) identified six global B2C segments by interviewing 1,000 consumers in 35 countries about core values.

BRANDING IN GLOBAL MARKETS

The firm's core branding choice is between *local* and *global*. When the firm provides the same or similar products in multiple countries, should it offer a single brand — *global branding*, or multiple *local brands*? Arguments for **global branding** include: Cross-border travel, leverage brand equity to new geographic markets, homogeneity of customer tastes across countries, and increased global media reach and lower costs.

Global brands offer specific advantages: Aspirational values, brand image, best-practice transfer, competitive advantage, global appeal, and help in recruiting and retaining better people worldwide.

Global branding does not imply identical implementation programs across countries. Differing national tastes often drive product design variations. In practice, global firms have global, regional, and local brands.

Marketing Question

Over many years, Toyota earned an enviable record for high-quality products. But in 2009, Toyota was forced to recall over seven million automobiles because of unintended acceleration. What actions would you suggest that Toyota take to repair the damage to its brand image?

COUNTRY OF ORIGIN

Country-of-origin (COO) effects add to (or subtract from) firm brands, forming customer attitudes and intentions and securing purchase. Country of origin researchers identify three effects:

- **Cognitive.** COO signals product quality but can be positive or negative depending on the product.
- **Affective.** COO has symbolic and emotional meaning for customers and confers attributes like authenticity, exoticness, and status.
- **Normative.** Customers view purchasing from certain countries as doing the *right* thing — domestic products to help the national economy or products from a developing country to help alleviate poverty.

IMPLEMENTING INTERNATIONAL, REGIONAL, AND GLOBAL MARKET STRATEGIES

The core challenge for international and global marketers is balancing the efficiency benefits of centralized corporate control versus addressing local market needs. Core problems are:

- **Excessive control.** Local managers must sell standard products, at standard prices, using standard communications and distribution systems. Lack of flexibility in meeting customer needs causes problems.
- **Excessive flexibility.** The firm offers a core product in multiple countries but allows country managers to make most other decisions. The firm gains few benefits from being a multinational firm.

For marketing-mix implementation decisions, we assume the firm has set market strategy centrally but provides significant autonomy to meet local needs.

PRODUCT

Degree of product standardization is the critical *product* decision for international, regional, and global marketers. Product standardization across national markets reduces costs and may allow the firm to offer lower prices. Conversely, standardization ignores local requirements and makes it easier for gray markets to form by shipping a standard product across national borders.

COMMUNICATIONS

Firms expanding internationally may have to adapt communications approaches to local conditions. Language differences across countries imply different communications. But the firm must be careful about translations; poor translations can cause problems. Also, in low-literacy countries, the firm should emphasize visuals, including graphs and diagrams, rather than words, but must be careful how customers interpret images and symbols (including logos).

DISTRIBUTION

The firm's distribution efforts should be appropriate to the local market. Domestic-type distribution systems from developed countries may not be available in foreign markets, so creativity is critical. Coca-Cola distributes products in over 200 countries by doing *whatever it takes*.

Marketing Question

Successful Spanish restaurant chain 100 Montaditos (inexpensive sandwiches and beer) entered the U.S. with a goal of opening 4,000 outlets in five years, via a combination of company-owned and franchised stores. Do you think 100 Montaditos will be successful? Why or why not? How would you advise 100 Montaditos?

PRICE

The firm should gear prices to target market segment(s) in specific countries. Firms may successfully offer mass-market products at similar prices in several developed countries. But in less-developed countries, similar product/price combinations may only address wealthy elites. To reach broader customer segments with the same product, the firm may have to reduce prices.

ORGANIZING FOR INTERNATIONAL, REGIONAL, AND GLOBAL MARKETS

Firms entering foreign markets must make critical organizational decisions. In part, organization structure depends on the number of foreign markets entered and firm investment.

EXPORT DEPARTMENT

Typically, an export department at head office directs initial firm efforts in foreign markets. This department interfaces with agents and brokers and develops intellectual capital about international marketing and sales.

INTERNATIONAL DIVISION

As foreign sales increase, the firm replaces its export department with an international division; country managers report to the international division head. The relationship between country managers and corporate varies widely from firm to firm: Corporate may impose critical decisions on the countries, or assign them broad decision-making autonomy. Local autonomy promotes entrepreneurship, initiative, and speedy adaptation to local needs.

GEOGRAPHIC REGION

The firm places individual countries in a regional structure, typically based on geographic proximity, and manages P&L at the country level. A typical structure comprises four regions: U.S. and Canada; Latin America; Europe, Middle East, and Africa (EMEA); and Asia Pacific (APAC).

Advantages of the geographic-region organization over the international division are:

- Allows the firm to integrate functions across countries, within regions
- Avoids duplication costs
- Offers greater ability to manage performance across several countries, and
- Provides promotion opportunities for upwardly mobile executives.

FUNCTIONAL

In the functional structure, all firm functions globally, report directly to corporate; corporate controls decision-making around the world. The downside may be unresponsiveness to local conditions like offering inappropriate products, pricing, and service in various countries.

GLOBAL PRODUCT DIVISION

The global product division (brand, business unit) focuses on global consistency and cost efficiency, and is appropriate when customer needs are *homogeneous* across geography. The global product-division structure promotes production rationalization and is popular among FMCG firms with large product lines.

GEOGRAPHIC REGION/PRODUCT DIVISION MATRIX

Matrix organizations attempt to balance both geographic and product concerns.

GLOBAL CUSTOMER MANAGEMENT

When firms expand operations to multiple countries they often evolve their procurement operations. These firms prefer to source some inputs locally, but global procurement is often more effective and efficient. To enable global contracts, these firms want global supplier relationships. Hence, suppliers must develop organizational structures to interface with their global customers — global customer management. The centerpiece of global customer management organizations is the global account manager (GAM).

TRUE / FALSE QUESTIONS

1. Gross domestic product is the annual market value of all final goods and services made within a country's borders. ❏ **TRUE** ❏ **FALSE**

2. NAFTA is a free-trade zone comprising Brazil, Argentina, Paraguay, and Uruguay — and several associate members. ❏ **TRUE** ❏ **FALSE**

3. Major options for active entry into foreign markets include exporting, local production, and franchising. ❏ **TRUE** ❏ **FALSE**

4. A firm constructs local facilities from scratch in a greenfield project. ❏ **TRUE** ❏ **FALSE**

5. Heterogeneity of consumer tastes across countries is a strong supporting argument for global branding. ❏ **TRUE** ❏ **FALSE**

MULTIPLE CHOICE QUESTIONS

1. The annual market value of all final goods and services made within a country's borders is referred to as _____.

   a. Gross National Product
   b. Gross Domestic Product
   c. Gross National Income
   d. Purchasing Power Parity

2. The _____ is an organization that consists of 186 member countries that works together to foster global monetary cooperation, secure financial stability, facilitate international trade, promote high employment and sustainable economic growth and reduce poverty.

   a. World Bank
   b. World Trade Organization
   c. International Monetary Fund
   d. NAFTA

3. All of the following represent forms of active entry for entering a foreign market EXCEPT:

   a. licensing
   b. importing
   c. local production
   d. franchising

4. All of the following are options that firms can use to set up production operations in a foreign country locally EXCEPT:

   a. exporting
   b. greenfield
   c. acquisition
   d. joint venture

5. The organizational structure that focuses on global consistency and cost efficiency and is appropriate when customer needs are homogeneous across geographically is referred to as _____.

   a. functional
   b. international division
   c. global customer management
   d. global product division

Answers on page 205

ANSWERS

CHAPTER 1

TRUE/FALSE QUESTIONS
1. (True, page 5)
2. (True, page 6)
3. (False, page 6)
4. (True, page 7)
5. (False, page 9)

MULTIPLE CHOICE QUESTIONS
1. (c, page 6)
2. (a, page 6)
3. (c, page 7)
4. (c, page 8)

CHAPTER 2

TRUE/FALSE QUESTIONS
1. (True, page 12)
2. (False, page 13)
3. (True, page 13)
4. (True, page 15)
5. (False, page 15)
6. (False, page 17)

MULTIPLE CHOICE QUESTIONS
1. (a, page 12)
2. (d, page 12)
3. (d, page 14)
4. (a, page 15)
5. (a, page 16)
6. (b, page 16)

CHAPTER 3

TRUE/FALSE QUESTIONS
1. (True, page 25)
2. (False, page 26)
3. (True, page 27)
4. (False, page 28)
5. (True, page 29)

MULTIPLE CHOICE QUESTIONS
1. (b, page 25)
2. (a, page 25)
3. (c, page 26)
4. (b, page 27)
5. (e, page 28)

CHAPTER 4

TRUE/FALSE QUESTIONS
1. (True, page 32)
2. (False, page 33)
3. (False, page 34)
4. (True, page 35)
5. (False, page 36)

MULTIPLE CHOICE QUESTIONS
1. (a, page 34)
2. (c, page 36)
3. (d, page 36)
4. (c, page 38)
5. (a, page 39)

CHAPTER 5

TRUE/FALSE QUESTIONS
1. (False, page 43)
2. (True, page 45)
3. (True, page 45)
4. (True, page 48)
5. (False, page 49)

MULTIPLE CHOICE QUESTIONS
1. (a, page 43)
2. (d, page 44)
3. (d, page 45)
4. (b, page 45)
5. (c, page 48)

CHAPTER 6

TRUE/FALSE QUESTIONS
1. (False, page 53)
2. (True, page 54)
3. (False, page 55)
4. (True, page 57)
5. (True, page 58)

MULTIPLE CHOICE QUESTIONS
1. (c, page 54)
2. (d, page 55)
3. (a, page 56)
4. (b, page 58)
5. (d, page 58)

CHAPTER 7

TRUE/FALSE QUESTIONS
1. (True, page 64)
2. (False, page 65)
3. (True, page 65)
4. (True, page 66)
5. (False, page 66)

MULTIPLE CHOICE QUESTIONS
1. (a, page 65)
2. (c, page 65)
3. (a, page 67)
4. (a, page 67)

CHAPTER 8

TRUE/FALSE QUESTIONS
1. (True, page 71)
2. (True, page, 72)
3. (False, page 73)
4. (True, page 73)
5. (True, page 74)

MULTIPLE CHOICE QUESTIONS
1. (d, page 71)
2. (c, page 72)
3. (a, page 72)
4. (d, page 73)
5. (d, page 75)

CHAPTER 9

TRUE/FALSE QUESTIONS
1. (True, page 78)
2. (True, page 79)
3. (False, page 80)
4. (True, page 81)
5. (False, page 82)

MULTIPLE CHOICE QUESTIONS
1. (d, page 78)
2. (b, page 78)
3. (a, page 80)
4. (b, page 80)
5. (d, page 82)

CHAPTER 10

TRUE/FALSE QUESTIONS
1. (True, page 85)
2. (False, page 85)
3. (True, page 85)
4. (True, page 87)
5. (False, page 87)

MULTIPLE CHOICE QUESTIONS
1. (c, page 86)
2. (b, page 87)
3. (b, page 88)
4. (d, page 88)
5. (d, page 89)

CHAPTER 11

TRUE/FALSE QUESTIONS
1. (True, page 94)
2. (True, page 95)
3. (False, page 95)
4. (True, page 97)
5. (True, page 97)

MULTIPLE CHOICE QUESTIONS
1. (d, page 93)
2. (d, page 93)
3. (a, page 94)
4. (a, page 95)
5. (d, page 96)

CHAPTER 12

TRUE/FALSE QUESTIONS
1. (True, page 103)
2. (False, page 105)
3. (False, page 106)
4. (True, page 106)
5. (True, page 107)

MULTIPLE CHOICE QUESTIONS
1. (d, page 104)
2. (b, page 104)
3. (b, page 105)
4. (d, page 107)
5. (d, page 107)

CHAPTER 13

TRUE/FALSE QUESTIONS
1. (True, page 112)
2. (False, page 114)
3. (True, page 114)
4. (False, page 116)

MULTIPLE CHOICE QUESTIONS
1. (d, page 113)
2. (a, page 113)
3. (c, page 115)
4. (a, page 116)

CHAPTER 14

TRUE/FALSE QUESTIONS
1. (False, page 118)
2. (True, page 120)
3. (False page 120)
4. (False, page 124)
5. (True, page 124)

MULTIPLE CHOICE QUESTIONS
1. (a, page 119)
2. (d, page 121)
3. (c, page 123)
4. (c, page 124)

CHAPTER 15

TRUE/FALSE QUESTIONS
1. (True, page 128)
2. (False, page 128)
3. (True, page 128)
4. (True, page 129)
5. (True, page 130)

MULTIPLE CHOICE QUESTIONS
1. (d, page 127)
2. (c, page 128)
3. (a, page 128)
4. (d, page 130)

CHAPTER 16

TRUE/FALSE QUESTIONS
1. (False, page 134)
2. (False, page 135)
3. (True, page 135)
4. (True, page 136)
5. (True, page 137)

MULTIPLE CHOICE QUESTIONS
1. (b, page 134)
2. (c, page 135)
3. (d, page 135)
4. (d, page 136)
5. (d, page 140)

CHAPTER 17

TRUE/FALSE QUESTIONS
1. (True, page 147)
2. (True, page 149)
3. (True, page 152)
4. (False, page 154)
5. (False, page 155)

MULTIPLE CHOICE QUESTIONS
1. (a, page 147)
2. (c, page 148)
3. (d, page 150)
4. (d, page 152)
5. (d, page 153)

CHAPTER 18

TRUE/FALSE QUESTIONS
1. (False, page 159)
2. (True, page 161)
3. (True, page 161)
4. (True, page 161)
5. (False, page 162)

MULTIPLE CHOICE QUESTIONS
1. (c, page 158)
2. (a, page 159)
3. (d, page 160)
4. (d, page 162)
5. (b, page 162)

CHAPTER 19

TRUE/FALSE QUESTIONS
1. (False, page 166)
2. (False, page 166)
3. (True, page 167)
4. (True, page 168)
5. (False, page 169)

MULTIPLE CHOICE QUESTIONS
1. (d, page 165)
2. (c, page 166)
3. (b, page 166)
4. (d, page 169)
5. (d, page 170)

CHAPTER 20

TRUE/FALSE QUESTIONS
1. (True, page 173)
2. (False, page 173)
3. (False, page 174)
4. (True, page 176)
5. (True, page 176)

MULTIPLE CHOICE QUESTIONS
1. (a, page 173)
2. (d, page 174)
3. (d, page 174)
4. (a, page 175)
5. (c, page 176)

CHAPTER 21

TRUE/FALSE QUESTIONS
1. (True, page 181)
2. (True, page 181)
3. (False, page 181)
4. (True, page 182)
5. (True, page 182)

MULTIPLE CHOICE QUESTIONS
1. (a, page 180)
2. (b, page 181)
3. (c, page 181)
4. (d, page 181)
5. (d, page 182)

CHAPTER 22

TRUE/FALSE QUESTIONS
1. (False, page 186)
2. (False, page 188)
3. (True, page 188)
4. (False, page 189)
5. (True, page 190)

MULTIPLE CHOICE QUESTIONS
1. (b, page 186)
2. (d, page 189)
3. (d, page 190)
4. (d, page 190)
5. (b, page 191)

CHAPTER 23

TRUE/FALSE QUESTIONS
1. (True, page 196)
2. (False, page 197)
3. (False, page 198)
4. (True, page 199)
5. (False, page 200)

MULTIPLE CHOICE QUESTIONS
1. (b, page 196)
2. (c, page 197)
3. (a, page 198)
4. (a, page 199)
5. (d, page 203)

CPSIA information can be obtained at www.ICGtesting.com
Printed in the USA
BVOW052126090413

317738BV00004B/6/P